OLD TESTAMENT PARALLELS

OLD TESTAMENT PARALLELS

LAWS AND STORIES FROM THE ANCIENT NEAR EAST

Fully Revised and Expanded Edition

VICTOR H. MATTHEWS
and
DON C. BENJAMIN

Paulist Press
New York/Mahwah, N.J.

Cover Design
Cover design is taken from a fresco in one of the thirty-nine large rock-cut tombs at Beni-Hasan, about fifteen miles south of el-Minya, Egypt today on the east bank of the Nile. It depicts thirty-seven members of the household of Absha arriving from Syria-Palestine in the sixteenth nome or province of southern Egypt during the reign of Pharaoh Senworsret II (1897-1878 BCE). See P.E. Newberry, Beni Hasan (London, 1893): 1: pls 28, 30-31; D. Kessler, *Studien zur altagyptische Kultur* 14 (1987), 147–66.

Cover design by Cindy Dunne

Book design by Saija Autrand/Faces Type & Design

Library of Congress Cataloging-in-Publication Data

Matthews, Victor Harold.
    Old Testament parallels : laws and stories from the ancient Near East / Victor H. Matthews and Don C. Benjamin. — Fully rev. and expanded ed.
      p.   cm.
    Includes bibliographical references and index.
    ISBN 0-8091-3731-3 (alk. paper)
    1. Bible. O.T.—Extra-canonical parallels.   2. Middle Eastern literature—Relation to the Old Testament.   3. Law, Ancient—Sources.   4. Law—Middle East—Sources. 5. Bible. O.T.—History of contemporary events—Sources.   6. Bible. O.T.—Antiquities. 7. Middle Eastern literature—Translations into English.   8. Middle East—History— To 622—Sources.   I. Benjamin, Don C.   II. Title.
    BS1180.M42   1997
    221.9′5—dc21   97-15575
                                                                                             CIP
                                                                                             r97

Published by Paulist Press
997 Macarthur Boulevard
Mahwah, New Jersey 07430

Printed and bound in the
United States of America

CONTENTS

Joshua, Judges

Ruth

Samuel, Kings

Chronicles, Ezra, Nehemiah

Job, Ecclesiastes

Psalms, Lamentations

For our parents

E. Harold and Lillie Mae Matthews
Don C. and Edith B. Benjamin

whose love gave us life

FOREWORD

The huge gap in time and experience between our time and theirs makes studying ancient cultures difficult. Reading documents produced by scribes 4,000 or more years ago is tough going at best. A pioneer in providing both ancient Near Eastern texts and artifacts to western scholars and students was James Henry Breasted (1865–1935). By 1907, he had published five volumes of *Ancient Texts,* including translations of virtually every document recovered to that time. In 1919, he founded the Oriental Institute at the University of Chicago whose museum today houses an impressive collection of ancient Near Eastern artifacts. Recent scholarly interest in this material sparked a project headed by Burke O. Long (Bowdoin College) and other members of the Society of Biblical Literature entitled *The Writings from the Ancient World,* which promises to be an exhaustive critical edition of texts from the epoch of Sumer through the age of Alexander the Great. For classroom use by teachers and students, the standard critical edition of parallels to the Bible has been James B. Pritchard's *Ancient Near Eastern Texts Relating to the Old Testament* (Princeton University Press, 1969). This anthology provides a virtual picture in English of the original words, but its translations are so text oriented that beginning students tend to become lost and frustrated. These translations retain so many linguistic and cultural conventions from the original languages that an English reader gets very little sense from them. The full volume is also too large and too expensive for ordinary classroom use. From time to time, affordable and portable anthologies have appeared, although not all are still in print and some are too selective for an introductory course. There is a two volume, paperback set of *ANET,* for example, as well as D. Winton Thomas, *Documents from Old Testament Times* (New York: Harper, 1958), Michael David Coogan, *Stories from Ancient Canaan* (Philadelphia: Westminster, 1978), and Klaas A.D. Smelik, *Writings from Ancient Israel* (Louisville: Westminster/John Knox, 1991). Finally, given the ongoing and exciting discoveries of more and more ancient Near Eastern texts since 1950, even in the third edition, *ANET* just does not have all the traditions teachers want their students to experience.

Students and teachers today still needed a readable, affordable and portable anthology of ancient Near Eastern laws and stories. Therefore, in 1991, we published *Old Testament Parallels: Laws and Stories from the Ancient Near East*. We were delighted with how well this first edition served so many students and teachers. As a continuing service to them, and with an interest in further increasing the use of Old Testament parallels in introductory courses, we have prepared this revised and enlarged edition. All the parallels and the introductions from the first edition have been revised, and some have been expanded. Seventeen new parallels have been added, enlarging the anthology from forty-four to sixty-one selections.

A. Leo Oppenheim, who died in 1974, was an outstanding philologist and Assyriologist, whose major contribution to scholarship was made as the editor of the *Chicago Assyrian Dictionary*. He, however, described himself as a cultural anthropologist. By expanding his interest from text to society, Oppenheim did much to make Mesopotamian texts as understandable in the modern world as those of Greece and Rome. In the introduction to *Ancient Mesopotamia: Portrait of a Dead Civilization* (1977:3), to which Oppenheim devoted more than twenty years of his life, he wrote:

> . . . translated texts tend to speak more of the translator than of their original message. It is not too difficult to render texts written in a dead language as literally as possible and to suggest to the outsider, through the use of quaint and stilted locutions, the alleged awkwardness and archaism of a remote period. Those who know the original language retranslate anyhow, consciously or unconsciously, in order to understand it. It is nearly impossible to render any but the simplest Akkadian text in a modern language with a satisfactory approximation to the original in content, style, or connotation. A step nearer to the realization of the legitimate desire to make the texts "speak for themselves" would bring us, perhaps, an anthology of Akkadian texts, with a critical discussion of the literary, stylistic, and emotional setting of each translated piece.

In preparing *Old Testament Parallels* we tried to meet Oppenheim's challenge. Our readings are not literal or visual, text-oriented, translations, but responsible, reader-oriented, paraphrases. The English vocabulary and idiom emphasizes the relationship between the ancient Near Eastern parallel and the Bible. It imitates commonly used patterns of speech today. It avoids awkwardness and archaism. It avoids as much sexism and racism as possible. There was certainly sexism and racism in the world of the Bible, and where it clearly appears in a tradition, we have left it in our readings. Where the traditions are indifferent to questions of gender and race, we have tried not to introduce it. Hopefully, *Old Tes-*

tament Parallels offers teachers and students readings that are dynamically equivalent to the way in which they were heard, and felt, and understood in their own worlds.

Clearly, *Old Testament Parallels* reflects our scholarship in reconstructing the world from which these traditions come, and our own understanding of the style and meaning of each parallel. Nonetheless, we have tried to keep our reconstructions consistent with scholarly work currently in progress, and avoid as much eccentricity as possible, by making our readings reflect the consensus of scholars working in the field.

Ancient Near Eastern texts are artifacts recovered by archaeologists. Some like those from the Dead Sea Valley between Jordan and Israel today and the city of Ebla in Syria dramatically change the way we reconstruct the world of the Bible. Establishing the correct connection between related biblical and non-biblical traditions is never easy. Simple solutions are generally misleading solutions. Parallels are a limited, not an exhaustive window on both their own culture and the cultures of their neighbors. We want to take advantage of all that these traditions have to offer to understand Israel and its culture, but not to blur the distinction between all the cultures in the world of the Bible, or to imply that the cultures of Mesopotamia, Asia Minor, Syria-Palestine and Egypt have value only insofar as they relate to the Bible. We also do not wish to destroy the distinctiveness of the Bible by overstating its similarity with the traditions of surrounding cultures.

Parallels between ancient Near Eastern traditions and the Bible can be based on their similarities as well as their contrasts. Some biblical and non-biblical traditions are parallels because they belong to the same genre. The Enuma Elish stories and the stories of the heavens and the earth in the book of Genesis (Gen 1:1—2:4a), for example, both belong to the genre: creation story. Other biblical and non-biblical traditions are parallel because they deal with the same topic. The annals of Mesha and the annals of Joram in the books of Samuel–Kings (2 Kgs 3:1–27), for example, both deal with a war between Israel and Moab that took place around 830 BCE. Some of the most important parallels come from the Middle Bronze period (2000–1500 BCE) and the Late Bronze period (1500–1250 BCE). For the books of Genesis (Gen 1—11), Psalms and Daniel, there are parallels from Ugarit in Syria whose liturgical traditions reflect Late Bronze period ritual and worship. For the books of Exodus, Leviticus, Numbers and Deuteronomy, there are parallels from Babylon in Iraq, whose legal library from the Middle Bronze period illustrates judicial systems like the gate-court as well as a wide variety of legal precedents. For the books of Joshua and Judges, there are parallels from El Amarna in Egypt, whose diplomatic communiqués document the unstable social and political conditions in Syria-Palestine during the Late

Bronze period. For the books of Samuel–Kings and the prophetic traditions in the Bible, there are parallels from Mari in Syria, whose government and diplomatic traditions illustrate social institutions like covenant, judge and prophet during the Middle Bronze period.

We offer our readers three tools for using parallels in the classroom. First, the table of contents and the body of the book itself arrange parallels according to the canonical order of the Old Testament found in most English translations of the Bible. Within each of these chapters, the parallels are arranged chronologically. Second, some of the most significant biblical parallels are identified in the introductions to our readings, and biblical references are cited next to the line numbers from the critical editions of the parallels. Third, a chart at the end of the book identifies six ways in which laws and stories from the ancient Near East can parallel the Bible. There are genre parallels, vocabulary parallels, motif parallels, social institution parallels, plot parallels and parallels in historical events.

Introductions to each parallel describe the physical appearance of the text, the language in which it was written, where it was recovered, and where it is preserved today. There is also a summary of its contents. Short explanations of those portions of parallels that we have not included are given to provide continuity, and to encourage students to read the entire text on their own. To that end, a selective bibliography directs readers to critical editions of the parallels. There are also outlines of the history of Mesopotamia, Egypt and Israel, which we hope will be helpful in the study of the ancient Near East and of the Old Testament.

A colleague who will take time from his or her own work to help you with yours is a blessing. There are no ancient Near Eastern parallels for this saying, but there are many modern examples. We have been helped repeatedly by colleagues who looked at drafts of *Old Testament Parallels* and made valuable suggestions in their reviews of the first edition. We want to thank them all, especially Robert J. Miller (Midway College), Robert Gnuse (Loyola University, New Orleans), J. Andrew Dearman (Austin Presbyterian Theological Seminary), Ronald A. Simkins (Creighton University), Bernard F. Batto (DePauw University) and Diedre Demsey (Marquette University). Frank S. Frick (Albion College) paid us a truly gracious compliment, and provided teachers with a fine model of how to teach comparative material in an introductory course, by his use of our *Old Testament Parallels* in *A Journey through the Hebrew Scriptures* (Harcourt Brace, 1995). We also want to thank Lawrence J. Boadt and the other members of the editorial staff at Paulist Press for agreeing to publish a second, revised and enlarged edition.

Victor H. Matthews, Ph.D.
Don C. Benjamin, Ph.D.

Genesis

HYMN TO PTAH

A hymn to Ptah that originally developed in Egypt's Old Kingdom
(2575-2134 BCE) at Memphis continued to be copied at least until
the end of the twenty-fifth dynasty (ca. 710 BCE). One version of the
hymn, copied on a slab of black granite known as the Shabaka Stone,
was recovered by British archaeologists in Egypt in the 1830s. It is
written in an archaic style similar to the Pyramid Texts and is preserved today in the British Museum in London.

The hymn celebrates Ptah, the divine patron of Memphis, as
the supreme creator, by contrasting the way Ptah creates with the
way Atum, the divine patron of Heliopolis, creates. When the
hymn opens, the Ennead, which is a divine assembly of the nine
most important divine patrons of Egypt, is ratifying the unification
of northern and southern Egypt as a single state. Horus, the divine
patron of northern Egypt, assumes the responsibilities of Seth, the
divine patron of southern Egypt, and becomes the absolute ruler of
Egypt. The hymn goes on to tell how Horus also assumes the responsibilities of Ptah to become the absolute ruler of the Ennead.

The dramatic quality of the hymn to Ptah is comparable to
the stories of the creation of the heavens and the earth in the book
of Genesis (Gen 1:1—2:4a). The hymn also authorizes the existing
political order of the Old Kingdom in which Ptah is the ruler of
the Ennead and Memphis is Egypt's sacred center and the capital of
a newly united state.

(Gen 1:3, 1:31—2:1; Prov 20:9, 22:11)

Geb the earth commanded the Ennead to assemble. At first, Geb
proposed to end the war between Horus and Seth by dividing Egypt
equally between them. Horus would rule over Lower Egypt in the north
and Seth would rule over Upper Egypt in the south. Then Geb proposed

The gods Seth and Horus extend the symbol of life,
the ankh, *to an Egyptian man.*

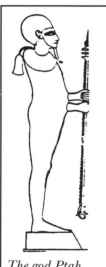

The god Ptah,
dressed as a
mummy to signify
that he is also
lord of the
underworld.

that the land of Horus should rule over the land
of Seth, and that Horus, son of Osiris, should unite
Upper and Lower Egypt into one land. Therefore,
Osiris marched in triumph through the gates of
death to rule over the land of the dead and his
son Horus sat in triumph on the throne of Upper
and Lower Egypt in the land of the living. Isis and
Nephthys then proposed that Horus and Seth end
their wars and become brothers.

Ptah gave life to every member of the Ennead
and to the soul (Egyptian: *ka*) of each. Each came
into being through the thoughts in his heart and
the words on his tongue. Horus came forth, and
Thoth came forth from the thoughts in the heart
of Ptah and the words on the tongue of Ptah. The
thoughts of the heart of Ptah and the words of the
tongue of Ptah guide all the thoughts and all the
words of the Ennead, and all the thoughts and all
the words of humans, and of all life. Ptah creates
the Ennead with only teeth and lips. Atum must
create with hands and semen. Atum had to mas-
turbate to bring forth the Ennead. Ptah had only

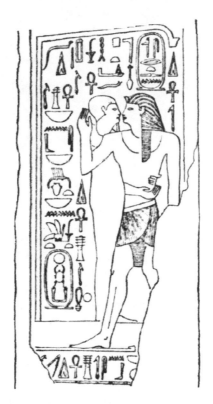

*Sesostris I honors the god Ptah in a relief
on a limestone pillar from Karnak
(12th dynasty, about 1930 B.C.E.).*

to speak, and the Ennead came forth. Ptah called the names of Shu the
wind and Tefnut the rain, who gave birth to Geb the earth and Nut the
sky. Just as all the senses of sight, of hearing and of smell all report to
the heart, and just as the heart is the source of all knowledge, and the
tongue speaks what the heart desires, so all the members of the Ennead
came forth . . . according to the thoughts of the heart of Ptah and the
words of the tongue of Ptah. . . .

   According to the thoughts of the heart of Ptah and the words of the
tongue of Ptah, the innocent are set free and the guilty are punished,
life is granted to the pure of heart and death to fools. According to the
thoughts of the heart of Ptah and the words of the tongue of Ptah, all
crafts came forth, all trades were created. Ptah is the creator of all and
the ruler of the Ennead. Ptah gave birth to the Ennead and from Ptah
comes forth all things. Ptah is the ruler of the Ennead. Having done all
these things, Ptah rested content with his work.

HYMN TO RA

A hymn to Ra, which is also spelled "Re," was recovered by British archaeologists in 1865 and is preserved today in the British Museum in London (Papyrus Bremner-Rhind, British Museum No. 10188). It is written in hieroglyphics on sheets of papyrus. Although the hymn originally developed during the Old Kingdom (2575-2134 BCE) at Heliopolis (Egyptian: iwnw) in the Cairo of today, this is a version as it was told after 400 BCE at Thebes in Luxor, which is some 300 miles south of Cairo.

Egyptians honored Ra as the creator and ruler who accompanied them, their pharaoh and their land from birth to death to rebirth. They honored pharaoh as "son of Ra." Heliopolis, Hermopolis and Edfu were the most important sanctuaries of Ra. Each day Ra sailed his boat along the clear blue body of Nut the sky toward the sunset horizon which was her mouth. At dusk, Nut consumed the sun. Throughout the night, Ra navigated his boat through the Nut's body, where the serpent Apophis waited to destroy it at the opening of her womb on the sunrise horizon. Like midwives, priests chanted a hymn to Ra as they waited for the creator to emerge. Having completed the voyage, Ra would recreate Egypt, thus allowing a new day to dawn and the pharaoh to continue to rule the land in peace. The sun, or its glyph which was a circle with a dot in the center, the cone-shaped benben stone, the pyramid, the obelisk, the sun temple and the scarab beetle (Egyptian: khepri) were among the artistic and architectural symbols connected with Ra. Beetles lay their eggs in balls of manure, and roll them from place to place while they gestate. Egyptians described Ra as a beetle rolling the sun from dusk to dawn. Every living thing emerged from the sun, just as the newly hatched beetles emerged from the ball of manure.

Parallels to a hymn to Ra appear in the stories of the heavens and the earth in the book of Genesis (Gen 1:1—2:4a).

Columns xxvi:21—xxvii:5 (Gen 1:1—2:4a; Exod 3:13–4)

As the sun dawned, Ra spoke:
  I am Khepri the beetle.
When I come, the day begins,
  When the almighty speaks, all else comes to life.
There were no heavens and no earth,
  There was no dry land and there were no reptiles in the land.

Then, I spoke and living creatures appeared.
  I put them to sleep in Nun the sea, until there was land where I could
    stand.

When I first began to create,
  When I alone was planning and designing every creature,
I had not exhaled Shu the wind,
  I had not spat Tefnut the rain,
  There was not a single living creature.
I planned a multitude of living creatures,
  All were in my heart, and their children and their grandchildren.

The goddess Shu supports the body of Nut over the body of Geb.

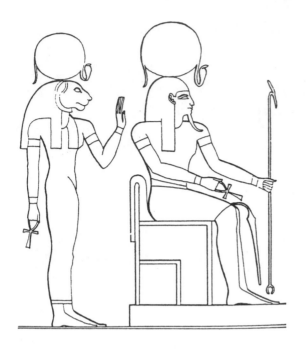

The goddess Tefnut behind the throne of the god Atum.

xxvii:1–15 (Gen 2:6–7)

Then I copulated with my own fist.
    I masturbated with my own hand.
    I ejaculated into my own mouth.
I exhaled Shu the wind,
    I spat Tefnut the rain.
Old Man Nun the sea reared them,
    Eye the overseer looked after them. . . .

In the beginning, I was alone,
    Then, there were three more.
I dawned over the land of Egypt.
    Shu the wind and Tefnut the rain played on Nun the sea. . . .

I wept and human beings appeared.
    With my tears, I created the reptiles and their companions.
Shu and Tefnut gave birth to Geb the earth and Nut the sky.
    Geb and Nut gave birth to Osiris and Isis, to Seth and Nephthys.
Osiris and Isis gave birth to Horus.
    One was born right after another.
    These nine (Greek: *ennead*) gave birth to all the people of the land.

ENUMA ELISH STORIES

In 1849, Austin Henry Layard, a collector of artifacts for the British Museum, recovered a copy of the Enuma Elish stories from Ashur, the Koujunjik, Iraq of today. Ashurbanipal (668–626 BCE) had the copy made for the Assyrian imperial library. They were written on baked clay tablets about 30 inches high in the Akkadian language using cuneiform script. A duplicate copy of Tablet V was found at Sultantepe, ancient Harran, on the upper reaches of the Euphrates River in modern Syria.

Between 1792–1750 BCE, the empire-building Hammurabi made Babylon the most important city in Mesopotamia and enthroned Marduk, Babylon's divine patron, as head of the divine assembly. Thus the previously minor city state of Babylon would grow in importance in both historical and epic terms for the next 1,200 years. Somewhere around 1100 BCE the story of creation found below was compiled from disparate Sumerian and Amorite traditions to celebrate the military and political accomplishments of the city and its rulers. It may not in fact represent normative religious thought in Mesopotamia since its purpose is more political than etiological.

Parallels to the Enuma Elish stories appear in the book of Genesis as well as in the books of Exodus and Psalms (Ps 8, 19, 50, 104). Like the Enuma Elish stories, these stories and psalms may have been part of the ritual reenactment (Akkadian: akitu) of creation at the new year. Israel's creation stories, however, are not directly dependent on any one parallel from Mesopotamia, Syria-Palestine or Egypt. Israel's understanding of Yahweh is particularly unique. The Hebrews celebrated Yahweh as the divine warrior whose armies, commanded by Moses, armed with a staff and the east wind, confront the armies of the Red Sea commanded by pharaoh. For the Hebrews, Yahweh both "...causes all things to be" and "...commands the divine warriors." Once they understood Yahweh both as the deliverer who liberates the Hebrews from slavery and the creator who calls the cos-

*Marduk in royal robes with the Mushashu
dragon, controlling the waters of chaos
(Babylonian cylinder seal; 9th century B.C.E.).*

mos from chaos, the technical cosmological language common in ancient Near Eastern creation stories began to appear in the Bible.

I:1–9 (Gen 1:1–2)

≋ *The crisis episode in the Enuma Elish stories describes the birth of the divine assembly of Mesopotamia out of a chaos of water and darkness through the merging of Apsu, divine patron of fresh water, with Tiamat, divine patron of salt water.*

When on high, no heaven had been named,
    When no earth had been called,
    When there were no *annunaki* elders . . .
When there was nothing . . .
    Nothing but . . .
Godfather Apsu and Mummu-Tiamat, godmother of all living,
    Two bodies of water becoming one,
When no reed hut was erected,
    When no marsh land was drained,
When there were no *iggigi* warriors,
    When no names had been called,
    When no tasks had been assigned.

I:10–9

Then, Lahmu and Lahamu were created,
    Their names were called.
Before they increased in wisdom and stature,
    Anshar and Kishar were created, surpassing their ancestors.
Before they increased in wisdom and in stature,
    Anu was created.
Anu, who was Kishar's heir, rivaling his ancestors,
    Anu, who was Anshar's first born, equaling his ancestors.
Anu made Nudimmud-Ea in his image;
    Surpassing his ancestors,
Ea, increasing in wisdom,
    Increasing in understanding, increasing in strength.

I:20

Ea, greater than Anshar, his ancestor,
    Unmatched among the brave *iggigi* warriors, his ancestors. . . .

≋ *Eventually, the increasing noise of the* iggigi *warriors disturbed Apsu and he made plans to destroy them. Apsu was prevented from carrying out his plans by Ea, who killed his father, and took his crown. After the assassination of Apsu, another generation of divine creatures was born. The pride of this new generation was Marduk.*

I:79–103

Then, in the Palace of Fates,
  Then, in the Temple of Destinies,
A brave *iggigi* warrior was created,
  The ablest and the wisest of the *iggigi*. . . .
Then, in the Heart of Apsu,
  Then, in the sacred Heart of Apsu,
  Marduk was created.
Ea was his father,
  Damkina, his mother.
Divine womb that bore him;
  Awesome the breasts he nursed.
Marduk's posture was erect,
  His glance inspiring.
Marduk's stride was commanding,
  His stature venerable.
Father Ea's voice sang,
  His face beamed,
  His heart filled with pride.
Ea declared Marduk flawless,
  His father endowed him with a double share of divinity.
Ea exalted Marduk above his ancestors,
  He exalted him above them all.
Marduk's head was incredible,
  It was incomprehensible, inconceivable in power.
No sight escaped his eyes,
  No sound evaded his ears.
Marduk's voice was strong,
  His words blazed like fire.
Marduk's hearing was acute,
  His eyesight sharp.
Marduk's body was unsurpassed.
  His physique was powerful.
Marduk's arms and legs were huge,
  His height dwarfed all others.

"My son," Ea sang,
  "My beloved son.
My son, who is the sun.
  He is the sun in the sky."
Clothed with the powers of ten gods,
  Marduk excelled them all. . . .

≋ *To become the ruler of the divine assembly, Ea murders Apsu. Tiamat then marries Kingu, who encourages her to revolt against the divine assembly for allowing Ea to kill her first husband. To help her overthrow the divine assembly, Tiamat creates a team of ferocious and monstrous creatures.*

I:132–38

Tiamat, the mother of all,
  Gave birth to peerless and hideous monsters.
Serpents with fangs for teeth,
  Snakes with venom for blood.
Terrifying dragons,
  Filled with divine power.
To see them was to die,
  Once prepared to strike, they were invincible.

≋ *Ea and the divine assembly are afraid to face Tiamat and these monsters. At this point, Marduk, divine patron of the storm and divine patron of Babylon, steps forward to serve as the divine warrior for the assembly. For his service, however, he exacts a price.*

III:116–22

"If I agree to serve as your deliverer,
  If I am successful defeating Tiamat,
  If I save your lives,
You must proclaim me the ruler of the divine assembly.
  My word, not yours, must determine all things.
What I create must not change,
  What I command must not be revoked or altered."

≋ *Rejoicing that it has found a warrior to challenge Tiamat, the divine assembly agrees.*

IV:3–32, 35–41 (Eccl 3:3; Jer 1:10)

"You will be the most honored member of this divine assembly . . .
  Your word shall not be challenged,
  Your word shall speak for all.
Your decree shall not be altered.
  Your word shall build up and tear down.
Your word shall be the law,
  Your command shall be obeyed.
No member of this assembly shall surpass you. . . .
  Marduk is Lord. . . .
This divine assembly approves your mission,
  We, the gods, swear allegiance to you as Lord. . . .
Go and destroy Tiamat,
  Scatter her blood to the winds. . . .

Marduk builds himself a bow,
  Designs it to his special needs.
He feathers the arrows,
  Ties the string.
Marduk raises his sword,
  Grasps it in his right hand.
Bow and quiver hang at Marduk's side,
  Lightning he carries as a shield.
Marduk dons a blazing fire for armor,
  He weaves a net big enough to trap Tiamat.

瓣 *Tiamat, disguised as a sea serpent (Ps 74:13-4), taunts Marduk as he*
  comes to the field of battle. Taunting before battle was a common
  part of military strategy in the ancient Near East (1 Sam 17:8-10;
  2 Sam 5:6-8; 1 Kgs 20:1-11; 2 Kgs 18:19-37). Marduk responds to her
  taunt with a retort.

IV:77–86 (1 Sam 17:8–10; 2 Sam 2:18–23)

"Why do you raise your hand against the divine assembly,
  Acting like its ruler?
You deceive yourself,
  You cannot disown your own children.
You cannot designate Kingu to be its divine warrior,
  You cannot give Kingu the power of Anu, who rules the sky.
You rebel against Anshar, who commands the dusk,

Combat between Marduk and a dragon (cylinder seal).

You are in revolt against the divine assembly.
Of your armor, I am not afraid,
  Of these monsters, I am not frightened.
I challenge you to come forward alone.
  I dare you to duel with me, one on one."

When Tiamat hears the retort of Marduk, she is infuriated. Out of her mind with anger, she rushes away from the other serpents and attacks Marduk by herself. As she opens her mouth to roar, Marduk inflates her with storm winds to incapacitate her. Then, he pierces her with an arrow of lightning (Isa 41:2). After his victory, Marduk processes triumphantly to the sacred mountain to be proclaimed ruler of the divine assembly. Here he builds his temple on the grave of Apsu, and names the temple for his slain ancestor. Outside the gate, Marduk erects Tiamat's monsters as statues to remind all who enter of his victory (based on the additions to Tablet V of the story found in the Sultantepe material).

V:71–6

Marduk rounded up the monsters of Tiamat,
  He brought them as trophies before the divine assembly.

Marduk trapped the eleven of Tiamat in his net,
   He shattered their weapons, and shackled their feet.
Marduk transformed these serpents into statues,
   He mounted them at the gate of his temple, the Apsu.
"Let these statues be a memorial," he proclaimed,
   "So that this revolt may never be forgotten."

Having remodeled his temple with the spoils of war, Marduk then uses Tiamat's body to build a new world. He crushes her skull with his club, and scatters her blood into the wind. He splits her body in two. He uses half to make the heavens, and half to make the earth. The body of Tiamat seals out the primeval waters at the mountains on the horizons (Gen 1:6-7). Marduk assigns the members of the divine assembly as constellations to mark each season of the year. He assigns the moon to guard the night and to mark the month with its phases (Gen 1:15-16). Finally, Marduk and Ea discuss a plan to create humans.

VI:5–8, 23–42

I will knead blood and bone into a savage,
   "Aborigine" will be its name.
These aborigines will do the divine assembly's work.
   These savages will set the divine assembly free.

*Sumerian cylinder seal showing the combat of Marduk
against the winged dragon Zu.*

≋ *Ea suggests that Marduk sacrifice one of Tiamat's allies to create the savage. So, Marduk convenes the divine assembly to discuss Ea's proposal.*

Who planned Tiamat's uprising?
　Who advised her to rebel?
Hand over the instigator of this revolt,
　Punish the conspirator for his crimes, and live in peace.
The divine assembly testified: "Kingu planned the uprising.
　Kingu advised Tiamat to rebel."

≋ *So the divine assembly binds Kingu and Ea slits his throat. They use his blood to fashion the aborigines (Gen 1:26-7; 2:7-15), whom Ea assigns to do the divine assembly's work in the new world.*

Marduk arrested Kingu, his rival,
　Ea arraigned him.
Marduk convicted him of conspiracy,
　Ea executed him by cutting his throat.
Ea formed the aborigines from Kingu's blood,
　Marduk set the aborigines to work.
Ea emancipated the divine assembly,
　The wise created the aborigines.

An artist's reconstruction of the Ziggurat of Ur
as it may have appeared about 2100, B.C.E.

Marduk put the aborigines to work,
   He set the divine assembly free.
   What an incredible accomplishment!
Nudimmud-Ea created.
   Marduk masterfully designed.
Ea the wise created the aborigines,
   Marduk ordered them to work for the divine assembly.
What an incomprehensible task,
   What a work of art.
The aborigine designed by Marduk,
   The savage executed by Nudimmud.
Marduk the king split the annunaki elders into groups,
   Appointed Anu their supervisor.
Marduk stationed three hundred *annunaki* in the heavens above,
   Three hundred more on the earth below.

➹ *To celebrate Marduk's coronation, the divine assembly builds the Esagila, a great ziggurat in the city of Babylon. Then they transfer their divine titles to Marduk and decreed a new year festival, the akitu, to annually celebrate Marduk as the divine warrior by retelling the Enuma Elish stories.*

STORIES OF
GILGAMESH

≋ In 1872, George E. Smith announced that during 1848-49 Austin Henry Layard had recovered baked clay tablets about six inches high from Nineveh in today's Iraq. They contained a version of the stories of Gilgamesh popular during the reign of Ashurbanipal (668-626 BCE). The stories were written in Akkadian cuneiform, with about 300 lines on each tablet. The full story covered ten to twelve tablets, and developed during the Early Bronze period (3000-2000 BCE). Today they are preserved in the British Museum. Because the tablets from Nineveh are damaged and incomplete, portions of the stories have been taken from an older Babylonian version from the Middle Bronze period (2000-1500 BCE) to fill in some of the lost material.

The stories of Adam and Eve (Gen 2:4b—4:2) and the stories of Noah (Gen 6—11) in the book of Genesis have the most parallels to the stories of Gilgamesh. Enkidu is parallel to Adam, Utnapishtim to Noah, and Dilmun to Eden.

HARIMTU SHAMHAT AND ENKIDU

≋ The stories of Gilgamesh celebrate this ruler of Uruk. When they open, Gilgamesh is a tyrant, so the divine assembly creates Enkidu to be his companion. The assembly hopes that Enkidu will take Gilgamesh on daring adventures and keep him from using his energies to oppress the people of Uruk. At first Enkidu has little interest in Gilgamesh and prefers to run with wild animals. To make him more interested in human friendship, the divine assembly dispatches a wise woman (Akkadian: **harimtu shamhat**) who teaches Enkidu how to be human.

Tablet I, col. iii:49–51

The hunter and the wise woman took up positions,
    For two days they waited by the watering hole.
Finally, the wild beasts came to drink,
    The animals came to splash in the water.

col iv:2–7

Enkidu, like a creature from the hills, came with them,
    Grazing with the gazelles,
Watering with the wild beasts,
    Splashing in the water with the animals.
The wise woman saw this creature primeval,
    This savage from deep within the treeless plains.

col iv:15–21

The wise woman bared her breasts,
    Enkidu took hold of her body.
She was not bashful,
    She welcomed his passion.
She spread her clothes on the ground,
    Enkidu had intercourse with her on them.

*A Sumerian cylinder seal showing mythical conflicts between
rampant lions and heroes, partly human and partly beast.
The bottom scene may represent Gilgamesh.*

*Gilgamesh, naked, fights with Enkidu, half man, half beast, on the left.
Ishtar stands on the far right. (Cylinder seal from the time of
Hammurabi, 18th century B.C.E.)*

She treated this savage like a man.
  Enkidu made love with her.
For six days and seven nights Enkidu took her,
  Every day and every night he had intercourse with the woman.

col iv:22–9, 33–45 (Gen 3:5)

Having satisfied himself with the woman,
  Enkidu turned to rejoin the animals.
Seeing him, the gazelles ran off,
  The beasts of the steppe shied away from him.
Enkidu felt weak, his body grew taut,
  His knees locked when the beasts began to run.
Enkidu became weak, unable to run as before,
  But his mind was filled with a new wisdom. . . .

Finally, the woman said: "Now you are wise, Enkidu,
  Now you have become like us.
Why do you run with the wild animals?
  Why do you run through the plains?
Let me lead you to Uruk, the city of great markets,
  Come with me to the sanctuary of Anu . . . where Gilgamesh rules. . . ."

OB Version Tablet II, col ii:31–5 (Gen 3:7, 20–1)

She took some of her own clothes and dressed Enkidu,
    Then she dressed herself.
The wise woman took his hand and led him like a child.
    They walked to the corral, where the herders gathered to stare.

col iii:1–25

Enkidu knew only how to nurse . . .
    To suckle the milk of wild animals.
When they placed beer and bread before him,
    He turned away, he sniffed, he stared.
Enkidu did not know how to eat bread.
    No one had taught him how to drink beer.
Then the woman said: "Eat the bread, Enkidu, it is the staff of life.
    Drink the beer, it is the gift of the land."

Enkidu ate bread until he was full.
    He drank beer from seven jars.
He became cheerful and playful.
    His heart rejoiced and his face glowed.
He bathed and oiled his body,
    He combed his hair.
Enkidu became a man.

GILGAMESH AND DEATH

≋ *The two heroes participate in a number of dangerous adventures,
which would have been impossible for normal humans. However,
when Enkidu begins to consider the danger in which they are plac-
ing themselves and talks with Gilgamesh about dying, the king does
not know what he means.*

Tablet III, col iii:96–115

One day, Gilgamesh said to Enkidu,

"Fierce Humbaba lives in the Cedar Forest.
    Let us kill him and thus deliver our land from evil. . . ."

Enkidu said to Gilgamesh:

"When I ran with animals, I learned that the Cedar Forest has no end.
   No one goes there.
Humbaba's roar is like a flood,
   His mouth is fire, his breath is death.
Why do you want to do this?
   It is impossible for us to destroy Humbaba the destroyer."

OB Version: Tablet III, col. iv:138–48 (Job 7:16; 14:5)

Nonetheless, Gilgamesh insisted:

"Who can climb to heaven and become immortal?
   Only the members of the divine assembly live forever.
The days of humans are numbered;
   Human deeds are like a breath of wind.
Here you stand afraid of death.
   What about your mighty arm? I will stand in front of you.
Encourage me, saying: 'Fear nothing!'
   If I die, I will at least have made a name for myself."

🪶 *Enkidu and Gilgamesh kill Humbaba and a divine bull, but they become arrogant (Greek:* hubris*). When Gilgamesh rejects the goddess Ishtar, who wants to have intercourse with him, the divine assembly sentences Enkidu to death. Enkidu hears his sentence in*

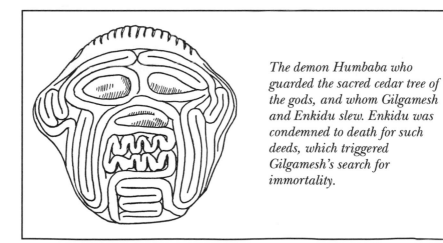

The demon Humbaba who guarded the sacred cedar tree of the gods, and whom Gilgamesh and Enkidu slew. Enkidu was condemned to death for such deeds, which triggered Gilgamesh's search for immortality.

a dream and subsequently falls ill. Gilgamesh is frightened by his prolonged death. He digs a grave for his friend, and erects a memorial over it. Enkidu's fate also drives Gilgamesh to seek a cure for his own mortality and he begins a quest that will ultimately take him to Dilmun.

GILGAMESH AND SIDURI THE BREWER

≈⦚ *Along the way to Dilmun, Gilgamesh encounters Siduri, a woman who brews beer, with whom he discusses his plan to become immortal.*

Tablet X, col. ii:1–14

Gilgamesh told Siduri, a woman who brews beer, his story:

"My friend . . . Enkidu . . .
    Was overtaken by the fate of all mortals.
For seven days and seven nights I wept for him
    Until a maggot crawled out of his nose.
Then I became afraid.
    Fearing death, I roamed the steppe. . . .
The friend I loved has become clay. . . .
    Shall I not also lie down like him, never to rise again?"

OB Version: Tablet X, col. iii:6–13 (Eccl 3:12–3)

≈⦚ *In one tradition, Siduri advises Gilgamesh to forget his quest for immortality and return home to enjoy life as a mortal.*

Siduri gave Gilgamesh this advice:

"Let your belly be full,
    Make merry day and night.
Turn each day into a feast of rejoicing,
    Dance and play day and night.
Put on fresh garments,
    Wash your hair and body clean in water.
Play with your children,
    Take pleasure in your wife."

A cylinder seal showing the sun god Shamash rising from behind the mountains. The goddess Ishtar stands over him and the god Adad (or Baal) pours out the rain to his right. On the left, Shamash is shown again as a hunter (Sumerian period).

Assyrian Version: Tablet X, col. ii:21–31

≋ *In another tradition, Siduri teaches Gilgamesh how to cross the Sea of Death and reach Dilmun safely.*

Siduri went on:

"From the beginning of time, no one has crossed the Sea of Death,
    No one, but Shamash, the divine patron of the sun. . . .
Even if you, Gilgamesh, cross the sea
    What will you do when you come to the Sea of Death?
If it is possible, cross with Urshanabi the boatman,
    If not, then return home."

GILGAMESH AND UTNAPISHTIM

≋ *Gilgamesh follows Siduri's instructions, obtains the aid of Urshanabi and crosses the Sea of Death to Dilmun. Here he asks Utnapishtim how he and his wife became immortal. The story that Utnapishtim tells Gilgamesh describes how the divine assembly tries to destroy every mortal with a flood. When it discovers that Utnapishtim and his wife survived in an ark, the divine assembly changes them into immortals, so that its decree ordering the destruction of all mortals by a flood could, at least technically, be fulfilled.*

Tablet XI, col. i:7–40 (Gen 6:14–21)

"Tell me, Utnapishtim, how did you and your wife become immortal
    And join the divine assembly?"
"Well, Gilgamesh, let me tell you the story of a divine conspiracy,
    A divine plot to exterminate humanity. . . .
Anu the godfather, Enlil, and Ninurta convened the divine assembly,
    Which decided to flood the earth. . . .
Ea, divine patron of fresh water, opposed Enlil.
    Ea repeated Enlil's plan aloud outside the reed walls of my house.

"'Listen to me, wall,' Ea whispered,
    'You reed mat, pay attention to me.
Pull down your house,
    Build a barge.
Abandon all your possessions,
    Save your life.
Take specimens of every living thing on board.
    Make the ark square with a roof like the dome of the heavens.'"

"I told Ea that I would obey,
    But asked: 'What shall I tell the people of Shuruppak?'
Say: 'Enlil, the divine patron of Shuruppak, has sentenced me to death,
    So I must move to the coast where Ea is lord. . . .'"

col. ii:58–94 (Gen 6:14–6; 7:2–4+7–9+13–6)

"I built the hulls of the ark one-hundred seventy-five feet high,
    And the decks one-hundred seventy-five feet wide.
I constructed a top deck and six lower decks,
    I separated the hull into compartments by nine bulkheads.
Then I caulked the ark with bitumen
    And asphalt thinned with oil.
I fed my workers as generously as if it were festival time
    And the ark was completed in seven days. . . .
We had a difficult time launching the ark,
    But we finally put it into the water using log rollers.
Then I loaded all my gold and silver into the ark,
    My entire household, domestic animals, wild beasts, and craftspeople.
Finally, at the precise moment set by Shamash, I boarded the ark,
    I battened down the hatch,
    I turned the ark and its manifest over to Puzur-Amurri the boatman."

col. iii:96–144 (Gen 7:11–12, 23–24, 8:3–4, 21–22; Isa 30:14, 42:14; Mic 4:9)

"At dawn . . . the horizons turned black with clouds,
    Adad, divine patron of thunder, roared.
Nabu and Sharru, the divine messengers,
    Flew before the wind.
Nergal, divine patron of the dead, unlocked the fountain of the deep.
    Ninurta, son of Enlil, opened the dikes.
The divine assembly strafed the earth with lightning,
    Adad turned the day into night; the land was smashed like a pot.
One person could not see the other,
    The heavens could not see the earth.
The flood ran the old Annunaki into the heavens,
    Frightened the divine assembly like stray dogs against city walls.
Ishtar, divine patron of love and war, shrieked,
    Cried out like a woman in labor.
'How could I kill my own people,
    Conspire against those to whom I gave birth?
Their bodies float on the sea, swell like schools of dead fish.'
    The old Annunaki sat humbled, the divine assembly wept.
For six days and six nights the winds blew.
    On the seventh day, the storm subsided, the sea grew quiet.
I felt the stillness.
    Every living thing had drowned.

I opened the hatch, sunlight fell on my face.
    I bowed my face to the deck and wept.
The ark ran aground on Mount Nisir.
    It remained grounded for six days."

col. iv:145–98 (Gen 8:5–22; 9:1–17)

"On day seven, I released a dove which flew, but returned.
    There was no place for it to rest.
I released a swallow, which flew, but returned.
    There was no place for it to rest.
I released a raven, which flew, cried out and flew away.
    The flood had subsided.
Then, I released all the creatures,
    Which scattered to the four winds.
I prepared a sacrifice,
    I poured a libation on the mountaintop.

I set out my sacred vessels,
    I kindled a sacred fire of reed, cedar, and myrtle.
The divine assembly smelled the aroma,
    They swarmed like flies around the sacrifice.
Ishtar arrived and removed her necklace of lapis-lazuli, saying:
    'By my necklace, I swear, I shall never forget these days.
Let every member of the divine assembly enjoy this meal,
    But let Enlil eat no sacrifice which mortals prepare.
Enlil thoughtlessly created a flood,
    He drowned the mortals who feed the divine assembly.'
But, when Enlil did arrive and saw the ark, he was furious.
    'Have some mortals escaped? Every last one was to be destroyed!'
Ninurta convened the divine assembly.
    He indicted Ea for revealing Enlil's plan . . .
For wanting to control population with wild animals, famine, plague . . .
    For not wanting to destroy every last mortal with a flood.
But Ea testified: 'I did not tell Utnapishtim of Enlil's plan,
    I did not warn him of the impending doom.
Subpoena Utnapishtim, and let the mortal speak.
    He dreamed alone.
    He interpreted the divine conspiracy for himself.'
Enlil boarded the ark, and told me and my wife to kneel.
    He laid his hands on our heads and announced:
'Utnapishtim and his wife have been mortal, now they are immortal.
    They shall live far away, they shall dwell at the mouth of the rivers.'
So, the divine assembly settled us at the mouth of the rivers.

"This concludes our story.
    Now, Gilgamesh, tell us who will assemble the gods for your sake."

GILGAMESH AND THE SERPENT

Tablet XI, col. vi:258–307

As Gilgamesh and Urshanabi prepared to cast off,
    the wife of Utnapishtim said to the Faraway One:
"Gilgamesh has worked and slaved to come here.
    What can you give him to take back to his land?"
When she spoke, Gilgamesh poled his boat back to shore.
    Utnapishtim said to Gilgamesh: "I will tell you a divine secret.
There is a plant like the buckthorn . . .
    It will prick your hands like a bramble.

*A statue of
Gilgamesh
holding a lion
cub (Louvre).*

If you can find the plant,
   You will find the secret of immortality."

No sooner had Gilgamesh heard the words of Utnapishtim
   Than he headed for the well cap at the bottom of the sea.
He tied heavy stones to his feet.
   They pulled him down to the bottom where he saw the plant.
Gilgamesh pulled up the plant;
   It pricked his hand;
He cut the heavy stones from his feet,
   And the sea cast him up upon its shore.

Gilgamesh said to Urshanabi: "This is the miraculous plant.
　　This is the plant which restores life.
I will take this miraculous plant to Uruk, the city of sheep,
　　Whose citizens will eat it. . . .
I will call it '. . . the fountain of youth.'
　　I will eat it myself, and regain my youth."

After fifty miles Gilgamesh and Urshanabi stopped to eat,
　　After seventy-five miles they dropped anchor for the night.
Gilgamesh saw a spring whose water was cool.
　　He went to bathe in the water.
A serpent smelled the fragrance of the plant.
　　It came up from the water,
And carried off the plant.
　　As it returned to the water, the serpent shed its skin.
Gilgamesh sat down and wept,
　　Tears ran down his face.
". . . for whom have my hands toiled,
　　For whom has my heart pounded?
I have nothing to show for my work.
　　I have worked for this serpent,
But the tide will have carried the serpent fifty miles away.
　　When I dove to the well cap at the bottom of the sea,
I found the miraculous plant which was a sign for me.
　　Let us finish the journey on foot, leave the boat on the shore."

After fifty miles they stopped to eat.
　　After seventy-five miles they stopped for the night.
When they arrived at Uruk, Gilgamesh said to Urshanabi:
　　"Climb up and walk the walls of Uruk.
Inspect their foundations, examine their brickwork,
　　Their brick is fired.
Seven sages laid their foundation.
　　Uruk is one part city, one part orchard, one part pasture.
The land of Ishtar consists of three parts,
　　Not counting the clay quarries."

STORIES OF ATRAHASIS

≋ *Copies of the stories of Atrahasis in the Babylonian and Assyrian dialects of Akkadian, written in cuneiform, have been recovered by archaeologists at various sites in Mesopotamia and Syria-Palestine. These tablets are housed today in the British Museum in London, the Archaeological Museum in Istanbul, Turkey, and in the Musee de'Art et d'Ilistoire in Geneva, Switzerland.*

The stories of Atrahasis begin in a world populated only by the warriors (Akkadian: iggigi) and the elders (Akkadian: anunnaki) of the divine assembly. Eventually the young warriors revolt, refusing to do all the work that is necessary to keep their world running properly. Ea-Enki negotiates a settlement with them, in which workers (Akkadian: lullu) will be created to take care of the world, especially by dredging its canals. The elders ratify Ea-Enki's proposal, but assign Nintu-Mami the actual task of carrying out the project. In time, these workers, too, revolt against the divine assembly and

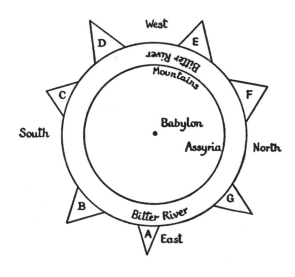

Clay tablet of about 2000 B.C.E. with a map of the world with Babylon at the center.

refuse to do their work. Initially, the divine assembly uses epidemics and famines to control these workers, but without lasting effect. Finally, they create a flood from which only the household of Atrahasis in its ark survives.

Parallels between the stories of Atrahasis and the Bible include the stories of the heavens and the earth (Gen 1:1—2:4a) and the flood stories (Gen 6:1—11:26) in the book of Genesis.

I:192–5

"Summon Nintu, the divine midwife!
  Let her create workers to labor for the divine assembly."
So, the divine assembly summoned Nintu-Mami,
  They called the wise woman before them.
"Midwife the *lullu*," they commanded,
  "Create workers to labor for us.
Let the *lullu* bear the yoke,
  Let them work for Enlil,
  Let them labor for the divine assembly."

≋〗 *The stories of Atrahasis describe the labor of Nintu-Mami with several different accounts of how the task was carried out. One account compares Ea-Enki with a menstruating woman, who bathes three times during the menstrual cycle: first when the new moon appears, then seven days later, and finally fourteen days later when the full moon appears. Intercourse is described as the mixing of the body of Ea-Enki, with the blood of We-ila. During pregnancy, Nintu-Mami massages the uterus of Ea-Enki just as a potter would shape a vessel. When Ea-Enki's labor comes to term, Nintu-Mami summons the workers from the womb with the command: "Live."*

I:200–30 (Jer 18:2–6)

Nintu said to the divine assembly: "I cannot do Ea-Enki's work.
  Only Ea-Enki has the clay to create."
Ea-Enki spoke: "I will bathe to mark my time . . .
  At the new moon, the seventh day, and the full moon, I will wash.
Let the divine assembly sacrifice We-ila.
  Let them bathe in his blood.
Let Nintu thin my clay with his blood.
  Let Nintu mix clay with blood, the human with the divine.

Let the drum mark off the days,
    Count down the time.
Let We-ila's blood give these workers life,
    Let the midwife call out to them: 'Live!'"
The divine assembly agreed,
    The *anunnaki* elders consented.

At the new moon, the seventh day, the full moon, Ea-Enki bathed.
    The divine assembly sacrificed We-ila the wise. . . .
Nintu thinned the clay . . . with his blood.
    The drum marked off the days . . . counted down the time.
We-ila's blood gave the workers life,
    Nintu-Mami called out to them: "Live!"

≋ *In another version, Nintu-Mami thins clay with the saliva of the anunnaki and the iggigi.*

I:235–40 (Gen 3:20)

The divine assembly gave Nintu-Mami moisture to thin the clay.
    She wet it with saliva from the *anunnaki* and the *iggigi.*
Nintu-Mami sang: "Praise to you who gave me this task,
    Praise to you who sacrificed . . . We-ila to help me complete my work.
I have created workers to labor for the *iggigi* warriors. . . .
    I have loosened your yoke, I have set you free."
The divine assembly heard the hymn which Nintu-Mami sang.
    The anunnaki and the iggigi kissed her feet.
"Yesterday, we called you 'Mami.'
    Today, you are 'Mother of the divine assembly.'"

≋ *Yet another version describes Ea-Enki as the godfather having intercourse with Nintu-Mami, while she sings. Nintu-Mami conceives seven sets of fraternal twins: seven males and seven females. Her midwife helps Nintu-Mami mount the birth stool, and prepare the room for her delivery.*

I:250–300 (Gen 2:7; 35:17; Exod 1:16; 1 Sam 4:20)

Ea-Enki and Nintu-Mami entered their birthing room,
    She summoned her midwife, he worked the clay.
She sang the sacred song,
    He prayed the special prayer.

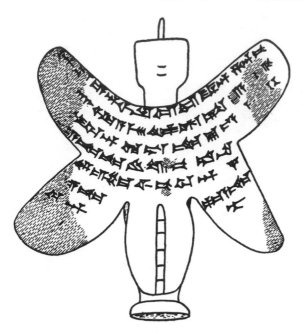

*Late clay amulet with an inscription to
the demon Pazazu across his body.*

*Small amulet of the
demon Pazazu,
the bringer of disease.*

When Nintu-Mami finished singing,
   She pulled off fourteen pieces of clay.
The midwife divided the clay into rows of seven,
   She set up a brick for a birth stool between them. . . .

The midwife helped Nintu-Mami mount the birth stool . . .
   She counted ten months to determine her date.
The tenth month came,
   Nintu-Mami went into labor.
Her face was beaming. . . .
   She was full of joy.
The midwife put on her cap,
   She donned her apron,
She began to pray.
   She scattered the flour.
On the birth stool, Nintu-Mami sang: "I have created life.
   Let the midwife rejoice in the labor room when a mother gives birth.
Erect the birth stool for nine days,
   Honor Nintu-Mami and her midwife. . . .
Praise Nintu-Mami,
   Praise her midwife, Kesh.

Let husband and wife lie together in their wedding room.
  Let them do what Ishtar commands in the house of her father-in-law. . . ."

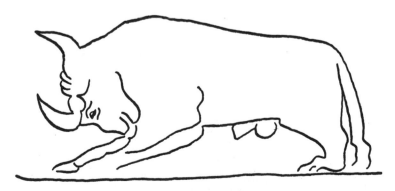 *Soon the workers begin to disturb the members of the divine assembly, and Enlil tries to control them with a plague.*

I:355–60

In less than twelve hundred years . . .
  there were more and more workers in the land.
  The workers multiplied.
The land bellowed like a bull,
  The uproar disturbed the divine assembly.
When Enlil heard the noise, he complained:
  "I cannot stand this uproar, I cannot sleep. . . .
  Send an epidemic upon the land."

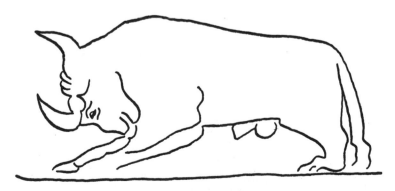 *Atrahasis prays to Ea-Enki, his divine patron, for help and Ea-Enki teaches him how to end the epidemic.*

I:375–83

"Command messengers to proclaim,
  Tell them to shout throughout the land:
'Do not feed the gods,
  Do not pray to the goddesses.'

A bull on a bas relief from the ancient city of Enink.

Go to the gate of the temple of Namtar.
  Place your finest bread on the threshold.
This grain will please Namtar,
  Your gift will shame him into withdrawing his hand."

⊇ *Atrahasis persuaded the elders to follow Ea-Enki's advice. They ren-*
   ovated the temple of Namtar, the divine patron of fate, placed offer-
   ings at the gate and Namtar stopped the plague. Over the next six
   years, Enlil tries other means of controlling the workers with drought
   and a famine. Each time, Atrahasis appeals to Ea-Enki, who advises
   the workers to stop feeding all the gods and the goddesses except
   the one member of the divine assembly responsible for their suf-
   fering. Each time, the strategy works and the workers survive and
   continue to multiply.

II.i:10–20; Isa 5:6; Hos 2:9

"I cannot stand this human uproar,
  I cannot sleep!
Reduce their food supply,
  Let plants become scarce.
Adad! Withhold the rain!
  Do not allow springs to rise from the deep.
Winds! Blow the earth dry!
  Clouds! Gather, but do not rain.
Let harvests be reduced,
  Let Nisaba, divine patron of grain, retard growth.
Let the joy of the harvest be gone. . . ."

iv:11–4

After three years . . . every worker's face was drawn with hunger.
  Every worker's face was crusted like malt.
  Every worker lived on the brink of death. . . .

Assyrian Recension: S.vi:7–12

After five years . . . a daughter stares as her mother goes into the house,
  . . . while her mother locks her out of the house.
A daughter stares while her mother is sold as a slave,

A mother stares while her daughter is sold as a slave.
After six years . . . a daughter is cooked and eaten,
  A son is served as food.

Every effort of the divine assembly to control the workers is blocked by Ea-Enki's advice to Atrahasis. Therefore, the divine assembly decides that only a flood will get the workers back into line. They order Ea-Enki to take an oath not to advise Atrahasis how to save the workers. Nonetheless, Atrahasis falls asleep in the temple of Ea-Enki, who sits behind his screen woven from reeds, talking to himself about the decision of the divine assembly. Atrahasis thinks the voice of his divine patron is a dream.

III.i:20–48 (1 Sam 3:3–4)

"If I were you, my woven lattice,
  My braided reed screen, I would pay close attention.
I would pull down my house,
  I would build a barge.
I would abandon all my possessions
  . . . to save my life. . . .

Place a roof over the barge,
  Cover it as Apsu, the heavens, covers the earth.
Do not let the sun see inside,
  Enclose it completely.
Make the joints strong,
  Caulk the timbers with pitch.
I will gather flocks of birds for you
  . . . and schools of fish."
Then, Ea-Enki filled the water clock,
  Set the time for the flood on the seventh night.

Atrahasis addressed the elders at his gate:
  "My god has had a dispute with your god.
Ea-Enki and Enlil are at odds,
  So I must leave this place.
Since I worship Ea-Enki,
  I am a partner in this conflict.
I can no longer live here,
  I can no longer dwell in the land of Enlil."

〰️ *With this as his explanation, Atrahasis proceeds to construct a barge and fill it with all sorts of animals. Once he has it loaded, he stages a banquet and sends his family on board. As he sits, saddened by the impending flood, it begins to rain.*

ii:48–55 (Gen 6:14)

The weather began to change. . . .
Adad roared within the clouds.
  Atrahasis heard Adad's voice,
He closed the door
  And sealed it with pitch.
Adad's roar filled the clouds,
  The winds blew fiercely.
Atrahasis cut the mooring rope,
  He let the barge float free.

III.iii:10–20, 23–40, 51–4

The noise in the land ceased,
  Like the silence following the breaking of a pot.
The flood rushed forward,
  The flood charged the people like an army.
One person could not see the other,
  In the water no one was recognizable.
The flood bellowed like a bull,
  The winds howled like a wild ass braying.
There was no sun,
  Only the darkness of the flood. . . .

The noise of the flood terrified the divine assembly.

Ea-Enki was furious,
  Seeing his children destroyed.
The lady Nintu
  Bit her lips in anger.
The *anunnaki* elders sat without food to eat,
  The mighty went without wine to drink.
The wise Mami wept at what she saw,
  The divine midwife broke into tears.
"How could I have agreed with the divine assembly?
  How could I have voted for a destruction so complete?

Enlil's evil decree has gone too far,
  His words are worse than the demon Tiruru. . . .

Where is Anu, our leader, now?
  Where are the humans to carry out his commands?
Where is he who so thoughtlessly decreed a flood?
  . . . who condemned his own people to destruction?"

For seven days and seven nights the flood covered the earth. Nintu and the divine assembly wept. Because the temples were flooded and the humans were dead, there were no sacrifices for them to eat or drink. Although the text is broken at this point, by comparison with the stories of Gilgamesh, it can be assumed that the flood subsided and Atrahasis disembarked to prepare a sacrificial meal for the divine assembly.

III.v:34–45 (Gen 8:21)

The divine assembly smelled the aroma,
  They swarmed like flies around his sacrifice.

After the divine assembly had eaten their fill,
  Nintu indicted them all:
"Where is Anu, Our leader, now?
  Why has this aroma not brought Enlil here?

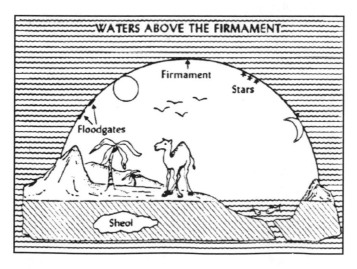

An artist's portrayal of the universe as understood by the ancient Semitic world.

Where is he who so thoughtlessly decreed a flood?
　. . . who condemned his own people to destruction?
You decreed complete destruction,
　You darkened every shining face on the earth. . . ."

III.vi:5–10

Enlil the warrior saw the barge.
Enlil was furious with the *iggigi* warriors:
　"The annunaki and the rest of the divine assembly all swore an oath.
How could anyone survive that flood?
　How did this human escape destruction?"

> *Anu immediately accuses Ea-Enki of once again interfering with the will of the divine assembly. Ea-Enki defends himself, but the final solution to human population explosion is achieved when Ea-Enki and Nintu create women who are sterile, whose newborns die from crib death, or who become celibate.*

III.vii: 1–8

Let there be three new kinds of women . . .
　Let some women be fertile,
　But let other women be sterile.
Let the demon prey on the newborn,
　Let Pashittu steal infants from their mothers' laps.
Let there be women who are taboo,
　Let them be priests forbidden to have children.

STORIES OF ADAPA

≋ The stories of Adapa are written on four clay tablets in the Akkadian language using cuneiform script. German archaeologists recovered one tablet (EA 356 = B) from the royal city of pharaoh Akhenaten (1353-1335 BCE) at Tel el Amarna in Egypt. British archaeologists recovered the other three tablets (A, C, D) from the library of the great king Ashurbanipal (668-626 BCE) at Nineveh in Assyria. The tablets are preserved today in the Vorderasiatishes Museum in Berlin and in the British Museum in London.

Adapa (Akkadian: a-da-pa) is a priest of Ea in the city of Eridu. He is human, but he inadvertently performs a divine act. Attacked by the south wind while fishing, he cripples the wind with a curse. Although the wind can do no further harm to those who fish on the lake, it also cannot bring rain to those who farm the land. The drought sets off an epidemic. Because Adapa has performed a divine act, Anu, the ruler of the divine assembly, gives Adapa the opportunity to become divine by offering him the bread of life. On the advice of Ea, his divine patron, Adapa refuses. He loses the opportunity for immortality, but returns to teach the people of Eridu how to cure human illness and stop the epidemic. People throughout the world of the Bible sang the stories to protect themselves from disease.

The gospels of Mark (Mark 4:35-41) and Luke (Luke 8:22-5) portray Jesus in the role of Adapa dueling with a windstorm on a lake. As he sinks below the raging waters, Jonah like Adapa calms the raging sea (Jonah 2:1-10). Using Augustine's long-standing interpretation of the stories of Adam and Eve in the book of Genesis, interpreters have often paralleled the role of Anu in the stories of Adapa to the role of the serpent. Both are understood to have tricked humans out of their opportunity to become immortal. In the stories of Adam and Eve, the serpent tricks the woman, whereas in the stories of Adapa, Anu tricks the man. The names "Adam" and "Adapa" are comparable. Ea does not wish to lose his servant and thus tricks him *into refusing the food that would have made him immortal. Another reading might understand Adapa to have wisely followed the advice of Ea, his divine patron, and chosen to remain mortal and enjoy the earth, rather than to become immortal and leave it. In contrast, Utnapishtim and his wife in the stories of Gilgamesh accept the invitation of the divine assembly and become immortal.*

A: Lines 4–5, 8, 15–22

Ea created Adapa to be wise,
    He had not created him to be immortal.
When the wise Ea began to create Eridu,
    He made Adapa to be a just man. . . .
Ea anointed Adapa to be his priest.
    He anointed him to sail the boats which fish for his temple in Eridu.

One day while Ea was asleep,
    Adapa went about his chores at the temple of Ea in Eridu.
He boarded his sailboat at the Harbor of the New Moon.
    The wind drove his boat far out into the lake. . . .

B: Lines 1–13

Suddenly, the south wind attacked the boat of Adapa,
    Waves swamped the boat with water.
As he sank into the water with the fish, Adapa prayed:
    "Give me the strength to break the deadly wing of this wind."
Suddenly, the wing of the south wind was broken,
    For seven days, no south wind blew across the land of Eridu.

    The damage to the south wind had grave consequences for the land of Eridu. When the south wind did not blow, there was no rain which brought drought and disease.

Then Anu, who rules the divine assembly, asked the wise Ilabrat:
    "Why has the wind not blown across the land for seven days?"
So Ilabrat told Anu:
    "Adapa, the priest of Ea, broke the wing of the south wind."
When Anu heard the charge, he stood and ordered:
    "Bring Adapa before this assembly."

*The second god from the right is probably Anu holding the waters of life,
which he hands to the naked Gilgamesh. The small objects and
animals represent the constellations of stars.*

B: Lines 14–32

To win the favor of the divine assembly, Ea advised Adapa:
   "Do not comb your hair, and do not wash your clothes. . . .
When you come before the divine assembly at the gate of Anu,
   Tammuz and Gizzida will question you.
'Mortal, for whom are you mourning?
   Why have you not combed your hair or washed your clothes?'
Answer their question with these words:
   'I am mourning for two gods who have left Eridu.'
When they ask: 'Who are these two gods missing from Eridu?'
   Tell them: 'Tammuz and Gizzida.'
Tammuz and Gizzida will be flattered.
   They will support your case before Anu.
   The verdict of Anu will be in your favor.

When Anu offers you bread to eat,
   Do not eat it.
When Anu offers you water to drink,
   Do not drink it.
When Anu offers you a garment and oil for your body,
   Clothe and anoint yourself."

The god Ea with two men wrestling and a fisherman.

〰️ *Events occur just as Ea described them. Adapa gains the support of Tammuz and Gizzida, and their support causes Anu, the ruler of the divine assembly, to decide that a mortal who has been given the knowledge to "...break the wing of the south wind" must join the divine assembly. Therefore he offers Adapa the bread and water of life.*

B: Lines 66–70 (Gen 3:22)

Anu handed down the verdict of the divine assembly;
   Anu pardoned Adapa for stilling the wind.
"Adapa, come join the divine assembly.
   Eat our life-giving bread. Drink our life-giving water.
   You, mortal, will become immortal."
But Adapa replied: "Ea, my divine patron, told me:
   'Do not eat their bread or drink their water.'"
So, the divine assembly decreed:
   "Send this mortal back home to earth."

D: Lines 4–6, 15–7

Then Anu laughed at the actions of Ea,
   "Let the assembly decide if another . . . has ever outsmarted the
      word of Anu.

"Whatever ill Adapa has brought upon the people of Eridu,
    The disease which he brought to their bodies,
Ninkarrak, the divine patron of physicians, will relieve.
    Let the illness be removed,
    Let the disease be turned aside!"

NUZI ARCHIVES

🔖 *Nuzi (Arabic:* **Yorghun Tepe***) is one-hundred fifty miles north of Baghdad, eight miles southwest of Kirkuk and ten miles east of the Zagros mountains in northeastern Iraq today. The city flourished for about one-hundred fifty years during the Late Bronze period (1500–1250 BCE), and was destroyed by the Assyrians. Nuzi was excavated between 1920-30 by R. F. S. Starr. Some three-thousand five-hundred tablets were collected from the house of the ruler (Akkadian:* **hazannu***) of Nuzi, from sanctuaries, from rich and poor neighborhoods in the city itself, and from its outlying villages. They are not written in the Hurrian language of Nuzi, but in the Babylonian dialect of Akkadian using cuneiform. Sumerian, Hurrian and Elamite are neither Indo-European nor Semitic languages. Hurrians appeared in both Syria-Palestine and northern Mesopotamia, where Nuzi was an important city in the state of Mittani. The Nuzi archives are preserved today in the Iraq Museum in Baghdad.*

The Nuzi archives provide some of the best social scientific evidence for the political, economic and legal practices in the stories of Abraham and Sarah (Gen 11:27—25:18), and of Jacob, Leah and Rachel (Gen 25:20—37:2) in the book of Genesis. The similarities between these two cultures may be due to the widespread distribution of Hurrian peoples throughout the ancient Near East.

Mitannian seals from Nuzi in Iraq.

CERTIFICATE OF ADOPTION

≋ *Technically, in the world of the Bible, a household could not sell its land. Nonetheless, with a certificate of adoption (Akkadian:* tuppi maruti*), the father of a household could adopt a member of another household, who then became eligible to "inherit" land from the household in return for a "gift." In the stories of Abraham and Sarah in the book of Genesis (Gen 15:2-3), Abraham uses this legal remedy to adopt Eliezer of Damascus as an heir because he and Sarah have no natural children. Similarly, when Sarah gives her slave Hagar to Abraham as a surrogate mother, the implication is that the child produced will be the legal son of Sarah (Gen 16:1-5). Also at Nuzi, only heirs could inherit the statues of the divine patrons of their households. Therefore, when Rachel lays claim to the statues of the divine patrons (Hebrew:* teraphim*) of her household in the book of Genesis (Gen 31:1-21), she is declaring that her son, and not the son of Leah or the sons of her brothers, will be heir to the household of Laban.*

C.J. Gadd xxiii (1929), 49–161, No. 51

Nashwi from the household of Ar-shenni hereby adopts Wullu from the household of Puhi-shenni. In return, Wullu must provide Nashwi with food and clothing for as long as he lives. When Nashwi dies, Wullu shall inherit his land. If, subsequently, Nashwi has a natural son, Wullu and this son must divide the land of the household equally. The natural son of Nashwi, however, shall receive the statues of the divine patrons of the household. If, however, Nashwi dies without a natural son, then Wullu shall receive the statues of the divine patrons of the household.

Nashwi hereby gives his daughter, Nuhuya, to Wullu in marriage. If, subsequently, Wullu divorces Nuhuya, he must return the land and houses of Nashwi, and pay a fine of eighteen ounces (Akkadian: *mina*) of silver and eighteen ounces of gold.

≋ *A list of witnesses and the name of the official who negotiated the covenant are attached.*

CERTIFICATE OF ADOPTION

≋ *Certificates of adoption often deal with various eventualities. If a father of a household adopts a son, and subsequently has a natural child, then the status of the adopted son is altered. If a mother of the household is infertile, she designates a slave to be her surrogate mother. The surrogate's children are adopted by the mother and father of her household. In addition, care was taken to prevent the transfer of the land and children of one household to another in the event that only daughters were born to the mother and father of the household. In such a case, the daughters become eligible to inherit like the daughters of Zelophehad in the book of Numbers (Num 36).*

HSS 5.67 (Gen 16:1–5; 30:1–8; Num 36:1–12)

Suriha-ilu hereby adopts Sennima, son of Zike, from the household of Akkuya and gives him his land, his houses, and all his possessions. If Suriha-ilu has a natural son, then this child will inherit twice as much as Sennima. As long as he lives, Sennima will honor Suriha-ilu as father of his household. When Suriha-ilu dies, Sennima will then become father of the household (Akkadian: *ewuru*).

Suriha-ilu hereby gives his daughter Kelim-ninu to Sennima as his wife. If she has children, then Sennima may not take another wife. If Kelim-ninu is infertile, then she is to give Sennima a slave as a surrogate mother for his child. Kelim-ninu will adopt the child born to her slave as her own. . . .

The sons of Kelim-ninu and Sennima will inherit my land, my houses, and all my other possessions. If Kelim-ninu has only daughters, then Kelim-ninu's daughters will inherit my land and houses.

Suriha-ilu hereby declares that he will not adopt any other sons than Sennima.

Whoever violates this covenant is required to pay a penalty of eighteen ounces (Akkadian: *mina*) of silver and eighteen ounces of gold.

Suriha-ilu hereby gives Yalampa to Kelim-ninu as her slave.

Suriha-ilu hereby appoints his sister, Satim-ninu, as to be the legal guardian of Kelim-ninu.

As long as she lives, Sennima shall honor Kelim-ninu as his wife. Satim-ninu may not abrogate this marriage covenant (Akkadian: "untie the knot").

If Kelim-ninu has children, and Sennima marries another wife, then he forfeits his authority over the land and children of Kelim-ninu (Akkadian: "tears the hem off his tunic"). . . .

No other son of Zike is to inherit the land or houses of Suriha-ilu.

▤ *A list of witnesses is attached.*

LAST WILL AND TESTAMENT OF ARIPPABNI, SON OF SHILWA-TESUB

≋ In patrilineal cultures like Nuzi and ancient Israel, the land and children of a household were inherited by males related to the father of the household. The beloved son or heir (Akkadian: maru rabu) received the largest share. Typically, the oldest son became the heir, received the statues of the divine patrons of the household, and cared for (Akkadian: "showed proper respect for") the mother of the household, its marriageable women and all its children. Wills (Akkadian: tuppi simti) from Nuzi, however, show that fathers of the household could designate heirs who were not their oldest sons, divide property as they chose, and make various stipulations about the use of property, the ownership of the statues of the divine patrons of their households, and the responsibilities of their wives and children. In the Bible, the blessing of Isaac (Gen 27:27-9) and the blessing of Jacob (Gen 48:15-20) are wills in which fathers designate heirs and distribute the land and children of their households without adhering to the age of the beneficiaries.

HSS 19.17

. . . all my lands, houses, and possessions . . . are to be divided equally between my three sons: Akibtashenni, Turrishenni, and Palteya.

I also appoint my daughter, Ukkie, as legal guardian of the land, houses, and possessions of my sons. As long as Ukkie lives, my three sons shall honor her as mother of their households. . . . If any of my three sons fails to obey Ukkie, then she may punish him in the same manner that she would her own son.

No other son of mine shall inherit any of my lands, houses, or other possessions.

≋ Witnesses and seal impressions appended here.

CERTIFICATE OF ADOPTION

≋ Twice Abraham called his wife, Sarah, his "sister" (Gen 12:10-9; 20:1-14). In the Nuzi archives, there are certificates of adoption (Akkadian: tuppi ahatuti) in which the father of the household adopts a woman as a sister, and becomes her legal guardian. The economic relationships of the father of a household to a sister, to a wife and to a daughter are similar, but not identical.

AASOR 16.54

I, Kuni-asu, daughter of Hut-tesup, declare before witnesses: "Previously, Akam-musni negotiated a marriage covenant for me and received thirteen ounces (Akkadian: forty shekels) of silver as a bride price. Akam-musni and my husband are now dead. Now, Akkiya, son of Hut-tesup, has adopted me (Akkadian: "seized me in the street") as his sister. As my legal guardian, he shall negotiate a marriage covenant for me and will receive three ounces (Akkadian: ten shekels) of silver as a bride price."

Whoever breaks this covenant shall pay a fine of eighteen ounces (Akkadian: *mina*) of gold.

COVENANT BETWEEN SHILWA-TESHUB AND URHIYA

Households with more livestock than they could herd themselves negotiated covenants with households of herders to graze and breed the animals for them. Owners negotiated to pay herders either a flat fee or a commission. A herder's fee might be a certain number of young stock or a weight of wool, dairy products, clothing or grain. Owners expected eighty percent or about twenty ewes in each herd of thirty-eight animals to bear lambs. They expected to lose fifteen percent or five to six animals to predators or disease. Consequently, some owners paid their herders with all the lambs over the projected eighty percent increase or with any animals that survived the projected fifteen percent loss. The Bible characterizes the household of Abraham and Sarah and the household of Jacob, Leah and Rachel as semi-nomadic herders who care for livestock from both their own villages and the villages of others.

HSS 9.64 (Gen 30:27–34)

Shilwa-teshub, the father of the household, has entrusted two fertile female sheep, seven castrated male sheep, one male lamb, eleven fertile female goats, seven male goats, two male kids and one female kid, a total of thirty-one livestock, to the herder, Urhiya, son of Ikkianni.

PROMISSORY NOTE OF HUTIP-APU, SON OF EHLIP-APU

Promissory notes (Akkadian: muddu) record a herder's commitments to repay the owner for any animals lost because of negligence. Herders were not responsible for animals lost due to an "act of God

Map of ancient Mesopotamia.

(Akkadian: lipit ilim*)," and they might be excused from repaying the loss if the livestock were killed by another animal, after the hides of the lost animals were studied by the owners. A sheep lost due to negligence cost the herder about three months' salary (Akkadian:* one and one-third shekels*).*

HSS 13.385

The herder, Hutip-apu, son of Ehlip-apu, acknowledges the receipt of . . . three fertile female sheep, five lambs, two castrated male sheep, four kids, a total of fourteen livestock. . . .

Annals of Hatshepsut

≋〗 *Hatshepsut (1504-1482 BCE) was the daughter of Thutmoses I (1525-1508) and the childless widow of Thutmoses II (1508-1504 BCE). When Thutmoses II died, Hatshepsut ruled Egypt initially as co-regent with Thutmoses III (1482-1450 BCE), who was the child of a secondary wife. She then took the unprecedented step of declaring herself pharaoh. Twice before in Egypt, queens had reigned for brief periods, but never had they taken the title of pharaoh. Hatshepsut, like many rulers in the world of the Bible, was celebrated as a child of God, conceived in a marriage between a human mother and a divine father. The annals of Hatshepsut, which tell her birth story, are taken from a group of reliefs and inscriptions found in the Deir el-Bahri temple in the valley of the pharaohs at Thebes. They were found during the excavations of the Egypt Exploration Fund, under the direction of the Swiss archaeologist Edouard Naville in 1894. The annals of Hatshepsut describing her care of Egypt are inscribed on the architrave of a temple to Pakhet that she built at Speos Artemidos (Arabic: Istabl Antar) fifteen miles south of El Amarna.*

The annals describe the intercourse between Amon Ra, her divine father, and Ahmose, her human mother. Then, Khnum shapes Hatshepsut and her ka (soul) as a young boy on a potter's wheel. When Ahmose goes into labor, she is led into a birthing room attended by Bes, divine patron of midwives, and gives birth under the divine protection of Thoth, Khnum and Heqet, a divine patron of childbearing. The annals of Hatshepsut describe her as an ideal ruler protecting Egypt from its enemies, and providing food for its people.

The annunciation to the wife of Manoah in the stories of Samson (Judg 13:1-23), the annunciation to Hannah in the books of Samuel-Kings (1 Sam 1:9-18), and the annunciation to Mary in the New Testament (Luke 1:26-38) parallel the annals of Hatshepsut's

52

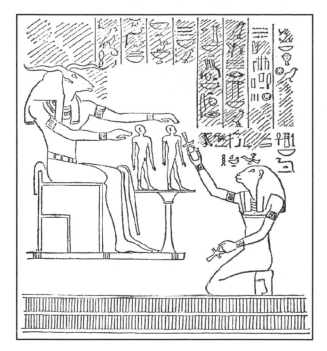

Ram-headed Khnum, the god of creation, forms the body of Queen Hatshepsut and her ka. *The* ka *is the immortal substance in humans that generally corresponds to our "soul." (From her mortuary temple at Deir 'el-Bahri at Thebes; 18th dynasty, about 1480 B.C.E.)*

description of her birth. The annals of Solomon in the books of Samuel-Kings (1 Kgs 3:1-15) parallel the annals of Hatshepsut's description of her care of Egypt. Both Hatshepsut and Solomon describe themselves as rulers with "...an understanding heart."

Deir el-Bahri, north colonnade

▤ *Hatshepsut's inscriptions at Deir el-Bahri have been badly damaged. Therefore, some restoration is based on the parallel inscription of Amenhotep III at Luxor.*

"I, Ahmose, dare to speak.
   The queen says to Amon Ra, the powerful,
To Amon Ra, the glorious,
   To Amon Ra, the divine patron of Thebes:

'How great is your power.
   How perfect. . . .

Your heart guides my heart.
　　Your breath is in all my limbs.
I am your servant.
　　Do with me what you will.'"

"I, Amon Ra, promise Ahmose,
　　The divine patron of Thebes says to the queen:
'I have given you a child,
　　You will name her Hatshepsut. . . .
She will reign over the land of Egypt. . . .'"

"I, Amon Ra, now command Khnum,
　　The divine patron of Thebes says to the divine potter:
'Go, create this child,
　　Give Hatshepsut my soul (Egyptian: *ka*).
Make her a child of God.
　　Give the daughter I have begotten life,
Give her strength, and happiness,
　　Endow her with the gifts and offerings of Amon Ra forever.'"

*A reconstructed drawing of the god Khnum modeling Hatshepsut
on his wheel, while the ibis-headed god Thoth records it.*

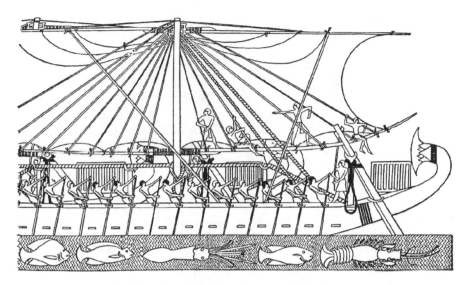

An Egyptian ship from the time of Hatshepsut.

≋ *Khnum affirms that he will do as Amon Ra commands and then
proceeds to fashion the child and her* ka *(soul) on a potter's wheel.
While he works, Khnum repeats the words of Amon Ra.*

"I, Khnum, say to Hatshepsut,
    The divine potter says to the child of Amon Ra:
'I have created you from the divine patron of Karnak.
    I have made you a child of God.
I have given you life,
    I have endowed you with strength and happiness.
You will reign over every land and all peoples.
    I have endowed you with all gifts and offerings. . . .
I will set you above the *ka* [souls] of all creatures,
    You will shine over Upper and Lower Egypt,
You will rule both south and north,
    You will govern according to the command of your loving father.'"

≋ *The actual birth of the child is represented in a relief depicting the
mother sitting enthroned and holding the child while four female
deities stand before her as midwives. They extend their arms to
receive the child while Meskhenet, the goddess of births, gives
instructions to the divine midwives. Their brief utterances are promises of happiness and a glorious reign.*

Speos Artemidos

Between 1640–1532 BCE, a Semitic people whom the Egyptians called "Hyksos" conquered Egypt and permanently destroyed its protective isolation from the rest of the ancient Near East. Hyksos pharaohs adopted Seth as their divine patron and replaced the households that had traditionally ruled Egypt with foreign bureaucrats. Eventually, Ahmose (1550–1525 BCE) led a successful revolt against the Hyksos and founded the New Kingdom (1550–1070 BCE) during which Hatshepsut ruled. The annals of Hatshepsut reveal Egypt's lingering indignation against them.

*Asiatic, Ethiopian and central African captives
brought before Pharaoh Ramses II.*

Let all the earth know that I have ruled with an understanding heart. I have not slept. I have not forgotten to do anything. I have rebuilt all the villages, cities and temples which those Asiatics at Avaris (Greek: *Tanis*; Arabic: *San el-Hagar*) in the north had destroyed or had allowed to fall into ruins and become haunted by criminals and fugitives. These Asiatics ruled without the consent of Ra, and their descendants refused his divine command to acknowledge me as pharaoh.

Now I am established upon the throne of Ra. I was born to be a divine warrior, striking out at my enemies like the uraeus serpent of Horus which rides upon my brow. I have driven the enemies of the divine assembly into exile. Their footprints have vanished in the sand.

I have done everything which Amon Ra, the father of my predecessors, has decreed. No one whom Amon Ra protects shall be harmed. My reign will endure like the mountains. My name will last as long as Amon Ra the sun shines, and as long as his rays illuminate my royal titles carved throughout the land. Horus the falcon will soar above the obelisks bearing my name for all eternity.

ANNALS OF DEDUMOSES

🏳 *Dedumoses was pharaoh in 1640 BCE when the Hyksos conquered Egypt. His annals were a source for a history of Egypt written in Greek by Manetho (323-245 BCE). This Egyptian priest wrote his history to instruct Greek-speaking peoples of the grandeur of Egypt from the days of the first pharaohs until the conquest of Egypt by Alexander the Great in 332 BCE. It is preserved only as quotations in the works of the Jewish historian Flavius Josephus (37-100 CE) and in the works of some early Christian writers, such as Eusebius (260-339 CE).*

The annals of Dedumoses, like the annals of Hatshepsut, portray the Hyksos as barbaric and merciless conquerors from the north, who swept through Syria-Palestine and turned a once fertile Egypt into a desert. Although the linguistic structure of the Hyksos' names clearly indicates they were a federation of more than one ethnic group, they were primarily a Semitic people. The Egyptians nicknamed them "Hyksos," which carried the same animosity as "damn Yankees" or "carpetbaggers" in the American South following the War between the States.

From 1720-1552 BCE, Hyksos pharaohs in Memphis and Avaris or Tanis opened the borders and government of Egypt to non-Egyptians like Joseph whose teachings close the book of Genesis (Gen 41:9—47:12). In 1552, Kamose and Ahmose, who were native

Serekh *(emblem)*
of King Amosis.

Egyptians from the south, drove the Hyksos back into Syria-Palestine, and degraded the social standing of all Semites in Egypt. These are the days and the conditions reflected in the opening of the book of Exodus (Exod 1:7—13:16).

Manetho, Aegyptiaca, *frag. 42 in Manetho*, Against Apion *1.75–92*

During the reign of pharaoh Dedumoses (Greek: *Tutimaeus*), the wrath of the divine assembly struck Egypt unexpectedly from the east. These Hyksos fanatics (Greek: *asemoi*) marched confidently to victory against our land. They easily overpowered pharaoh and his governors. They ruthlessly burned our cities, and razed the temples of Egypt's divine assembly to the ground. They treated the people of Egypt with hostility and cruelty. They massacred our soldiers. They enslaved our women and children. Finally, they appointed Salitis, one of their own, to be pharaoh. From his palace in Memphis, Salitis dispatched Hyksos soldiers and officials to the most strategic locations in the land to collect financial restitution from both southern and northern Egypt.

The first priority of Salitis was to fortify the eastern border of the Delta, in anticipation that the Assyrians, as they grew stronger, would one day covet and attack Egypt. So, in the name of Sais, Salitis restored the ancient city of Avaris situated at a commanding site on the east bank of

An Egyptian chariot of pharaoh.

Bubas, a branch of the Nile. To defend the border, he reconstructed its buildings, surrounded it with a massive wall, and stationed two-hundred forty thousand of the best Hyksos soldiers there. Salitis would spend summers at Avaris meeting with government officials and military commanders, and conducting military maneuvers designed to paralyze his enemies with fear of the army. Salitis reigned thirteen years. He was succeeded by Beon, who reigned for forty-four years. . . . The first six Hyksos rulers never stopped making war on the Egyptian people, whom they were committed to exterminate. . . .

Eventually, the native Egyptian rulers of Thebes declared their independence of the Hyksos, and a long and hard-fought revolt quickly spread across the rest of Egypt. Finally . . . all the Hyksos were driven into a small area around Avaris . . . fortified with a massive enclosure wall. . . . An army of four-hundred eighty thousand Egyptian soldiers laid siege to Avaris. Having realized there was no hope, the Hyksos negotiated a treaty that guaranteed them safe conduct out of Egypt. . . . Two-hundred forty thousand Hyksos left Egypt for Syria. . . .

STORIES OF
ANUBIS AND BATA

≋ *Stories of the two brothers, twins or rivals, were popular throughout the ancient Near East. In Egypt, their names were "Anubis" and "Bata" or "Seth" and "Horus." The Hebrews called them "Cain" and "Abel." Before 1860, French archaeologists had recovered a copy of the stories of Anubis and Bata, as they were being told during the nineteenth dynasty (1307-1196 BCE). The stories were written on papyrus, not in hieroglyphic characters, but in a hieratic or cursive style of writing. This D'Orbiney manuscript is preserved today in the British Museum (#10183).*

The stories of Anubis and Bata tell of two brothers who work together successfully to graze and farm their land. Their rivalry for children, however, leaves them both infertile.

The twin-motif in creation stories reflects two important convictions developed by cultures along the Nile and Euphrates. They believed that life and death were present right from the beginning. Twins came into the world not only bringing twice the life of a single birth, but also the death brought on by sibling rivalry. Twins appear again and again in Egypt's world-view. There is Upper Egypt or the Nile Valley and Lower Egypt or the Nile Delta; the desert under the protection of Seth and the farmland under the protection of Horus; the growing season and the flood season; the world of the living to the east and the world of the dead to the west. Like all creation stories, those with twins explain how humans learned to use divine power to herd, to farm, to bear children, to pray and to wage war. Agriculture, sexuality, worship and combat all appear in the stories of Anubis and Bata. Twins, brothers or rivals like Anubis and Bata, also appear in the stories of Cain and Abel (Gen 4:3-16), the stories of Jacob and Esau (Gen 25:19—33:20), and the stories of

Joseph and his brothers (Gen 37:1—45:28). The propositioning of a slave by the master's wife also has a parallel in the teachings of Joseph (Gen 39:1-21). The talking animal who saves the life of its master in the stories of Anubis and Bata is parallel to the ass that talks with Balaam in the book of Numbers (Num 22:28-30).

Once there were two brothers: Anubis was the older, Bata the younger. Anubis was a villager, who was married and owned his own house. Bata was under the care of his brother and lived with him like a son. In return for living in the household of Anubis and wearing the clothes that Anubis bought for him, Bata tended the cattle of Anubis, plowed his fields, tended his crops, brought in his harvests. Bata was young, but he was righteous and blameless in his generation, so the divine assembly of Egypt often let him use their power.

i:5–10

Every day, after Bata finished grazing the cattle, he headed back to the village loaded down with vegetables, milk and firewood, everything he needed to prepare supper for Anubis and his wife. After supper, Bata went out to the barn to sleep with the cattle.

Every morning, Bata got up, cooked the morning meal for Anubis and his wife, and packed a meal for his brother to eat at noon. Then Bata drove the cattle out into the pasture to graze. As he walked alongside the cattle, they would say to him: "The grass in this pasture is excellent," and Bata would listen to them and drive them to whatever pasture they wanted to graze, so Anubis' cattle became prime livestock, calving twice as often as the livestock from any other village.

Egyptian farmers plowing with oxen.
(From tomb 2, Beni Hasan, 19th century B.C.E.)

Harvesting flax, and other agricultural chores.
(Tomb 2, Beni Hasan; 19th century, B.C.E.)

ii:1–5 (Gen 30:40–2)

Now when it was time to plow, Anubis told Bata: "Tomorrow is the first day of plowing. Be sure the oxen are ready to be yoked and the seed is ready to be planted, first thing in the morning."

The younger brother did everything his older brother told him to do. At the break of dawn, Anubis and Bata hurried to the fields with their seed in order to start plowing. They were delighted with how well the work was going.

After a while, they ran short of seed. So Anubis sent his younger brother to the village to get more. When Bata got to the house, the wife of Anubis was sitting there combing her hair. Bata said to her: "I need seed for the field; my older brother is waiting for me. Hurry!"

iii:1–5 (Gen 39:7–12)

Then she said to him: "Go and open the bin and take what you want. I am not finished combing my hair."

Bata went to the barn, took a large jar and filled it with barley and emmer seed and hoisted the jar on his shoulders.

When the wife of Anubis saw Bata, she said: "How much seed are you carrying?"

Bata answered: "Three measures of emmer, two measures of barley: five in all."

Then she said: "My, you are certainly strong. Every day I notice your bulging muscles." To convince Bata to have intercourse with her, the wife of Anubis jumped up and threw her arms around him. "Sleep with me just this once, and I will sew some new clothes for you," she pleaded.

Bata became furious as a leopard at the very thought of sleeping with his brother's wife. His anger terrified her. "You have got to be crazy!"

Leading cattle back to the barns. (Tomb 3, Beni Hasan, 19th century, B.C.E.)

he shouted at her. "You and your husband are like a mother and father to me. Because he was older than I, he reared me. How can you possibly suggest I commit a crime like this against him? Listen, if you promise never to proposition me again like this, I won't tell anyone what you said."

iv:1–5

Then Bata shouldered the seed and left for the field. He rejoined his brother, and they worked hard all day together. When the sun set, Anubis left for home, while Bata tended to the cattle and picked up all the equipment. Then he drove the cattle home so that they could sleep in their own barn in the village.

Meanwhile, the wife of Anubis was afraid of getting into trouble for what she had done. So she drank grease to make herself sick. . . . She neither trimmed nor lit the lamps when it got dark. She did not bring Anubis any water to wash his hands when he got home. She just lay there vomiting. . . .

v:1–5 (Gen 39:17–9; Num 22:28–30)

When Anubis returned, she told him: ". . . When your brother came back for some seed, I was here alone. He propositioned me: 'Let your hair down and sleep with me just this once!' I would not pay any attention to him. 'Aren't I like a mother to you?' I pleaded. 'Isn't your older brother like a father to you?' But he panicked and beat me so that I would not tell you. Now, if you let him live, I will kill myself. . . ."

Anubis became as furious as a leopard. He fetched his spear, sharpened it and stood behind the barn door to wait for Bata to return with the cattle later that evening.

. . . when the first cow went into the barn, she warned Bata: "Your older brother is waiting to kill you with his spear. Run!"

vi:5–10 (Ps 7:11)

. . . as soon as Bata looked under the door of the barn and saw his older brother's feet . . . he dropped the tools he was carrying and ran. His older brother chased him with his spear.

Bata began to pray: "Ra-Harakhti, you are my divine patron . . . only you can judge between the just and the unjust."

The moment Ra heard his prayer, he created a lake full of crocodiles around Bata to protect him from his older brother. . . .

vii:5–10 (Num 30:12; 2 Chron 6:22)

When it was dawn and Ra-Harakhti rose over the horizon, Bata argued his case with his older brother in broad daylight. "Why are you hunting me? Why do you want to kill me without giving me a chance to speak in my defense? I am still your younger brother. You and your wife are like father and mother to me. . . ." Then Bata told him everything that had happened. He swore to the truth of his story with an oath and an ordeal.

"So help me Ra-Harakhti, only an unfaithful wife could get you to take up your spear and try to kill me for no reason at all." Then, he took his knife, cut off his penis and threw it into the lake where a catfish swallowed it. . . .

viii:7–10 (2 Kgs 9:36)

Bata went into exile in Lebanon, the Valley of the Cedars, and Anubis set off for home in the morning. He struck his forehead with his hand and smeared his face with dirt. When he got home, he killed his wife, and fed her body to the dogs. Then he mourned his younger brother. . . .

≋ *The story concludes when the divine assembly provides Bata with a wife. Eventually he becomes pharaoh. Later Bata is reconciled with his elder brother, who succeeds him as pharaoh.*

STORIES OF AQHAT

⌘ *Ugarit was an important commercial center on what is today the northern coast of Syria. It connected the trade lanes between Egypt to the south, islands like Crete to the west and Mesopotamia to the east. Culture followed Ugarit's prosperity especially between 1500-1250 BCE. Among this period's magnificent works of art and tradition, recovered by a French excavation directed by C.A. Schaeffer during twenty-two seasons between 1929-1960, are the stories of Aqhat. They are written on three baked clay tablets (CTA 17-19) in Ugaritic, a Semitic language like Hebrew. Ugaritic uses wedge-shaped, cuneiform characters, but the characters represent individual sounds from an alphabet, rather than syllables, which was the earlier method used in Mesopotamian cuneiform writing and the hieroglyphics of Egypt as well. They are preserved today in the Louvre Museum in Paris.*

The stories of Aqhat portray him as a wise son and a wise hunter. Danil is Aqhat's father, Danatiya is his mother, Paghat is his sister. Danil and Danatiya are unable to have a son until Ba'al, their divine patron, helps them. When he reaches puberty, Kothar-wa-Hasis, the divine metalworker, makes the boy a unique and powerful bow and arrows. Jealous that Aqhat will not sell her his weapons, Anat, divine patron of love and war, hires Yatpan to assassinate him. Paghat subsequently avenges his death.

There are parallels to the barren-wife motif in the stories of Aqhat in the books of Genesis (Gen 15:1-4, 16:1-15, 18:9-15, 25:21, 30:1-24), of Judges (Judg 13:2-3), and of Samuel-Kings (1 Sam 1:2-17; 2 Kgs 4:8-17). The motif describes a couple who want, but cannot have a child. Yahweh intervenes to announce the impending birth of a child. Miraculous events highlight the birth of their child who is destined to deliver the people. Some of the episodes from the stories of Aqhat also appear in a story of Hagar (Gen 21:9-21) where Ishmael plays Aqhat's role of the great hunter whose life is threat-

*ened by Sarah, playing the role of Anat, and whose life is saved by
Hagar, who plays the role of Paghat. In the stories of Jacob and Esau
(Gen 27:1-45), it is Esau who plays Aqhat the hunter, whose mother
Rebekah, playing the role of Anat, tries to take away his inheritance.*

*A i:1–42 (Gen 1:1—2:4a; Deut 14:26; 32:38; 2 Sam 12:15–18;
Neh 8:18; 9:20–3; Isa 51:17–18; Hos 7:5)*

≋ *The stories of Aqhat open with Danil engaged in a ritual of incubation during which he sleeps in the sanctuary and prays that he
and Danatiya will be able to have a son. For seven days, Danil feeds
the members of the divine assembly. Then, on the seventh day,
Ba'al, the divine patron of Ugarit, stands and addresses El, the ruler
of the divine assembly.*

On the first day, Danil prepared food for his divine patrons to eat,
  The powerful one mixed wine for the divine assembly to drink.
Then the protégé of Harnam unrolled his mat in the sanctuary,
  Danil lay down and went to sleep. . . .
On the seventh day, Ba'al stood up before El.
  The divine patron of Ugarit addressed the divine assembly.
"The once-powerful Danil is now powerless,
  He is shamed for lack of a son.
Surely he should have a son like his brothers,
  He needs an heir like his covenant partners.
He has blessed the divine assembly with food,
  He has filled their sanctuaries with drink.
Bless Danil with a son and show that you are El the Bull.
  Build Danil a house with a child and show that you are my father.
Raise up a son for his household and show that you are father of all.
  Establish an heir in his palace.
Give Danil a son to erect a stele for the divine patrons of his ancestors,
  To build a shrine for the household of Danil in their sanctuary.
Name Danil a son to free him from death,
  To walk beside him to the grave.
Lift up Aqhat to punish those who revolt against his father,
  To drive out those who invade his land.
Make Aqhat strong enough to support Danil, when he drinks at the
      sanctuary,
  To put Danil's arm over his shoulder, when he is filled with spirits,
To eat his funeral meal in the sanctuary of Ba'al,
  To offer sacrifice in the house of El,

To patch Danil's roof after it rains,
    To clean his soiled clothing."

El took his servant by the hand
    He blessed Danil the powerful,
    He showed favor to the protégé of Harnam.
"Let Danil enjoy the bliss of his bed.
    When he kisses Danatiya, she will become pregnant.
    When he holds her in his arms, she will conceive.
Let Danatiya conceive and give birth.
    Let there be a son in the household of Danil.
    Let there be an heir in his palace. . . . "

A ii:8–15, 25–42 (Gen 17:17; Exod 34:29–35)

Danil lifted up his face.
    His skin was shining.
Danil put his head back and laughed,
    Put his feet up on his footstool and roared.
Danil began to sing: "Now I can sit and rest.
    Now my spirit can be at ease.
For a son like those my brothers have will be born to me.
    I will have an heir like those of my covenant partners."

≊ *For seven days, Danil entertains the midwives (French:* femmes sages*),*
    who will assist him and Danatiya with the birth of Aqhat.

Danil went home,
    He entered his palace.
On the first day, the midwives arrived,
    The singers and the chanters entered the household of Danil.
The powerful one roasted an ox for the midwives,
    The protégé of Harnam threw a feast for them.
He gave wine to the skillful midwives,
    He provided food for the singers and the chanters. . . .
On the seventh day, the midwives left his house,
    The singers and the chanters departed.
Then Danil and Danatiya experienced the joy of sex,
    They enjoyed the bliss of bed. . . .

Parts of the tablet are missing. When the story picks up again, Aqhat has reached puberty and is about to become a man. Kothar-wa-hasis, the divine metalworker, is talking about making a bow and arrows for him.

A.v:2–28 (Gen 18:2, 6–7; 19:1; Judg 4:5; Ruth 4:1; 2 Sam 15:2; 1 Kgs 22:10)

. . . Kothar-wa-hasis announced: "I will deliver a bow to Aqhat."
  The divine metalworker will present him with his arrows.
On the seventh day, Danil was in the gate,
  The powerful one sat at the threshing floor beneath a great tree.
Here, Danil judged the widow's complaint,
  Here, he heard the orphan's case.
In the distance, Kothar-wa-hasis appeared running with giant strides.
  Danil saw him carrying a bow and a quiver of arrows.
The powerful one called to Danatiya: "Prepare a lamb from the flock.
  Cook Kothar-wa-hasis his favorite meal.

*An Egyptian stringing his bow
(tomb painting).*

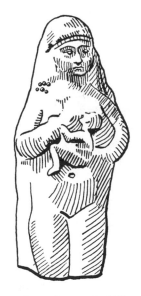

*A mother and child
(late 3rd millennium;
Sumero-Akkadian period).*

Kothar-wa-hasis is hungry,
   The master craftsman wants something to eat. . . ."
Kothar-wa-hasis put the bow in Danil's hands,
   He laid the arrows in his lap. . . .

❁ *Aqhat uses his divine bow and arrows to become a mighty hunter*
   (Gen 10:9; 21:20–1). Anat, the divine patron of love and war, tries to
   woo Aqhat and win his bow and arrows.

A.vi:18–45 (Ps 10:6; Isa 14:25; 41:25)

Anat promised Aqhat: "Ask for silver and I'll give it to you.
   Ask for gold and it will be yours.
Just give the divine patron of love and war your bow.
   Let the virgin have your arrows."

"No, Anat," Aqhat replied.
   "I will bring you yew trees from the mountains of Lebanon,
I will harvest sinews from wild oxen,
   And horns from mountain goats.
I will collect tendons from the legs of bulls,
   And reeds from the marshes.
You can give them to Kothar-wa-hasis.
   Let the divine craftsman build a bow and arrows for Anat."

Anat continued: "Ask for life without end, and I will give it to you,
   Ask for immortality and I will grant it to you.
Your years will be as countless as the years of Ba'al,
   Your months like the son of El.
Ba'al will bestow on you immortality,
   He will feast you at his table forever.
Ba'al will give you the bread of life,
   He will serve you the wine of everlasting life.
Ba'al will honor your name in endless song,
   Storytellers will sing of you forever."

"Do not lie to me, Anat," Aqhat replied.
   "Do not waste your lies on humans like me, Virgin.
Mortals cannot become immortals.
   What becomes of mortals?
We are faces to be masked with plaster,
   We are skulls to be daubed with lime.

All mortals die,
   And death is my mortal end.
My bow is the weapon of a man at war,
   Can it arm a woman on the prowl?"

Anat roared, "Listen to me, Aqhat."
   The Virgin exclaimed: "Listen for your own good.
Your arrogance will cross my path again,
   Your presumption will lead you back to me.
I will overthrow you,
   I will trample you under my feet, my darling he-man."

Anat storms off to the divine assembly where she tries to get El to punish Aqhat. El refuses, but also agrees not to stand in Anat's way of getting revenge. So, Anat designs a plan to gain Aqhat's confidence so that she can murder him and take his bow. Anat sets her plan in motion by showing Aqhat a good place to hunt. Leaving him there to enjoy himself, she goes off and changes Yatpan, her accomplice, into a vulture. While Aqhat is field-dressing one of his kills, Yatpan, now disguised as a vulture, approaches him without arousing his suspicion (Gen 15:11). Swooping in behind him, Yatpan changes back into a human, and stuns Aqhat with a single blow to the head. He then murders him with three surgically placed blows to the temple.

B.iv:28–40

Anat hired Yatpan as an accomplice,
   She disguised him as a vulture. . . .
When Aqhat was dressing his kill in the field,
   When the son of Danil was preparing his meal in the open,
Vultures circled over his head,
   Birds of prey soared in the sky above.
Anat hid Yatpan among the birds of prey,
   Camouflaged him among the vultures swooping down on Aqhat.
Yatpan struck Aqhat twice on the head,
   He hit him three times behind the ear.
The blood of Aqhat ran down the arms of his assassin,
   Drenched the legs of his murderer.
The breath of Aqhat departed like the wind,
   He exhaled his last breath like a gentle breeze,
      The vapor clung to his face like a wisp of smoke.

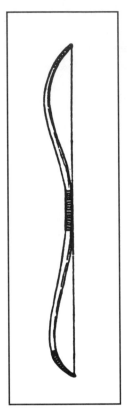

A double convex bow used by Semitic warriors. (From an Egyptian tomb painting of the 12th dynasty.)

As she watched Aqhat die,
   Anat began to weep. . . .

With Aqhat dead, there are no harvest rains. The crops of Ugarit wither from drought.

C.i:32–8 (2 Sam 3:31; Job 1:20; Ps 68:4; 104:3)

Vultures began to soar above the palace,
   Buzzards coasted in the wind.
Deep within her heart Paghat began to weep,
   Unnoticed, the sister of Aqhat began to cry.
She tore the garments of Danil the powerful,
   She rent the robe of Danil the judge.

≋ *Neither Danil nor Paghat was yet aware that Aqhat had been assassinated. By tearing Danil's garments, Paghat is not mourning the death of her brother, but officially filing a gloomy economic forecast with the head of state. Danil accepts her analysis, and predicts the drought will last for seven years.*

C.i:40 – C.ii:55 (Deut 33:26; Ps 104:3; Prov 31:15)

Then Danil officially declared that the land was cursed,
    The powerful announced that a prolonged drought had begun.
"For seven years Ba'al will disappear,
    For eight years the Rider of the Clouds will dispatch no dew and no
        rain.
Rivers and springs will dry up,
    There will not be a single thundershower. . . ."

Danil called to Paghat, who rises early to water the herds,
    Who feeds the livestock their barley while stars are still in the sky.
"Saddle an ass, harness my mount.
    Use my reins of silver, my bridle of gold."

≋ *After Paghat saddles an ass, she and Danil set off to survey the drought damage.*

C.ii:89 – C.iii:127 (Deut 21:1–9; 2 Sam 1:27)

Suddenly, Paghat saw two messengers appear.
    They began to weep and lament.
"Hear our words, Danil the powerful,
    Aqhat the hunter is dead.
Anat made the breath of Aqhat depart like the wind,
    The Virgin made him exhale his last breath like a gentle breeze. . . ."

Danil saw vultures appear in the clouds.
    He began to lament: "May Ba'al break their wings.
May Ba'al pluck the feathers from their wings,
    Let them fall at my feet.
I will split them open,
    To find Aqhat's flesh and bone.
I will mourn for him and will bury him.
    I will lay him in his grave at the sanctuary."

≋❙ *Paghat asks Danil to appoint her to avenge her brother's death.*

C.iv:190–8 (Gen 4:3—5:32; 27:38)

"My father," Paghat said, "you have completed your sacrifices,
   You have left food and drink for the divine assembly,
   You have fulfilled your vows to Harnam.
Now, bless me, father, and I will be blessed.
   Choose me, and I will be chosen.
I will kill my brother's killer,
   I will avenge my household."

≋❙ *Danil commissions Paghat by breathing into her nostrils (Gen 2:7;*
   Ezek 37:9).

C.iv:203–9 (Judg 5:24–7)

In the sea, Paghat bathes,
   With mollusks, she dyes her skin a rich purple.
Paghat puts on the clothes of a warrior,
   She thrusts a knife into her belt.
Paghat hangs a sword on her side,
   She covers her weapons with a woman's clothes.

≋❙ *At dusk, Paghat enters Yatpan's camp and asks to be taken to his*
   tent, where she finds him drunk.

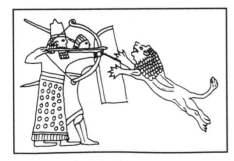

A scene of the king hunting lions.
(From the palace of Ashurbanipal of Assyria, 7th century, B.C.E.)

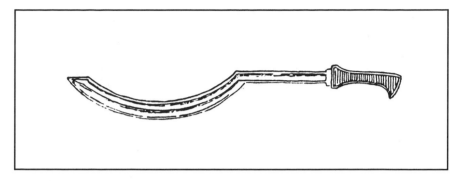

Canaanite sickle sword from Gezer (14th century, B.C.E.).

C.iv:210–24 (Gen 4:23–4, 9:20–23; Judg 4:19)

A messenger said to Yatpan: "A lady has come to your camp,
   Paghat is outside your tent."

Yatpan replied: "Let Paghat come into my tent."
   Anat's accomplice boasted: "She can serve me wine.
Paghat can take the cup from my hand,
   She can fill the drinking horn in my right hand."

Paghat entered the tent of Yatpan,
   She began to serve him wine.
Paghat took the cup from his hand,
   She filled the drinking horn in his right hand.

Then Yatpan began to brag:
   "This hand which killed Aqhat the hunter has killed a thousand."
Paghat served Yatpan more and more wine. . . .

🔖 *The end of the tablet is missing. However, there are two similar stories from the Bible, which may suggest conclusions for the stories
of Aqhat. The book of Judges (Judg 4:17-22) recounts that as Sisera
was lying fast asleep, Jael took a tent peg and hammer and drove
the peg into his temple. The book of Judith (Judt 13:2+6+9) tells how,
when Holofernes was stretched out on his bed, overcome with wine,
Judith went up to the bedpost, took down his sword, struck his neck
twice with all her might, and severed his head from his body.*

STORIES OF KERET

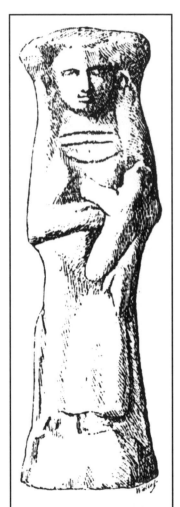

The stories of Keret or Kirta, like the stories of Aqhat, were recovered at Ugarit in Syria by C.A. Schaeffer and his French team between 1929-1960. They are written on three clay tablets (CTA 14-16; KTU 1.14-16) in the Ugaritic language using an alphabetic cuneiform script. They are preserved today in the Louvre Museum in Paris. Although the stories of Keret probably developed as early as 2000 BCE, this version is signed by Ilimilku, a scribe during the reign of Niqmaddu II (1360-1330 BCE).

Keret is a monarch who faces childlessness, sickness and revolt. The stories of Keret open with Keret engaged in a ritual of incubation during which he sleeps in a sanctuary of El to ask his divine patron to restore his household. In his dream, El tells him to go to war, capture a bride and begin a new household. Keret obeys, but fails to thank the godmother Asherah for her help in rebuilding his household. To punish Keret for his lack of humility (Greek: hubris), Asherah destroys his health. Nonetheless, El once again intervenes and Keret recovers only to have his own son, Yassib, revolt against him.

Terra-cotta statuette of the mother-goddess (from the Louvre).

The death of Keret's first household and its replacement with a second is parallel to the book of Job. Keret's dreams are like those of Jacob in the book of Genesis (Gen 28:10-7), and those of Solomon in the books of Samuel-Kings (1 Kgs 3:4-15). The revolt of his son, Yassib, parallels the revolt of David's son, Absalom, in the books of Samuel-Kings (2 Sam 15:1-6).

I.i:8–42 (Gen 28:10–7; 2 Sam 7:14; Mic 5:5; Job 1·13–9)

The household of Keret, once home to seven, to eight,
    All sons of a single mother, was ruined.
Keret's soul was despondent,
    His palace vacant.
His wife had died,
    His companion was gone.
Three sons died at birth,
    A fourth son of disease,
    A fifth son of fever,
    A sixth son was lost at sea,
    A seventh son died in battle. . . .
Keret sealed himself in the sanctuary and mourned,
    Going over each tragedy again and again. . . .
Exhausted from weeping, he fell asleep,
    Soaked with tears he began to dream. . . .

El appeared to Keret in his dream,
    The godfather came to him in a vision. . . .

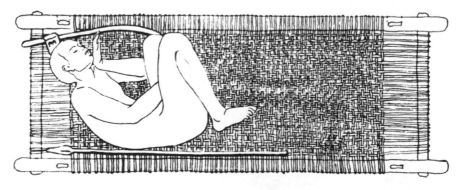

Reconstruction of a Syrian burial in which the warrior has a spear behind him and an axe before him.

"Keret, why are you crying?
  Why is the son of El in tears?
Act like your father, El the Bull,
  Be strong like the father of all. . . ."

I.ii:5–24 (Exod 29:4)

"Give me sons," Keret pleaded.
  "I need a household," he begged.

El replied: "Stop your mourning, Keret,
  Dry your tears, son of El.
Wash your face with water,
  Anoint your face with oil.
Bathe your arms to the elbow,
  Scrub the dirt from your fingertips to your shoulders.
Go to the shade of your tents.
  Prepare for a sacrifice.
Pick out the sheep with your right hand,
  Select a lamb with each hand.
Assemble all the food needed for a sacrifice.
  Find a bird suitable for sacrifice,
Pour wine from a silver cup,
  Drip honey from a golden bowl.
Climb to the top of the tower,
  Climb to the heights of the wall.
Raise your hands to heaven,
  Sacrifice to your father, El the Bull."

Sumerian seal showing offerings brought to a shrine.

A Phoenician city pictured on an Assyrian wall relief. It shows a lower rampart, high mound and walled inner city on top.

After El teaches Keret how to offer sacrifice, he tells him to gather a six-month supply of food for an army of 300,000 soldiers and lay siege to Udum. The army is not to attack the walls of the city, but cut them off for seven days until Pabil, the ruler of Udum, sues for peace (Josh 6:1-16). El tells Keret to seal the covenant between Ugarit and Udum by marrying Hurriya, a daughter of Pabil. Keret follows the instructions of El but, on the third day of the march, Keret stops at a sanctuary of Asherah and makes a vow (Judg 11:30-1; 1 Sam 14:24).

I.iii:38–49

"May Asherah give me what the household of Keret lacks,
    May Asherah give me the virgin Hurriya. . . .
Let her bear the children of Keret,
    Let her give birth to sons for the son of El."

I.iv:38–43 (Judg 8:19; Ruth 3:13; 1 Sam 19:6)

"By the power of Asherah, divine patron of Tyre,
    By the power of the divine patron of Sidon,
If I can marry Hurriya,
    If I can bring this woman into my palace,

Then I will give Asherah double her bride price in silver,
  I will endow you with three times the value of Hurriya in gold."

≋ *Keret and Hurriya celebrate their marriage before the divine assembly.*

II.ii:12–iii:16 (Ruth 4:11–2; Isa 32:5; Job 42:10–5)

When the divine assembly convenes
  The mighty Ba'al proposes a toast.
"May El the kind, the compassionate, bless Keret the powerful . . .
  Show favor to the son of El."

El takes his cup in his hand,
  He takes his goblet in his right hand.
El blesses his servant, Keret the powerful . . .
  He shows favor to the son of El.
"Keret, you have obtained a wife,
  You have taken a woman into your household,
  You have brought a virgin into your palace.
She will bear you seven sons,
  Eight sons she will bear you, and daughters. . . .
Even to the youngest daughter,
  I will give the first-born's possessions. . . ."

≋ *Hurriya gives birth to many sons and daughters. Keret, however, does not fulfill his vow to endow the sanctuary of Asherah. To remind him of his vow, Asherah inflicts Keret with a fever no one can cure. Royal officials and the household of Keret go into mourning to prepare for his death. Finally, El hears their prayers and responds by polling the other members of the divine assembly to see if any of them will cure Keret. None of the divine assembly wishes to undertake so dangerous a mission, so El commissions Shataqat to cure him (2 Kgs 4:34–7; 5:10–4).*

III.vi:1–18 (2 Kgs 20:1–11)

"Death, be vanquished!" El orders.
  "Shataqat, be strong!" he commands.
Shataqat sets out from the divine assembly,
  She arrives at the household of Keret.
She enters to the sounds of mourning,

Weeping fills the palace.
Shataqat wipes the sweat from Keret's brow,
   She lets his appetite return,
   She returns his taste for food.
Death is vanquished.
   Shataqat is victorious.

Then Keret the powerful commands,
   He shouts in a mighty voice:
"Hear me, Hurriya,
   Butcher a lamb for me to eat,
   Prepare a sheep for my supper."

   Keret once again sits upon his throne and all appears to be well. Keret's illness, however, gave his son, Yassib, a chance to seize the throne, so he challenges Keret to abdicate (2 Sam 15:1–14).

III.vi:31–8 (Deut 10:18; Isa 1:17; 10:2; Ezek 22:7; Amos 2:6–7; 5:12; Ps 68:5; Prov 29:14–6)

Yassib indicts Keret:
   "If enemies had invaded the land while you were ill,
They would have driven you out,
   They would have forced you into the hills.
Your illness made you derelict.
   You did not hear the case of the widow.
You did not hear the case of the poor.
   You did not sentence the oppressor.
You did not feed the orphan in the city.
   You did not feed the widow in the country.
The sickbed has become your brother,
   The pallet is your best friend.
Step down from the kingship,
   Allow me to reign.
Relinquish your power,
   Let me sit on the throne. . . ."

   The story breaks off with Keret pronouncing a curse on his rebel son. The failure to keep his vow to Asherah cost him his family and his health, and, if the prediction came true, he was left with his youngest daughter as his heir (Josh 6:26).

Exodus

A bronze head of King Sargon of Akkad, from the Old Akkadian Period. It is one of the finest pieces of third millennium Mesopotamian art.

ANNALS OF SARGON I

Sometime after 3000 BCE, the state of Akkad was founded near the current city of Baghdad, Iraq. Agriculture, trade and war soon made Akkad an empire, and Sargon of Agade (ca. 2371-2316 BCE) one of its greatest rulers.

By 1900, British archaeologists had recovered three copies that comprise the annals of Sargon I celebrating the humble beginnings of this great king. All three were written in cuneiform. Two were written in the Assyrian dialect of the Akkadian language and one in the Babylonian dialect. They are preserved today in the British Museum in London.

A parallel to the annals of Sargon I appears in a story of the birth of Moses in the book of Exodus (Exod 1:22—2:10), which celebrates the humble beginnings of Moses as one of ancient Israel's greatest leaders.

Call me Sargon. I am the child of a priest and an unknown pilgrim from the mountains. Today, I rule an empire from the city of Agade.

Because my mother did not want anyone in the city of Asupiranu to know that she had given birth to a child, she left me on the bank of the Euphrates river in a basket woven from rushes and waterproofed with tar.

The river carried my basket down to a canal, where Akki, the royal gardener, lifted me out of the water and reared me as his own. He trained me to care for the gardens of the great king.

With the help of Ishtar, divine patron of love and war, I became king of the black-headed people and have ruled 55 years. I blazed trails through the mountains with bronze axes. I scaled high peaks. I crossed deep valleys. I conquered every land from Dilmun on the Persian Gulf to Dor on the Mediterranean Sea. Three times I marched from the Persian Gulf to the Mediterranean Sea. I conquered ports like Dor and cities like Kazallu.

To my successors I leave this legacy.

TREATY BETWEEN RAMSES II AND HATTUSILIS III

For more than one hundred years, Egypt and Hatti struggled for control of the eastern Mediterranean. The conflict drained the resources of both superpowers. About 1280 BCE, following a famous, but inconclusive, battle at Kadesh, located in Syria today, the treaty of Ramses II and Hattusilis III was negotiated. This treaty was a remarkable political and military accomplishment. It was motivated both by Egypt's and Hatti's need for economic recovery, as well as the increasing military threat of the Sea Peoples migrating across the islands of today's Greece and into the eastern Mediterranean. The treaty kept the peace for virtually the next fifty years and brought the Late Bronze period to an end.

In the early 1900s archaeologists recovered both Egyptian and Hittite editions of the treaty. In the Egyptian edition, Ramses II flamboyantly elaborates on the role that he played in negotiating the treaty in order to use it as a public relations tool. He had one copy carved in hieroglyphics on the walls of the temple of Amon in Karnak and another on the walls of his own funeral chapel, the Ramesseum, in the valley of the pharaohs, both located near today's Luxor in central Egypt. The Hittite edition is a more sober legal document written on clay tablets in cuneiform, using Akkadian, which was the diplomatic language of the ancient Near East. German archaeologists recovered the tablets from the archives of Hattusas, the Hittite capital, located in today's Turkey. They are preserved in the Ankara Museum in Ankara, Turkey.

The Hittites developed the treaty form, which other cultures

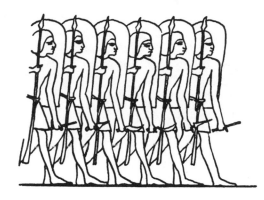

*The infantry of Pharaoh
Ramses II on the march.*

*used. Standard Hittite treaties contained at least six components.
They opened by giving the credentials of the signatories to the treaty
and issued a new and official history of the partners. Then they
laid out the terms in careful legal language. These were followed
by a list of witnesses to the treaty, a litany of curses for treaty vio-
lations and blessings for treaty compliance, and finally provisions
to record and promulgate the treaty. Covenants in the Bible today
parallel Hittite treaties. Simple covenants appear in negotiations
between Jacob and Laban in the book of Genesis (Gen 31:44-54).
The Covenant Code in the book of Exodus, the Holiness Code in
the book of Leviticus and the Deuteronomic Code in the book of
Deuteronomy are more complex examples of the genre.*

CREDENTIALS

Inscribed on this silver tablet is the treaty creating peace and eternal alliance between Hattusilis, the great king of Hatti, son of Mursilis,
a great king of Hatti, grandson of Suppiluliumas, a great king of Hatti,
and Ramses, the pharaoh of Egypt, son of Seti, a pharaoh of Egypt, son
of Ramses, a pharaoh of Egypt.

HISTORY

In the beginning, the divine assembly decreed that there be peace
between the pharaoh of Egypt and the great king of Hatti. Then
Muwatallis, my brother and a great king of Hatti, declared war on Ramses. From this day forward, Hattusilis will observe the decree of Ra and
Seth, which prohibits war between Egypt and Hatti forever.

*Pharaoh Ramses II
in his war chariot at
the battle of Kadesh
in Syria.*

TERMS
(Deut 23:15–6; 2 Kgs 9:16–26)

Current Relations

Hattusilis agrees to this treaty with Ramses, creating peace and an eternal alliance between us. We are brothers and are at peace with each other forever. I, Hattusilis, came to the throne of Hatti, when Muwatallis died. Therefore, I agree to this treaty with Ramses, creating peace and an alliance between us. The state of peace and alliance between our lands is now better than in former times. I, Ramses, agree to peace and an alliance. The successors of the great king of Hatti will be allies with the successors of Ramses. The relationship between Egypt and Hatti shall be like our relationship, one of peace and eternal alliance. There will never again be war between us.

Mutual Non-Aggression

In the future, the great king of Hatti shall neither invade nor raid Egypt, and Ramses shall neither invade nor raid Hatti.

Reaffirmation of Former Treaties

I, Hattusilis, reaffirm the treaties of Suppiluliumas and of Muwatallis, great kings of Hatti. I, Ramses, affirm the treaty I make with Hattusilis this day, and will observe it and act accordingly from now on.

Defensive Alliance

If a foreign army invades the lands of Ramses, and he sends a message to the great king of Hatti, saying: "Come and help me against this enemy," the great king of Hatti shall come and fight against the enemy of Egypt, his ally. If the great king of Hatti does not wish to come personally, he may send infantry and chariots to fight against the enemy of Egypt, his ally. Likewise, if Ramses is trying to put down an armed revolt, the great king of Hatti shall help him until all the rebels have been executed. If a foreign army attacks the great king of Hatti, Ramses shall come and fight against the enemy of Hatti, to aid his ally. If Ramses does not wish to come personally, he may send infantry and chariots, as well as word to this effect, to Hatti. If the officials of the great king of Hatti break their oaths of loyalty to him, Ramses. . . .

Orderly Succession

When Hattusilis dies, the son of Hattusilis shall be crowned great king of Hatti in his father's place. If the people of Hatti revolt against his son, Ramses shall send soldiers and chariots to protect the son of Hattusilis. Once order has been restored in Hatti, they shall return to Egypt. If the people of Egypt. . . .

Extradition

The great king of Hatti shall not grant asylum to any fugitive from Egypt. The great king of Hatti shall have fugitives extradited to Ramses. Likewise, any runaway slave, who escapes to Hatti in search of a new master, shall be extradited to Ramses. The pharaoh of Egypt shall not grant asylum to any fugitive from Hatti. The pharaoh of Egypt shall have fugitives extradited to the great king of Hatti. Likewise, any runaway slave who escapes to Egypt in search of a new master shall be extradited to the great king of Hatti.

LIST OF WITNESSES
(Gen 31:51–3)

All the divine patrons of Hatti and Egypt are witnesses to this treaty between the great king of Hatti and Ramses inscribed on this silver tablet.

Ra, divine patron of the sky
Ra, divine patron of Arinna
Seth, divine patron of the storm
Seth, divine patron of Hatti
Seth, divine patron of Arinna
Seth, divine patron of Zippalanda

Seth, divine patron of Pettiyarik
Seth, divine patron of Hissashapa
Seth, divine patron of Sarissa
Seth, divine patron of Aleppo
Seth, divine patron of Lihzina
The divine patron of Zitharias
The divine patron of Karzis
The divine patron of Hapantaliyas
The divine patron of Karana
The queen of the sky
The divine patrons of oaths
The divine patron of the earth
Ishara, the lady of oaths
Ishara, the lady of mountains and rivers of Hatti
The divine assembly of Kizuwanda
Amon Ra
Seth
The divine patrons of the mountains and rivers of Egypt
The sky
The earth
The sea
The winds
The clouds

LITANY OF CURSES
AND BLESSINGS
(Gen 31:50–4)

Cursed by the divine assembly of Hatti and Egypt be the homes and lands and slaves of those who do not observe the treaty between Hatti and Egypt inscribed on this silver tablet. Blessed by the divine assembly of Hatti and Egypt with prosperity and long life be the homes and lands and slaves of those Egyptians and Hittites who observe and carry out faithfully the treaty between Hatti and Egypt inscribed on this silver tablet. . . .

The Hittite god Teshub.

ANNALS OF MERNEPTAH

In 1896, Flinders Petrie from England recovered a stele or column of granite almost seven and one-half feet high and three and one-quarter feet wide from the funeral chapel of Merneptah (1224-1214 BCE) in the valley of the pharaohs (KV8) at Thebes or Luxor today. The stele itself was originally inscribed by Amenhotep III (1391-1353 BCE), but was recycled by Merneptah to celebrate his victory over Libya to the west and Syria-Palestine to the east in the fifth year of his reign (ca. 1221-1219 BCE). The victory hymn is written in hieroglyphics on twenty-eight lines. The stele is now in the Egyptian Museum in Cairo (34025 verso).

The victory hymn of Merneptah contains the only mention of Israel during the New Kingdom (1550-1070 BCE) yet discovered in Egypt. It is one argument for dating the emergence of Israel by 1250 BCE and ascribing the Exodus event to the reign of Ramses II (1290-1224 BCE). Merneptah refers to the Israel who was his enemy as a people, rather than as a state. The historical character of this document is still in dispute since it is so similar to earlier victory hymns (Kadesh Battle Poem from the reign of Ramses II) and its bragging style is typical of the propagandistic nature of this genre.

Parallels to the victory hymn of Merneptah appear in the conquest narrative in the books of Joshua and Judges (Josh 10:40-1; Judg 1:4-11), and in the annals of Israel's rulers in the books of Samuel-Kings (2 Sam 8:1-12).

The rulers of my enemies now lie prostrate before me and beg for peace. Not one of my enemies raises his head in revolt. I have devastated Tehenu and put down a revolt against the great king of Hatti. I have plundered Canaan from one end to the other, taken slaves from the city of Ashkelon, and conquered the city of Gezer. I have razed Yanoam to the ground. I have decimated the people of Israel and put their children

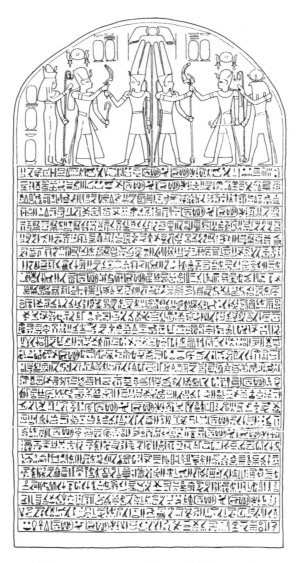

The Victory Stele of Pharaoh Merneptah.

*The name "Israel" as it appears in hieroglyphics
on the Victory Stele of Merneptah.*

to death. Hurru is a widow. All Canaan has been pacified. Every rebel is
now prostrate before Merneptah, pharaoh of Upper and Lower Egypt,
the divine presence of Amon Ra (Egyptian: *Ba-en-Ra*), beloved of the
divine assembly (Egyptian: *Meri-Amon*), who dawns each day like Amon
Ra the sun.

LEVITICUS, NUMBERS, DEUTERONOMY

CODE OF UR-NAMMU

Ur-Nammu (2112-2095 BCE) and Shulgi (2094-2047 BCE) were rulers of Sumer, in southern Iraq today. They authorized the publication of the code of Ur-Nammu, which is the oldest system of laws recovered by archaeologists from the world of the Bible. Two fragments of the code were recovered at Ur (Arabic: **tell al-Muqayyar***) during the 1922-34 excavations sponsored by the British Museum and the University of Pennsylvania and directed by C. Leonard Wooley (1880-1960). Both tablets, including only articles #7-37, are written in Sumerian using the cuneiform script. There were originally eight columns of writing, four on each side of the tablets. They are preserved today in the British Museum in London. The first ten articles contained in the code have been reconstructed from tablets discovered at Nippur, also housed in the British Museum.*

The code of Ur-Nammu established an enduring legal tradition that applies uniform principles of justice to a wide range of social institutions, from the standardization of weights and measures to the protection of widows and orphans. Sentences in the code of Ur-Nammu are generally determined by the principle of restitution paid to the victim, rather than by the principle of revenge taken on the convict.

Seal of Namu, servant of king Shulgi.

In the Bible, the covenant code (Exod 21—3), the holiness code (Lev 17—26) and the Deuteronomic code (Deut 12—26) are parallel to the code of Ur-Nammu.

art 1 (Exod 20:13)

If a citizen commits murder, then the sentence is death.

art 6 (Deut 22:23–4)

If one citizen rapes a woman, who is marriageable and is engaged to another citizen, then the sentence is death.

art 8 (Lev 19:20–1)

If one citizen rapes the slave of another, who is marriageable, then the fine is one and two-thirds ounces (Akkadian: five shekels) of silver.

art 17 (Deut 23:15–6)

If a slave flees the household and the city of one citizen, and another returns the slave, then the owner shall pay a reward of two-thirds ounces of silver.

art 25 (Gen 16:4–6)

If a slave shames the mother of her household by speaking insolently to her, then her mouth is scoured with . . . salt.

art 28 (Deut 19:16–9)

If a citizen is guilty of perjury, the fine is five ounces of silver.

SUMERIAN CODE

≋ *The Sumerian code is the remnant of a student exercise. The site where the tablets were found is unknown. It is currently housed in the Yale Oriental collection at Yale University (YOS 1.2).*

The code dates to ca. 1800 BCE, but it represents a much older legal tradition. Texts such as this were copied by students and were among the most important subjects studied by candidates for government jobs in Sumer and Babylonia. Candidates wrote out, again and again, the technical terms and phrases that would appear in the examinations at the end of their training.

Parallels to the Middle Assyrian code appear in the covenant code in the book of Exodus (Exod 21–3), in the holiness code in the book of Leviticus (Lev 17–26) and in the Deuteronomic code in the book of Deuteronomy (Deut 12–26).

art 1 (Exod 21:22)

If one citizen accidentally strikes the daughter of another, and she miscarries, then the fine is three and one-third ounces of silver.

art 4 (Deut 21:18–21)

If a son disowns the father and mother of his household with the oath: "You are not my father. You are not my mother," then he forfeits his right to inherit their land and property, and can be sold as an ordinary slave at full market value.

art 5

If the father and mother of a household say to their son: "You are not our son," then. . . .

*Plaque of Sumerian King
Ur-Ninu of Lagash showing
his cupbearer and four sons.*

art 7 (Gen 34:1–12)

If one citizen rapes the daughter of another, while she is in the street without the knowledge of the father and mother of her household, and he swears: "I will marry her," then her father and her mother, without her consent, give her to the man who raped her as a wife.

art 8 (Gen 34; Exod 22:16; Deut 22:23–4)

If one citizen rapes the daughter of another, who, with the knowledge of the father and the mother of her household, is walking about the city, then the citizen, if he swears at the sanctuary gate that he did not know she was the daughter of a household, is not guilty.

CODE OF HAMMURABI

The code of Hammurabi is a treatise on legal theory, political science and social organization. Hammurabi, great king of Babylon from 1792-1750 BCE, published this classic to endorse the legal thinking and moral values of his government. In 1901, French excavators recovered a copy of the code of Hammurabi at Susa on the border between Iraq and Iran where it had been taken by the Elamites, who were Babylon's enemies. The code was inscribed in cuneiform on an eight foot pillar of black diorite, and is preserved today in the Louvre Museum in Paris.

A catalog of Hammurabi's military victories and political endorsements introduces two hundred eighty-two case laws. In both the code of Hammurabi and the Middle Assyrian code, prologues place the promulgation of a code of law within the context of a ruler's rise to power. Within the code itself, each case law has two parts. First, a dependent clause introduced by the conjunction "if" describes a situation: "If one citizen charges another with murder, without the evidence to prove it...." Second, a main clause introduced by the adverb "then" imposes a sentence: "...then the sentence is death (CH 1)." Distinct social groups, like slaves, citizens and priests, appear in the laws. An essay on the role of law in a state concludes the code.

In ancient Israel, the covenant code (Exod 21—3), the holiness code (Lev 17—26) and the Deuteronomic code (Deut 12—26) are parallel to the code of Hammurabi.

art 1 (Exod 23:1–3; Deut 19:16–9)

If one citizen charges another with murder, but has no evidence, then the sentence is death.

Cylinder seal from Alalakh in Syria. The owner says he is a subject of the king of Karana, but the arrow-shaped spade between the figures suggests the symbol of Marduk and probably indicates both cities were subject to king Hammurabi of Babylon.

art 2

If one citizen charges another with witchcraft, but has no evidence, then the defendant is tried by ordeal in a river. If the defendant drowns, the plaintiff inherits the defendant's household. If the defendant survives, then the sentence is death for the plaintiff, and the defendant confiscates the plaintiff's household.

art 3 (Deut 19:16–9)

If a citizen commits perjury before the city assembly in a case involving the death penalty, then the sentence is death.

art 5 (Exod 23:6–8; Lev 19:15; Deut 16:19)

If a judge accepts a bribe to render and seal a decision, then the judge is fined twelve times the settlement ordered in the decision, is expelled from the bench, and cannot serve as a judge again.

art 8 (Exod 20:15; Lev 19:11 + 13; Deut 5:19; 22:1–4)

If a citizen steals an ox or a sheep from a state or temple official, then the citizen is fined thirty times the value of the stolen livestock. Likewise, if one citizen steals an ox or a sheep from another, then the fine is ten times the value of the stolen livestock. If a citizen fails to pay a fine for stealing livestock, then the sentence is death.

art 14 (Exod 21:16; Deut 24:7)

If a citizen kidnaps and sells a member of another citizen's household into slavery, then the sentence is death.

art 15 (Deut 23:15–6)

If a citizen helps state slaves or household slaves to escape, then the sentence is death.

art 16 (Deut 23:15–6)

If a citizen harbors slaves who have run away from the state or from a household, and if the citizen disobeys a court order to extradite them, then the sentence is death.

art 17

If a citizen captures a runaway slave in the open and returns the slave to the owner, then a reward of one-third ounce (Akkadian: one shekel) of silver is paid by the owner to the citizen.

art 21 (Exod 22:2–3)

If one citizen tunnels through the wall of another's house and robs it, then the citizen is sentenced to death. The execution shall take place outside the tunnel, and the body used to fill in the tunnel.

art 24 (Deut 21:1–9)

If a murderer is not caught, then a fine of eighteen ounces (Akkadian: one mina) of silver is paid by the state to the household of the victim.

art 25

If one citizen steals property from the house of another while fighting a fire in that house, then the sentence is death.

art 57 (Exod 22:5)

If a herder does not have a covenant with the owner of a field to graze his sheep on it, but has grazed his sheep on the field without the consent of its owner, when the owner of the field harvests it, then the fine is one-hundred forty bushels (Akkadian: *kur*) of grain for every sixteen acres (Akkadian: *iku*) of land.

art 71 (1 Kgs 21:1–2)

If a citizen is renting land adjoining his own, and decides to purchase it, then, before negotiating a covenant to purchase the land, the citizen must abrogate the covenant to rent the land, forfeit the grain, silver or goods paid as rent, and certify that the land is not mortgaged to any other household.

art 94 (Deut 25:13–5; Amos 8:5)

If bankers use a light scale to measure the grain or the silver that they lend and a heavy scale to measure the grain or the silver that they collect, then they shall forfeit their investment.

art 117 (Exod 21:2–11; Deut 15:12–8)

If a citizen sells his wife, his son, his daughter or himself into slavery to pay a debt, then the creditor cannot keep them as slaves for more than three years and must free them at the beginning of the fourth year.

art 125 (Exod 22:7–8)

If one citizen stores property in the warehouse of another, and if the property is stolen by a thief who tunnels through the wall or climbs over it, then the owner of the warehouse, whose carelessness allowed the robbery to take place, must make every effort to find the thief and recover the stolen property. In any case, the warehouse owner must make full restitution of the value of the stolen property to its owner.

art 129 (Deut 22:22)

If the wife of a citizen commits adultery, then she and her partner are to be tied up and tried by ordeal in a river. If, however, the woman's husband pardons her, then the monarch can pardon her partner.

art 130 (Deut 22:23–7)

If a citizen rapes a woman, who is marriageable, engaged and still living with her parents, then the man is sentenced to death, but the woman is exonerated.

art 131 (Num 5:12–22)

If a citizen falsely accuses his wife of adultery, and she swears an oath of innocence before the divine patron of her household, then she may return home.

art 132 (Num 5:11–31; Ur-Nammu 10–1)

If a citizen charges a woman with adultery, but has no evidence, then she is to be tried by ordeal in the river to restore the honor of her husband. If she survives, then she must pay a fine.

art 141 (Deut 24:1–4)

If the wife of a citizen leaves the house of her husband on her own business, and if she neglects the house and shames her husband, then her husband may either divorce her without paying a fine, or may marry another woman while his former wife is to live in the house as a slave.

art 142–3

If a woman so hated her husband that she spoke the words: "You may not have intercourse with me!" and if the elders conclude that she is a faithful wife, despite the false accusations of her husband, then the woman may take her dowry and return to the household of her father. If the elders conclude that the woman is unfaithful, that she leaves the house of her husband on her own business, that she neglects the house and shames her husband, then she is to be drowned in the river.

art 146 (Gen 16:1–15; Gen 21:9–21)

If the slave, with whom a Naditu priest negotiates a covenant to bear her husband's children, considers herself to have the same status as the Naditu priest, once she has borne children, then the Naditu priest may pierce her ear and downgrade her status in the household, but the Naditu priest may not sell her.

art 154 (Lev 18:6–18; 20:10–21; Deut 27:20 + 22–3)

If a citizen has sexual intercourse with his daughter, then he is exiled from the city.

art 155 (Lev 18:15; 20:12)

If the father of a household chooses a bride for his son, and if his son has had intercourse with her, but later the father of the household also has intercourse with her, then the father of the household is to be drowned in the river.

art 156 (Lev 19:20–2)

If the father of a household chooses a bride for his son, and if his son does not have intercourse with her, but the father of the household himself does have intercourse with her, then a fine of nine ounces of silver is paid to the household of her father, her dowry is returned, and she may marry the man of her choice.

art 157 (Lev 18:8; 20:11; Deut 27:20)

If a citizen has intercourse with his mother after the death of his father, then both are to be burned at the stake.

art 170 (Gen 21:9–21)

If a citizen, who has children by his wife and by his slave, adopts the slave's children, then his household shall be divided evenly between the children of both, after his wife's first-born son receives the preferential share.

art 195 (Exod 21:15)

If a citizen strikes his father, then his hand is to be cut off.

art 196

If a citizen blinds an eye of an official, then his eye is to be blinded.

art 197

If one citizen breaks a bone of another, then his own bone is to be broken.

Drawing of the top of Hammurabi's Stele showing the king before the sun god Shamash.

art 198

If a citizen blinds the eye or breaks the bone of someone who is not a citizen, the fine is eighteen ounces of silver.

art 199 (Exod 21:26; Lev 24:19–20; Deut 19:21)

If one citizen blinds the eye or breaks the bone of another citizen's slave, the fine is one-half the price of the slave.

art 206–7 (Exod 21:18–9)

If a citizen accidentally hits another citizen and causes injury, then that citizen must swear: "I did not strike this citizen deliberately," and must pay for the cost of a physician. If the victim dies from the blow, then the citizen must swear the same oath, but if the citizen is a member of a royal household, then the fine paid to the household of the victim is nine ounces of silver.

art 209 (Sumerian Laws 1; Exod 21:22–3)

If one citizen beats the daughter of another and causes her to miscarry, then the fine is six ounces of silver.

art 233 (Deut 22:8)

If a builder constructs a house and does faulty work resulting in an unsafe wall, then the builder must pay to strengthen that wall at his own expense.

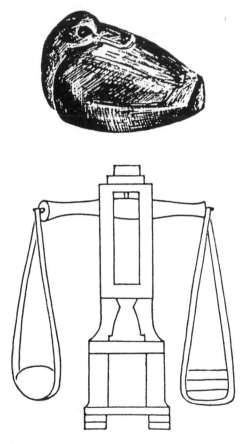

Assyrian balance scales and a duck weight.

art 244 (Exod 22:14–5)

If a citizen rents an ox or an ass, and if a lion kills it while it is out in the open, then there is no fine.

art 249 (Exod 22:14–5)

If a citizen rents an ox and a member of the divine assembly strikes it with lightning and it dies, then the citizen who had rented the ox must swear in the name of a member of the divine assembly that the death of the ox was an act of God, and then there is no fine.

art 251 (Exod 21:28–36)

If the ox of a citizen, who has neither tethered, nor blunted the horns of the animal, even after the city assembly has put the owner on notice that it was dangerous, gores a state official, then the fine is eighteen ounces of silver.

art 266 (Gen 31:39; Exod 22:10–3)

If an act of God occurs in a sheepfold or a lion makes a kill, then the shepherd must take an oath of innocence before his divine patron, and turn the remains of the animal over to its owner.

HITTITE CODE

After 1893 archaeologists excavated some 10,000 baked clay tablets from Hattusas, the four-hundred and nineteen acre site of the Hittite capital, now in central Turkey. They included samples of the Hittite code. These two-hundred case laws were written on two baked clay tablets in Neshili Hittite using cuneiform script. By 1915, Bedrich Hrozny, a Czech scholar, was able to translate the language.

The Hittite code represents legal thinking in Hatti between 1450-1200 BCE. It prefers sentences that compensate victims for loss, rather than sentences that punish convicts for crime. It also regularly commutes death sentences to corporal punishment and reduces corporal punishment sentences to fines. To make these changes, the Hittite code simply inserts "Formerly..." at the beginning of the old law and then introduces the new law with "...but now...."

Parallels to the Hittite code in ancient Israel appear mainly in the book of Deuteronomy (Deut 12—26) and in the book of Leviticus (Lev 17—26). These parallels are especially clear in each code's use of similar technical terms. The terms "brother" and "brother-in-law" identify citizens who are covenant partners, rather than simply individuals who are kin to one another by birth. For example, in the book of Deuteronomy (Deut 25:5-10), a "brother-in-law" is a legal guardian. The same legal connotations appear in the English use of "sons" in the title of a business like "J.R. Everitt & Sons." Although the terms "sister" and "daughter" in English are used only to identify members of one's family of origin, in Semitic languages the same words often carry important legal connotations as well. Another strong parallel appears in the practice of sealing a covenant, which exchanges food and weapons, with a marriage. The most valuable women for such marriages are named in a twelve-point decalogue in the book of Leviticus (Lev 18:6-18).

art 10 (Exod 21:18–9)

If one citizen beats another so that the victim becomes an invalid, then the assailant shall take care of the victim. The assailant shall also pay someone to look after the victim's house until he recovers. When the victim recovers, the assailant shall give him three and one-half ounces of silver and pay his medical bills.

art 17 (Exod 21:22–3)

If a man causes a free woman to miscarry, he shall pay a fine of six ounces of silver if she is in her tenth month, and three ounces of silver if she is in her fifth month. He shall also put his own land and children up as collateral.

art 67 (Exod 21:37 [Heb], 22:1–4)

If a citizen steals a cow, the thief formerly was fined twelve head of cattle; now the thief will be fined six head: two two-year-old calves, two one-year-old calves, and two calves who have just been weaned. He shall also put his own land and children up as collateral.

art 94 (Exod 22:1 [Heb], 22:2–3, 7)

If a citizen breaks into a house, then the fine will be based on how much is stolen. Formerly the fine was thirteen ounces of silver, but now it is four.

Bulls in a frieze made of shell inlay from the Sumerian temple in Ubaid.

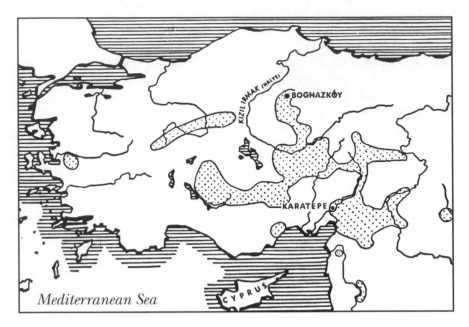

A map of Turkey with dotted areas showing where Hittite ruins were found.

art 98 (Exod 22:6)

If a citizen sets fire to a house, then the house must be rebuilt, and the household compensated for every animal or person who perished.

art 111 (Exod 22:18; Deut 18:10–14; 1 Sam 28:3)

If a witch creates a clay figurine and uses it to make magic, then the ruler determines the sentence.

art 189 (Lev 18:6–18)

A citizen may not have sexual intercourse with his mother, his daughter or his son.

art 193 (Gen 38; Deut 25:5–10; Ruth 4)

If a citizen dies, then his legal guardian (Hittite: brother) marries his widow.

If a citizen and his legal guardian die, then the citizen's father marries his widow.

If a citizen, his legal guardian and his father die, then one of his brother's sons marries the widow. . . .

art 195 (Lev 18:6–18)

If a citizen sexually abuses his brother's wife while his brother is still alive, then the sentence is death.

If a citizen sexually abuses the daughter of his wife, then the sentence is death.

If a citizen sexually abuses his mother-in-law or his sister-in-law, then the sentence is death.

art 197 (Deut 22:22–7)

If a citizen rapes a woman while they are in the mountains together, then the sentence for the man is death, the woman is not guilty. If a citizen rapes a woman while they are in her house together, then the sentence for the woman is also death. If the woman's husband discovers them in the act, then he may execute them without a trial.

MIDDLE ASSYRIAN CODE

≋ *Tiglath-Pileser I, great king of Assyria from 1115-1077 BCE, published the Middle Assyrian code. In 1903, German archaeologists found part of it at Ashur in Iraq today. It was written in the Assyrian dialect of the Akkadian language in cuneiform script on fifteen baked clay tablets. They are preserved today in the Staatliches Museum in Berlin.*

The Middle Assyrian code may have been four thousand lines long and probably followed the same literary pattern as the code of Hammurabi. An inspiring recitation of the military and political accomplishments of Tiglath-Pileser I introduces a major section of case laws aimed at clarifying guilt and responsibility.

Parallels to the Middle Assyrian code appear in the covenant code in the book of Exodus (Exod 21—3), in the holiness code in the book of Leviticus (Lev 17—26) and in the Deuteronomic code in the book of Deuteronomy (Deut 12—26).

A, art 1

If the wife or daughter of a citizen enters a temple, steals something, and it is found in her possession, then she is charged before the divine patron of the temple from which it was stolen, and the divine patron determines the sentence.

A, art 2 (Lev 24:16; Deut 24:16)

If the wife or daughter of a citizen blasphemes or gossips, then she alone is guilty. Her husband, sons and daughters are not guilty.

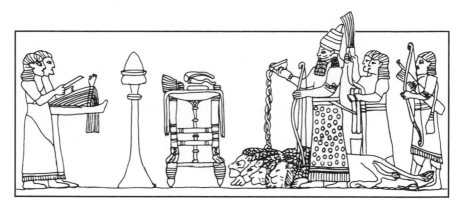

King Ashurbanipal pours out a libation over the lions killed in a hunt.
Musicians play before the altar and the king's attendants stand behind him.

A, art 8 (Deut 25:11–2)

If a woman ruptures one of the testicles of a citizen during a fight, then one of her fingers is amputated.

If a woman ruptures one of the testicles of a citizen during a fight and, even after medical treatment, his other testicle also ruptures, then both of the eyes of the woman are gouged out.

A, art 9

If one citizen forces the wife of another to let him fondle her like a child, then, following due process, one of his fingers is amputated.

If one citizen forces the wife of another to let him kiss her, then his lower lip is drawn along the edge of an ax blade and cut off.

A, art 12 (Deut 22:23–7)

If one citizen forces himself on the wife of another when she is outside her house and says, "Have intercourse with me," and has intercourse with her, even though she resists him and does not consent, regardless of whether he has been caught in the act or has been accused by witnesses, the man is executed. The woman is not guilty.

A, art 13 (Deut 22:22)

If the wife of one citizen leaves her own house, visits the house of another and he has intercourse with her, knowing that she is another's wife, then both are executed.

A, art 14

If one citizen has intercourse with the wife of another in a temple or outside their houses, knowing that she is another's wife, then both are to receive similar punishments.

If a citizen did not know that the woman with whom he had intercourse was another's wife, then the man is not guilty. The woman's husband shall charge his wife and punish her as he sees fit.

A, art 15 (Deut 22:22)

If one citizen catches another having intercourse with his wife, then, after due process, both the man and the woman are executed. The woman's husband is not guilty.

If one citizen catches another having intercourse with his wife, then the plaintiff is to charge the defendant before the ruler or the elders.

If, following due process, the plaintiff asks to have his wife executed, then the ruler or the elders are to also execute the defendant.

If the plaintiff asks to have his wife's nose cut off, then the ruler or the elders are to castrate the defendant and mutilate his face.

If the plaintiff asks to have his wife go free, then the ruler or the elders shall let the defendant go free.

A, art 16

If the wife of one citizen asks another to have intercourse with her, then the man is not guilty. The husband of the woman is to punish his wife as he sees fit.

If one citizen forces the wife of another to have intercourse with him, then, following due process, both are to receive similar punishments.

A, art 17 (Num 5:11–31)

If one citizen says to another: "Men are repeatedly having intercourse with your wife," but there are no witnesses, then the woman is tried by ordeal in the river.

A, art 18

If one citizen says to another, either in private or during a brawl: "Men are repeatedly having intercourse with your wife and I will charge her myself," but there are no witnesses, then the plaintiff is flogged forty times with staves, is to serve as a slave (French: *corvee*) for the state for a month, be castrated and be fined fourteen pounds (Akkadian: one talent) of lead.

A, art 19

If one citizen starts a rumor against another: "Men are repeatedly having homosexual intercourse with him," or says to him during a brawl in the presence of other people, "Men are repeatedly having homosexual intercourse with you and I will charge you myself," but there are no witnesses, then the plaintiff is flogged fifty times with staves, is to serve as a slave for the state for a month, be castrated and be fined fourteen pounds of lead.

A, art 20 (Lev 18:22; 20:13)

If one citizen has homosexual intercourse with another, then, following due process, the defendant is castrated.

A, art 21 (Exod 21:22)

If one citizen physically abuses the daughter of another until she has a miscarriage, then, following due process, he is fined sixty-two pounds (Akkadian: two talents, thirty minas) of lead, flogged fifty times with staves and is to serve as a slave for the state for a month.

A, art 24 (Lev 20:10–21)

If the wife of one citizen runs away, enters the household of another, whether in the same city or in a neighboring city, stays with the mother of the household, spending the night three or four times, without the knowledge of the father of the household, and later that woman is caught, then the husband of the fugitive woman is to cut off her ears and take her back. The husband of her accomplice is to cut off the ears of his wife, and either pay a fine of seventy-six pounds (Akkadian: three talents, thirty minas) of lead or divorce her.

If the father of the household knew that the fugitive wife was staying in his house, then he is fined one and one-third times her bride price.

If the father of the household pleads not guilty and swears: "I did not know there was a fugitive in my house," then he is tried by ordeal in the river.

If the father of the household refuses to go to the river, then he is fined one and one-third times the bride price of the fugitive wife.

An Assyrian winged bull-man called a cherubim in the Bible.
These gods were protectors of gates and doorways.

If the citizen whose wife deserted him refuses to go to the river, then the father of the household does not have to undergo the ordeal.

If the citizen whose wife deserted him does not cut off her ears and takes her back, then the father of the household and his wife are not guilty.

A, art 30

If a father of a household has paid the bride price for one son, but the wedding has not yet been celebrated, and another son who is already married dies, then he is to appoint the still unmarried son as the widow's legal guardian.

If, after he has accepted the bride price, the father of a woman's household becomes unwilling for his daughter to be married to a man who is a legal guardian for another woman, then the father of the man's household may either ignore the objections and marry the woman to his son, or abrogate the covenant and take back the lead, silver, gold and inedible part of the bride price. He must not take back any part of the bride price that was edible.

A, art 33 (Gen 38:1–30; Deut 25:5–10)

If the husband of a woman still living in the household of her father dies and she has sons, then she is to live in whichever of their households she chooses.

If the husband of a woman still living in the household of her father dies and she has no son, then the father of her husband's household is to appoint one of his sons as her legal guardian . . . or serve as her legal guardian himself.

If the husband of a woman still living in the household of her father dies, and the father of her household and the father of her husband's household are also dead, and she has no sons, then she becomes a widow and she may go wherever she wishes.

A, art 37 (Deut 24:1)

If a citizen wishes to divorce his wife, he may do so with alimony or without alimony.

A, art 40 (Gen 38:14–5)

Mothers of households, widows and other free women are to wear veils when they go out of their households. Marriageable women are to wear veils . . . when they go out of their households. Secondary wives are to wear veils when they go out with the mothers of their households. *Qadiltu* women, who are married priests, are to wear veils when they go out of their households.

Unmarried *qadiltu* women are not to wear veils when they go out of their households. Prostitutes are not to wear veils.

If a citizen sees a prostitute wearing a veil, then she is arrested, witnesses are subpoenaed, and she is charged before the assembly at the palace gate. Her jewelry is not confiscated, but the plaintiff is to confiscate her clothing. She is flogged fifty times with staves, and tar is poured into her hair.

If a citizen sees a prostitute who is wearing a veil, and does not charge her at the palace gate, then he is flogged fifty times with staves, his clothes are confiscated, his ears are pierced and tied with a cord behind his head and he is to serve as a slave for the state for one full month.

Slaves are not to wear veils.

If a citizen sees a slave wearing a veil, then she is arrested, charged before the assembly at the palace gate, her ears are cut off and her clothes are confiscated by the plaintiff.

If a citizen sees a slave wearing a veil and does not arrest her and charge her at the palace gate, then, following due process, he is flogged fifty times with staves, his ears are pierced and tied with a cord behind his head, his clothes are confiscated and he is to serve as a slave for the state for one full month.

A, art 41

If a citizen wishes to marry a captured woman, then he is to ask five or six of his neighbors to be present and he shall veil her in their presence while swearing: "She is my wife," and she becomes his wife.

If a secondary wife is not veiled in the presence of witnesses and the father of her household does not swear: "She is my wife," then she is still a secondary wife and not a mother of the household.

If a citizen dies and his wife has no sons, then his sons by concubines become eligible for a share of the household.

A, art 45

If the husband of a married woman becomes a prisoner of war, and the father of her household and the father of her husband's household are both dead, and she has no son, then she is to remain faithful to her husband for two years. . . .

If, during those two years, the woman swears before witnesses that she does not have enough to live on, then the state is to appoint a legal guardian to support her, and for whose household she is to work. . . .

If, during those two years, the woman swears before witnesses that she does not have enough to live on, but that her husband will inherit a field and a house in the city, then the ruler and the elders of the city are to accept his field and house as collateral and pay for her support. . . .

. . . after two years, the ruler and the elders are to declare her a widow; then she may go to live with the husband of her choice.

If a husband who becomes a prisoner of war returns after his wife has been declared a widow and has remarried, then he is to take her back. He may not claim the sons whom she has had with her second hus-

Symbolic rendering of Asshur giving rain to maintain living vegetation on earth.

band. Their sons belong to his household. Unless he remains in the army, he is to repay the ruler and the elders of the city for everything they spent to support his wife, and recover his right to inherit a field and a house in the city.

If a husband who becomes a prisoner of war dies in a strange land, the ruler is to reassign his field and house to whomever he wishes.

A, art 47 (Exod 22:18; Lev 20:27; Deut 18:10–4; 1 Sam 28:3)

If a man or woman works magic, or if a man or woman has magical potions or objects in his or her possession, then, following due process, the defendants are sentenced to death.

If a citizen witnesses a man or woman working magic, or if a citizen hears of it from an eyewitness who swears: "I have seen it myself," then he is to come forward and testify before the ruler. . . .

A, art 50 (Exod 21:22–5)

If one citizen physically abuses the wife of another until she has a miscarriage, then her husband is to physically abuse the wife of the defendant until she has a miscarriage. The defendant is to also compensate the victim by giving her household a child from his household.

If one citizen physically abuses the wife of another until she has a miscarriage and dies, then the defendant is executed, and his household is to compensate the victim by giving her household a child.

If one citizen physically abuses the wife of another until she has a miscarriage and her husband has no sons, then the defendant is executed and, even if the fetus is female, his household is to compensate the victim by giving her household a child.

A, art 53

If a woman has an abortion, then, after due process, she is impaled on a stake and left unburied.

If a woman has an abortion and dies, then her body is impaled on a stake and left unburied.

If a citizen hides a woman so that she can have an abortion, and does not charge her before the ruler. . . .

A, art 55 (Deut 22:23–7)

If a marriageable woman, who is the daughter of a citizen, who is living in her father's house, who is not engaged or married, and who is not collateral for any of her father's debts, is kidnaped and raped by another citizen, either in the city, in the country, in the street at night, in a granary or at a city festival, then the father of her household is to kidnap and rape the wife of his daughter's assailant.

If the assailant has no wife, the father of the daughter who was kidnaped and raped may also give his daughter to her assailant in marriage, and the assailant is to pay one-third more than the standard bride price in silver to her father as the bride price for a marriageable woman, and marry her without the opportunity for divorce.

If the father does not wish to marry his daughter to her assailant, he is to accept one-third more than the standard bride price in silver as a fine and marry his daughter to whomever he wishes.

A, art 56 (Exod 22:16–7; Deut 22:28–9)

If a marriageable woman freely consents to have intercourse with a married man, then the man is to swear that he did not force himself on her, and the father of the woman is not to touch the man's wife. The man is to pay one-third more than the standard bride price in silver for a marriageable woman, and the father of her household may punish his daughter as he wishes.

A, art 58

Only state officials may carry out prescribed sentences against a citizen's wife, like gouging out her eyes or cutting off her ears.

A, art 59

Although a husband may not carry out any prescribed sentences against his wife, he may, without liability, pull out her hair, mutilate or twist her ears, if she deserves it.

STORIES OF BALAAM

≋ *Hendricus Jacobus Franken excavated Deir 'Alla in the Jordan valley in 1967. First, a bit of plaster with writing in red and black ink on it, and then two large, fragmentary inscriptions were recovered. The plaster may have been applied to a stele or the walls of a sanctuary dedicated to the members of the divine assembly who are named in the stories and intended to protect the people of Deir 'Alla from the natural disasters which the stories describe. These traditions are written in a dialect of the Aramaic language common in the southern part of Canaan. The artifacts found with the plaster and the style of writing date it to 700 BCE.*

The fragments have been reassembled in more than one sequence. In one combination, Balaam has a dream that the divine assembly is planning to destroy his city by turning nature upside down. Tame animals would become wild and wild animals would become tame. Poor women would use myrrh as though they were rich. The next morning Balaam goes into mourning. When the people ask him why he is mourning, he tells them about the dream. The people repent, and the divine assembly spare the city, but condemn Balaam to death for thwarting their plans.

The world-turned-upside-down motif in the book of Lamentations is parallel to this story of Balaam from Deir 'Alla. The motif in which a divine patron warns a human protégé of an impending disaster also appears in the stories of Atrahasis, the stories of Gilgamesh and the flood stories in the book of Genesis. Balaam also appears in the book of Numbers (Num 22:5—24:25).

lines 5–10 (Exod 6:3; 30:23–33; 1 Sam 9:9; Lam 2:10; 3:2; Joel 2:10)

This is a story of Balaam, son of Beor and a seer. The divine assembly appeared to Balaam, son of Beor, at night. He dreamed he heard El

A painting around a Canaanite vase found near Ziklag showing antelopes grazing on shrubs (late Bronze Age).

pronounce a death sentence on his city. He watched as the divine assembly announced the beginning of a drought that would burn the land of his city like a raging fire. When Balaam got up the next morning, he began to fast and to lament bitterly.

The people of the city asked: "Balaam, son of Beor, why do you fast? Why do you mourn?" So Balaam agreed to tell them about his dream.

"Sit down and let me tell you what the Shadday have done,
    Let me show you what the divine assembly has decided.
The Shadday convened as a divine assembly,
    They decreed. . . .
Lock up the heavens,
    Bolt the doors of the clouds.
Bring darkness,
    Instead of light.
Seal the doors,
    Bolt them shut forever!
Let the sparrow hunt carrion like a vulture,
    Let the vulture chirp for its food like a sparrow. . . .
Let the stork steal the young of the cormorant,
    . . . claw the marsh bird and the sparrow.
Let shepherds herd rabbits instead of sheep. . . .

Let the hyena become tame,
    Let the pups of a fox run wild.

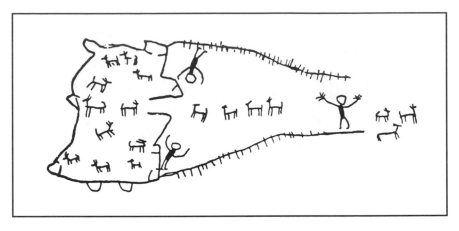

A sheepfold made from brambles and perhaps mud, used to hold sheep at night while on the move. (From a stone graffito found in Jordan.)

Let poor women perfume themselves with myrrh,
    Let priests smell of sweat. . . .

    Let princes wear rags. . . .
Let the respected now show respect,
    Let those who once showed respect now receive respect.
Let the deaf hear long distance,
    Let fools see visions. . . ."

JOSHUA,
JUDGES

STORIES OF SINUHE

Stories of Sinuhe are preserved today on five papyri in the Berlin Museum, and at least seventeen ceramic ostraca elsewhere.

The stories are told by Sinuhe, an official of pharaoh Amenemhat I (1991-1962 BCE). Sinuhe served the pharaoh's daughter, Neferu, and her husband, Senwosret. When Amenemhat dies, Sinuhe inadvertently witnesses a plot to take over Egypt. Afraid that the traitors will assassinate him to protect themselves, he goes into exile in Syria-Palestine, where he lives most of his life, away from the Egypt he loves. When the story ends, pharaoh Senwosret I (1971-1926 BCE) and Neferu invite Sinuhe, who is now an old man, to return to Egypt.

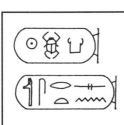

*Royal cartouches showing the names of King Senusret I (*Kheperkara *and* Senusret*).*

The stories of Sinuhe have parallels in the stories of Abraham and Sarah (Gen 11:27—25:18), the stories of Jacob, Leah and Rachel (Gen 25:20—37:2), and the teachings of Joseph (Gen 41) in the book of Genesis, which describe many of the same places and customs. The adoption of Sinuhe by Asiatic bedouin and his marriage to the chief's daughter are parallel to Moses' experience with Jethro the Kenite in the book of Exodus (Exod 2:11-22). Sinuhe describes his duel in Syria-Palestine in much the same language as the story of how David delivers Israel from Goliath in the books of Samuel-Kings (1 Sam 17:17-58).

B:20—35

. . . I traveled away from Egypt throughout the night, and by dawn I had reached Peten. I collapsed on an island in the Bitter Lakes (Egyptian: *Kem-wer*). My throat was so dry and parched that I thought I was going

129

to die from thirst. . . . I told myself: "I am about to taste death!" Suddenly, I heard the sounds of livestock, so I got control of myself and pulled myself to my feet. Some Asiatic bedouin were approaching. The head of their household, who had come to Egypt before, recognized me. He gave me water and yogurt and I traveled with his tribe. They were goods hosts to me. I was the guest of one household after the other until I reached Byblos (Egyptian: *kpny*) on the coast of Syria. I lived there in the eastern desert (Egyptian: *qedem*) for one and one-half years.

Then, Ammunenshi, who was ruler of northern Syria-Palestine (Egyptian: *retenu*), invited me to live in his land. "You shall be happy with me," he said, ". . . because you shall hear the language of Egypt again!" Ammunenshi extended this invitation to me because the other Egyptians in his land had told him that I was both honest and wise.

> *Sinuhe married the oldest daughter of Ammunenshi, and settled in his land. He lived like the bedouin, and became famous for his wealth and the strength of his household. He also served as host to travelers as repayment for the hospitality he had received in his flight from Egypt.*

78–100

Ammunenshi took me into his family and gave me his oldest daughter as my wife. He let me choose my own land from among his holdings within the land of Yaa. It was a land overflowing with figs and grapes. It had more wine than water, honey and oil in abundance. . . .

Every messenger and all those from Egypt who traveled through my lands were invited to my house. I gave water to the thirsty, directions to the traveler, help to those who were robbed. I counseled the Asiatic bedouin during times of unrest.

110–50

One day, a strong man from Syria-Palestine pushed his way into my tent and challenged me to a duel. He was a warrior without equal. He had never lost a duel. His household had encouraged him to pick a fight with me, and, once he had shamed me, to plunder all my livestock.

Ammunenshi asked me how I had caused the strong man to lose face. I swore to him: "I do not even know this man. I am not his covenant partner, and I have never raided his camp. I have never been a guest of his household, and I have never stolen livestock from his pens. He is angry with me for being your obedient servant. . . ."

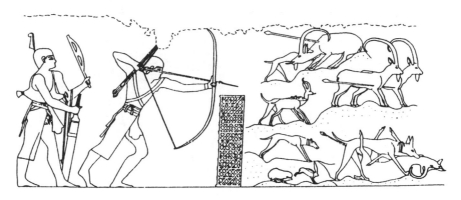

Desert hunting scene showing the owner, attendant, and hounds, from the Egyptian tomb of Senbi at Meir (12th Dynasty).

That night I strung my bow (Egyptian: *pdt*), and I practiced shooting my arrows. I took my knife (Egyptian: *b3gsw*) out of its scabbard and sharpened it. By dawn, half of all Syria-Palestine had arrived and pitched camp to watch the duel.

Each time the strong man advanced, I backed out of range. Everyone wanted me to win. Men and women groaned. Every heart embraced me as the underdog. Everyone wondered: "How can anyone defeat such a strong man?" He was armed with a shield, an ax (Egyptian: *minb*) and a whole armful of javelins (Egyptian: *nywy*). One after the other, I dodged the javelins, and sidestepped the arrows. I waited until finally the strong man rushed me, then I shot him in the neck with an arrow. With a loud cry he fell on his face mortally wounded. I finished him off with his own ax, and then stood on his back and let out my battle cry while all the Asiatic people thundered their applause. I sang hymns to Montu the divine warrior, while the household of the strong man sang their laments.

≋ *In spite of the wealth, the respect and the adventure that Sinuhe enjoyed in Syria-Palestine, he was homesick. In response to discreet inquiries, Senwosret (Sesostris) I invites him to come home to Egypt.*

248–84

At dawn, I was escorted by ten elders and ten soldiers to the palace of pharaoh. I prostrated myself between the long rows of sphinxes, while pharaoh's children watched from a balcony in the pylon gate overhead. The elders and soldiers escorted me as far as the grand hall, and then told me to present myself to pharaoh in his private chambers. I found

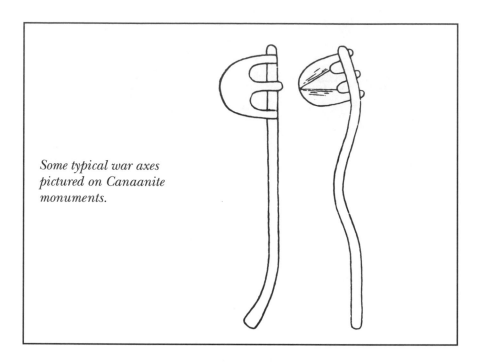

Some typical war axes pictured on Canaanite monuments.

pharaoh seated on a great throne in a room paneled with gold and silver. At once I prostrated myself before him. I had forgotten how to behave in his presence. Nevertheless, pharaoh the divine addressed me kindly. Immediately, I began having seizures. My ba-soul left my body. My arms and legs trembled. I fell unconscious.

At that moment, pharaoh ordered one of the soldiers: "Wake him up. I want to speak with him." Then pharaoh said to me: "Look, you have just made a frightening journey through strange lands. Old age is your enemy. Feebleness has caught up with you. Your burial is no small affair. You should not be buried like a miserable nomad. No, no indeed. . . . Why do you not answer, when I speak to you?"

I was almost too terrified to answer. "I do not understand what my lord is saying to me. I want to answer, but I cannot. I am possessed with terror. . . . I can only stand here in front of you. My life is in your hands. Pharaoh may do with me as he wishes."

Then, pharaoh sent for Queen Neferu and his children. "Look, this is Sinuhe, disguised as one of the Asiatic people, a nomad." Neferu shouted with joy, and all the children began to laugh.

Neferu and the children kept asking pharaoh: "Is this really Sinuhe?"

Pharaoh kept reassuring them: "It really is he."

≋◲ *A hymn is sung to the accompaniment of rattles and sistra, acknowledging Sinuhe's return to Egypt and his restoration to royal favor.*

285

I left the audience chamber with the pharaoh's children taking me by the hand. I was given a luxurious house with a bath, fit for a prince. I was also given robes of purest linen, myrrh, and the scents used by pharaoh and his court. I had slaves to perform my every wish. My years melted away as I was shaved and my hair combed. . . . I was clothed in the finest linen and anointed with the choicest oil, and I slept on a bed. I returned the sand to those who dwell in it and the wood oil to those who grease themselves with it.

≋◲ *To complete his transition to life and eternal life in Egypt, Sinuhe prepared his tomb and made arrangements with the mortuary priests to prepare his body after death. He had come full circle and was content.*

Egyptian clothing pictured during the period of the 12th Dynasty.

ANNALS OF
TUTHMOSES III

Several important copies of the annals of Tuthmoses III (1479–1425 BCE) have been discovered by German archaeologists and first published by C.R. Lepsius. Tuthmoses had ordered that the annals be carved in hieroglyphics on the walls of his section of the great temple at Karnak, an area on the north wall of the eastern hall in the precincts of the temple of Amon. The temple and its inscriptions remain in their original location on the east bank of the Nile in Luxor, Egypt. Subsequently, German archaeologists recovered a granite stele from Jebel Barkal near the fourth cataract of the Nile on which a portion of the annals of Tuthmoses were also carved. The Barkal

Head of Tuthmoses III.

stele is preserved in the Cairo Museum. While examining the temples at Armant in Upper Egypt, British archaeologists recovered a red granite stele on which was carved still another copy of the annals of Tuthmoses. The Armant stele is preserved today in the Cairo Museum.

Annals are the reports which rulers in the world of the Bible make as evidence that they have protected the land and provided for the people with whom they have been entrusted by the divine assembly. The primary audience for these annals is the ruler's divine patron. In his annals, Tuthmoses III reported to his divine patron, Amon Ra, that he had rebuilt Egypt's empire in Syria-Palestine, where he waged sixteen campaigns during a twenty-year period. The battle for Megiddo in 1468 BCE was Tuthmoses' greatest victory. According to the Jebel Barkal stele, the battle of Megiddo lasted seven months. During this time the Egyptian army harvested some 400,000–1,000,000 bushels of wheat from Megiddo's fields. Among his war trophies from Megiddo were 924 chariots.

Parallels to the annals of Tuthmoses appear in the books of Samuel-Kings where similar reports are filed by the rulers of Israel and Judah before Yahweh.

Armant Stele:8–11 (1 Kgs 15:16–22)

TENTH DAY OF MONTH TWO, SECOND SEASON, YEAR 22 OF THE REIGN OF TUTHMOSES III

His majesty, Tuthmoses III, marched immediately into Syria-Palestine (Egyptian: crossed the River) to crush the cities along its borders, utterly destroying them with fire. He erected a victory stele on its eastern bank. . . . He also marched to Djahi to punish the traitors (Egyptian: *retenu*) and reward those who were loyal to Egypt. After each victorious campaign, he returned to Egypt, which prospered as it did during the epoch primeval when Ra, its divine patron, ruled the land alone.

SECOND DAY OF MONTH FOUR, SECOND SEASON, YEAR 22 OF THE REIGN OF TUTHMOSES III

Armant Stele: 12–5 (2 Kgs 23:29–30)

His majesty, Tuthmoses III, won a great victory when he marched from Memphis into Syria-Palestine to punish the traitors. After his army had regained control of all the roads, the traitors took refuge in Megiddo.

*Mural from the tomb of Sebekhotep at Thebes, showing Syrian princes
bringing tribute (18th dynasty, about 1400 B.C.E.).*

His majesty led his army through the narrow pass along the Wadi Ara
against the traitors from all over Syria-Palestine who were waiting for him
on the plain of Megiddo . . . but the traitors fled like birds into the city
with their leader. . . . They bargained for their lives with everything they
owned. His majesty jubilantly returned to Egypt with every ruler of
Syria-Palestine bringing him tribute.

Hebsed Festival Hall at Karnak

TWENTY-FIRST DAY OF MONTH ONE, THIRD SEASON, YEAR 23

. . . when Tuthmoses III led his army to victory over the traitors, they
fled in terror into the city of Megiddo. They had to be pulled up over
the walls of Megiddo from their gold and silver inlaid, horse-drawn chariots by the clothes they were wearing, and holding to garments thrown
over the walls because the gates of the city had already been bolted shut.
If the soldiers of Tuthmoses III had not been so interested in plunder-
ing everything the traitors had abandoned on the plain of Megiddo, they
could have captured the city itself on that first day of battle while the traitors from Kadesh and Megiddo were being hauled up over the walls
paralyzed by fear of the great serpent *uraeus* riding on the forehead of
his majesty.

EL AMARNA LETTERS

The first three-hundred tablets containing the El Amarna letters were found in 1887 by a woman from an Egyptian village, who sold them all for about one dollar. Eventually, five-hundred forty tablets and fragments would be recovered by archaeologists through excavation or purchase. So far, three-hundred eighty-two tablets have been published, of which three-hundred fifty are diplomatic communiqués. Today they are preserved in the Vorderasiatishes Museum in Berlin, the British Museum in London, the Cairo Museum and the Louvre Museum in Paris. They were written in a dialect of Akkadian using cuneiform script, but they include many Canaanite words and expressions.

Akhenaton (1352–1335 BCE) built the royal city of El Amarna to replace Thebes as the capital of Egypt. The site he chose was about one-hundred fifty miles south of today's Cairo, and seems to have been at the exact geographical center of the Egypt of his day. Thebes was still some one-hundred fifty miles further south of El Amarna. The El Amarna letters were written to Amenophis III (1398–1361 BCE) and Akhenaton by their governors in Syria-Palestine. Neither pharaoh managed Egypt's domestic or foreign policy well. Consequently, governors throughout Egypt itself and its trade empire in Syria-Palestine seized the herds and crops of villages for raw materials and caravans for trade goods. In the El Amarna letters, governors protest their loyalty to pharaoh, and repeatedly ask for soldiers to protect themselves from their fellow governors, whom they label as rebels (Akkadian: 'apiru).

There is little evidence today for identifying the 'apiru in the El Amarna letters with the Hebrews in the Bible. Nonetheless, this social unrest in Syria-Palestine during the New Kingdom (1500–1250 BCE) is comparable to the social unrest in Syria-Palestine during the Iron I period (1250–1000 BCE) described in the books of Joshua–Judges.

An Egyptian tomb drawing of typical men from Syria and Canaan, from whence the Amarna letters originated.

An Egyptian soldier with shield honoring the king.

Letter 244: 1–30 (Est 3:2; Isa 45:23)

To: Pharaoh, ruler of the heavens and earth
From: Biridiya, governor of Megiddo

I am your slave, and I renew my covenant with you as my pharaoh by bowing before you seven times seven times.

Pharaoh should know that, since he recalled his archers to Egypt, Labayu, the governor of Shechem, has not stopped raiding the land of Megiddo. The people of Megiddo cannot leave the city to shear your sheep for fear of Labayu's soldiers.

Because you have not replaced the archers, Labayu is now strong enough to attack the city of Megiddo itself. If pharaoh does not reinforce the city, Labayu will capture it.

The people of Megiddo are already suffering from hunger and disease. I beg pharaoh to send one-hundred fifty soldiers to protect Megiddo from Labayu or he will certainly capture the city.

Letter 254: 1–40

To: Pharaoh, ruler of the heavens and earth
From: Labayu, governor of Shechem

I am your slave, who is less than the dust under your feet, and I renew my covenant with you as my pharaoh by bowing before you seven times seven times.

I have received pharaoh's letter. Your fears are unfounded. I am far too insignificant to be a threat to the lands of pharaoh in Canaan.

I am, and always have been, loyal to pharaoh. I am neither a traitor nor a rebel. I pay tribute on time, and I obey every order which the representative of pharaoh here in Canaan gives me. If pharaoh will personally look into the case, he will see that I am the victim of malicious lies.

My only crime is that I invaded the land of Gezer to replace the land of Shechem, which pharaoh confiscated from me. Milkilu, the governor of Gezer, has committed even worse offenses than I, and pharaoh has not confiscated his land.

Pharaoh has also indicted my heir as a rebel (Akkadian: *'apiru*). I had no idea that my son was consorting with rebels. I have since handed him over to Addaya. Even if pharaoh had indicted my wife, I would hand her over for trial.

I would not even refuse your order to thrust a dagger of bronze into my own heart.

Letter 286:1–64 (1 Kgs 11:26; Micah 6:3)

To: Pharaoh, ruler of the heavens
From: 'Abdi-Heba

I am your slave, and I renew my covenant with you as my pharaoh by bowing before you seven times seven times. What have I done to displease pharaoh? The charge circulating in your court that: "'Abdi-Heba is a rebel" is destroying my good name. I am well aware that I owe my authority to the mighty hand of pharaoh, and not as an inheritance. Why should I rebel against pharaoh, my lord?

Over and over I have asked the representative of pharaoh: "Why do you support the rebels who raid the lands of your governors in Canaan?" Now he charges me with treason. Enhamu blames me for failing to protect the lands of pharaoh, but it was he who recalled the soldiers which pharaoh sent to protect these lands. Today there are no soldiers left to

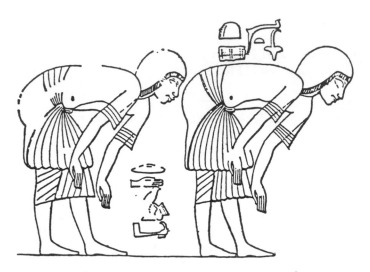

Officials of the royal harem bow before King Akhenaton.
(From the tomb of Ramose at Thebes; 19th Dynasty.)

protect the lands of pharaoh. It is now entirely up to pharaoh to deal with the rebels whom Milkilu, the governor of Gezer, has incited to seize pharaoh's lands.

On many occasions I have asked for an audience with pharaoh, but the hostility against me has prevented me from coming. Only if the pharaoh sends soldiers to protect his lands will I be able to come to court to speak with him. I swear by the life of pharaoh that soon all the lands of pharaoh in Canaan will be lost, and not a single governor will remain loyal to pharaoh.

May it please the pharaoh to send the archers needed to reinforce the garrison. Without opposition, the rebels will continue to plunder the lands of pharaoh at will. The only hope pharaoh has to keep his lands under control is if archers are sent this year.

(Note to the scribe of pharaoh: Be sure that at least this much of my message is brought to the immediate attention of pharaoh, ruler of all the earth: "The lands of pharaoh, my lord, in Canaan will be lost.")

ANNALS OF RAMSES III

When Napoleon invaded Egypt (1798-1803), his expedition included one-hundred sixty-seven scholars to study and catalog its antiquities. Dominique Vivant Denon recorded Medinet Habu in the valley of the pharaohs at Luxor, Egypt. A high pylon or gateway opens into a broad courtyard beyond which rises the ninety-foot pylon leading to the holy of holies. Emphatically carved on both sides of the entrance pylon more than eight inches deep into the walls are the annals of a pharaoh conquering his enemies. Jean François Champollion was only eight years old when Denon sketched these reliefs, but in 1822, at the age of thirty-two, he deciphered hieroglyphics for the first time. By 1829, he had conclusively identified the pharaoh of Medinet Habu as Ramses III (1194-1163 BCE) and translated his annals describing the defense of Egypt under attack by Sea Peoples including the Philistines.

Parallels to the annals of Ramses III appear in the stories of Samson in the book of Judges (Judg 13:1—16:31), in the stories of Samuel (1 Sam 1:1—4:1+7:3—8:13) and in the stories of David's rise to power in the books of Samuel-Kings (1 Sam 8:4—2 Sam 8:13). The most famous Philistine in the Bible is Goliath (1 Sam 17:17-58). The Philistines and the Hebrews were peoples brought together in the same land at the same time by Egypt, their common enemy. The Philistines settled in the land, which others would call "Philistia" or "Palestine." The Hebrews settled in the land called "Israel." The Philistines were from the western Mediterranean, the Hebrews were from the east. Philistines and Hebrews appear here for the first time at the end of the Late Bronze period (1500-1250 BCE), when the empires of Mycennae, Hatti and Egypt collapsed. As the Iron Age (1250-1000 BCE) opened, these two peoples would share a common border in a common land, which led to competition and conflict. This struggle between Dagon, the divine patron of the Philistines, and Yahweh, the divine patron of the Hebrews, would last 250 years.

*King Ramses III shown entering the temple slaughterhouse,
carrying the Hrp baton. The king carried this scepter when
he acted as "feast-leader" while making the great
offerings of animal sacrifice.*

a:1–26 (Jer 21:1–10)

YEAR 8 OF THE REIGN OF RAMSES III . . .

. . . strangers from the Islands formed an alliance with one another. Suddenly, their warriors were invading and destroying every land. No land could defend itself against them. In one campaign, they cut down Hatti, Kode and Arzawa in Turkey, Carchemish in Syria, and Alashiya in Cyprus. They pitched their battle camp at Amor, and began slaying the peoples of Syria-Palestine and devastating their lands as no one has ever done before. Then they turned toward Egypt, whose fire was preparing to devour them. In this alliance were the Philistines, the Tjekker, the Shekelesh, the Dannuna and the Weshesh. They attacked every land on the face of the earth, confidently boasting: "We will be victorious!"

Now my divine heart was plotting how I was going to snare them like birds. . . .

I, ruler of the divine assembly, ordered my governors and commanders in Syria-Palestine to deploy their soldiers and *maryanu* chariots at Djahi on the coast. I ordered them to outfit every warship, freighter and transport from stem to stern with heavily-armed, hand-picked troops, and to blockade the mouth of every river along the coast. These ships were the pride of Egypt, and they roared like lions in the mountains. Runners led the chariots manned by the best, hand-picked soldiers. The bodies of the horses quivered as they waited to crush these strangers under their hooves. As Montu, the divine warrior, I led them into battle, so that they could see my outstretched hand. . . .

Sea battle between the forces of Ramses III and the Sea Peoples.
(20th Dynasty, 12th century, B.C.E.)

Those who reached the border of Egypt by land were annihilated. Their hearts and souls will never rise again. Those who attacked by sea were devoured at the mouths of the rivers, while the spears of the soldiers on shore tightened like the wall of a stockade around them. They were netted, beached, surrounded, put to death and stacked, head to foot, in piles. Their ships and cargo drifted aimlessly on the water.

I decreed that no one in the lands of these strangers was to even say the word: "Egypt." Whoever pronounced the word was burned alive. Since the day I ascended to the throne of Ra-Harakhti, the divine patron of pharaohs, since the first day the divine power of the *uraeus* serpent rode like Ra upon my brow, I have not let a single stranger see the border of Egypt, or any of the Nine Bows even boast of having fought against it. I have seized their lands, and crossed their borders. Their rulers and their people all sing my praises, for I have walked in the ways of Ra, ruler of all the earth, my incomparable godfather, who rules the divine assembly.

GEZER ALMANAC

The coast highway (Latin: **via maris**) was an important north–south trade lane that ran along the Mediterranean Sea from Egypt to the Carmel mountains. An east-west cut-off connected that highway to Jerusalem. The ancient city of Gezer guarded the intersection. Here, around 925 BCE, a student practiced writing Hebrew on a piece of soft rectangular limestone about four inches long and four inches wide. R.A.S. Macalister recovered the text during his excavation in 1908.

The student copied an almanac identifying each month of the farmer's year with specific chores. In Syria-Palestine, the agricultural year begins in the fall, when olives are harvested and the October rains soften the sun dried soil enough to plant.

Parallels to the Gezer almanac appear in the books of Exodus (Exod 9:31), Deuteronomy (Deut 24:20, 26:5-11), Joshua (Josh 2:6), Ruth (Ruth 2:23), Samuel-Kings (1 Sam 6:13; 1 Kgs 19:19), Isaiah (Isa 5:6, 18:5, 24:13, 28:25), Amos (8:1), Jeremiah (Jer 40:10), Ecclesiastes (Eccl 11:6), and Proverbs (Prov 20:4).

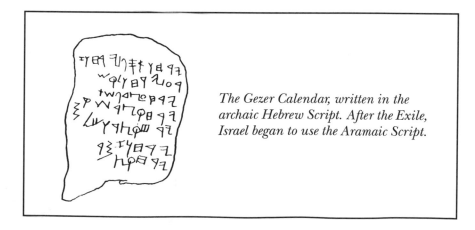

The Gezer Calendar, written in the archaic Hebrew Script. After the Exile, Israel began to use the Aramaic Script.

Egyptian scene of harvesting the grain (upper) and plowing (lower)
from Beni Hasan tomb 3 (19th century, B.C.E.).

August and September to pick the olives,
   October to sow the barley,
December and January to sow the wheat,
   February to pull the flax,
March and April to harvest the barley,
   April to harvest the wheat and to feast,
May and June to prune the vines,
   July to pick the fruit of summer.

RUTH

Cast of a female head found at Petra.

ARCHIVES OF BABATHA

⚋ *Near the end of the second war between Judah and Rome (132-135 CE), Jews from Ein Gedi took refuge in a cave on the cliffs above the Dead Sea, which archaeologists today call the "Cave of Letters." These refugees were eventually discovered and killed by the Romans. Among them was a widow named Babatha. She and other civilians left Ein Gedi with the Jewish troops commanded by her brother-in-law, Jonathan. Babatha brought with her a packet of legal documents that she had filed in courts of law between 93-132 CE.*

The archives of Babatha were recovered during 1960-61 by an Israeli archaeological expedition led by Yigael Yadin. They were written in Greek, Nabataean, and Aramaic. There were twenty-six documents in Greek, which was the official language of the eastern provinces of the Roman empire. Some had been annotated in Aramaic and Nabataean. There were six documents in Nabataean, which is the language of the people of Petra in the south of Jordan today. Three documents were written in Aramaic, which was the everyday language spoken by Jews throughout the Roman provinces of Judaea and Syria at the beginning of the common era. The archives are a unique source from which to reconstruct the everyday life of this region in antiquity, shedding light on such subjects as the legal system, economics, religious observances, geography, agriculture, and linguistics.

The archives are also fascinating testimony to the legal tenacity of a widow before courts of law. Like Tamar in the book of Genesis and Ruth and Naomi in the book of Ruth, Babatha was a persistent widow dedicated to protecting the legal rights of her household. In the book of Genesis, Mahoza or Zoar (Arabic: es-Safi), the village of Babatha, grants Lot and his daughters asylum.

DEED TO A PLANTATION IN ZOAR (JULY 13, 120 CE)

≋ *Babatha was born into a wealthy household in Zoar, south of the Dead Sea. A deed to a plantation in Zoar, dated July 13, 120 CE, is part of a trust created by Simeon for his wife, Miriam, and his daughter, Babatha. Simeon provides that if Babatha becomes a widow she may live in one of the houses on the plantation until she remarries.*

. . . on the third of Kislev, in the twenty-eighth year of Rabael . . . in the lifetime of Obdath the son of his majesty, Rabael, ruler of the Nabataeans who provided for his people and protected them from their enemies, and in the times of Gamilath and Hagru, his sisters, queens of the Nabataeans, children of his majesty, Maniku, ruler of the Nabataeans, the son of Naretath, ruler of the Nabataeans, who loved his people

. . . in the second consulship of Lucius Cailius Severus and Marcus Aurelius Antoninus, in the third year of Imperator Caesar Traianus Hadrianus Augustus, and on the twenty-fourth of Tammuz in the year fifteen in this province of Arabia. . . .

. . . issued in Zoar of Agalatain

. . . of my own free will, I, Simeon, son of Menahem, who live in Zoar, give to you, Miriam, my wife, daughter of Joseph, son of Manassah, and to the heirs of Joseph, son of Dormenes, all that I possess in Zoar

. . . water rights: one hour and one-half of three hours . . .

. . . water rights: Sunday, one-half hour of stream water

. . . Monday, one-half hour

. . . water rights: Wednesday, one hour

. . . all that I shall purchase and that shall be mine in the future. . . .

A TRIAL OF JONATHAN EGLA (OCTOBER 12, 125 CE)

≋ *Babatha was married twice. Her first husband was Joshua. They had one son and named him Joshua. After the death of her husband, the senate of Petra appointed two guardians for her son: Jonathan Egla who was Jewish, and Abdobdas Illoutha, a Nabataean. This action followed the tradition that a widow's care lay in the hands of her legal guardians. Several of Babatha's archives document her legal battle against Egla and Illoutha for control of her deceased husband's land. On October 12, 125 CE, Babatha filed suit against Egla and charged him with failing to pay her child support. She wanted the land held in trust by her son's guardians to be turned over to her and, in return, she would pay her legal guardians a higher rate of interest on it than the guardians could get in the open market.*

. . . since you, Jonathan Egla, did not pay adequate child support for my orphaned son, Joshua . . .

. . . Abdobdas Illoutha has given me . . . power of attorney over Joshua's inheritance and allowed me to use my own property as a bond. I shall pay him an interest of one and one-half days' wages in silver (Latin: *denarius*) a month for every one hundred days' wages in silver in the inheritance. This ingenious arrangement to provide for my son was negotiated during the happy days when Julius Julianos was governor.

. . . therefore, in the presence of Julius Julianos, I, Babatha, charge you, Jonathan, my son's legal guardian, for failing to pay child support. . . .

TAX RETURN OF BABATHA (DECEMBER 2, 127 CE)

≋ *When he was governor (127–129 CE), Florentinus, whose tomb is in Petra, promulgated a decree ordering a tax census of the Roman province of Arabia. The gospel of Luke describes a similar census taken by Quirinius in the Roman province of Syria (Luke 2:1–7). On December 2, 127 CE, Babatha filed her return in Rabbath-Moab in central Jordan today. Judah, her husband to be, was her legal witness.*

. . . in compliance with the decree ordering a census of Arabia promulgated by T. Aninius Sextius Florentinus. . . .

. . . I am Babatha, daughter of Simeon of Zoar, in the subdistrict of Zoar, in the district of Petra, living on my own property in Zoar. . . .

. . . I, Babatha, have declared everything I own in Zoar. Judah, son of Eleazar of Ein Gedi, in the district of Jericho, in the province of Judaea, who lives on his own property in Zoar, is my witness. . . .

. . . I swear by the Tyche of Caesar, my lord, that this declaration is true, correct and complete.

PRE-NUPTIAL AGREEMENT OF JUDAH AND BABATHA

≋ *After the death of her first husband, Babatha remarried. A pre-nuptial agreement (Hebrew: ketubba) between Babatha and Judah negotiates this second marriage, which was officially celebrated on February 2, 127 CE. Judah died almost immediately after the wedding, leaving Babatha a large estate. His relatives contested the agreement.*

Painted pottery
bowl from Petra.

lines 5–6

. . . a pre-nuptial agreement with Babatha, the daughter of Simeon
. . . who will be my wife, according to the law of Moses and the Jews. Based
on this pre-nuptial agreement, I will feed you and clothe you and I will
bring you into my house. I will pay your father fifty ounces of silver as a
bride price. . . .

lines 15–6

. . . if I die before you, you may continue to live in my house and be
supported by the income from it and from my other possessions, until
my heirs pay you the settlement stipulated in our pre-nuptial agreement. . . .

SAMUEL, KINGS

ANNALS OF
TIGLATH-PILESER I

≋ *The annals of Tiglath-Pileser I (1115-1077 BCE) are written in cune-iform using the Assyrian dialect of the Akkadian language. The inscription was recovered by a team of German archaeologists and is preserved today in the Vorderasiatisches Museum in Berlin (VAT 13833).*

The annals asks: "Is it possible for an ass to escape from a hun-ter for long when the divine assembly intervenes!" The protagonist in the parable is Tiglath-Pileser I (1115-1077 BCE) who is cast as a hunter (Akkadian: ba'iru). The antagonist is the ruler of Murattash and Saradaush, who is a wild ass (Akkadian: imeri sadi). The hunter stalks the ass into the mountains (Gen 16:12), where a ferocious battle takes place. The graphic description of ripping open the bellies of pregnant women is typical of annals and the military tactic of psy-chological terrorism. A more standard version of this account is found in the Assyrian king's cylinder inscription from his fifth regnal year (ARI 2.25).

There are parallels to the annals of Tiglath-Pileser I in the book of Genesis (Gen 10:9), the books of Samuel-Kings (2 Kgs 8:11-2, 15:16), and the book of Amos (Amos 1:13).

Obv. 21–22; Rev 1–4, 6–7

. . . after the hunter consulted the prophets,
  He hitched his horses to his chariots as fast as Adad the storm and
    Shamash the sun.
He set out before the sun rose.
  He marched three days' distance before dawn. . . .

Drawing of wall relief showing the Assyrian army defeating an enemy.

The hunter cut open the wombs of the pregnant,
    He blinded infants.
He slit the throats of warriors. . . .
    Whoever offended Ashur was destroyed.
Sing of the power of Assyria,
    Ashur the strong, who goes forth to battle. . . .

ANNALS OF MESHA

Mesha of Moab inscribed his annals on a curved topped, rectangular block of basalt three feet high and two feet wide. The thirty lines of text are written in the Moabite language using the Hebrew alphabet. The grammar, syntax and vocabulary of Moabite and Hebrew are similar. The stele was located in Dibon, Jordan in 1868 by F.A. Klein, a German missionary. Subsequently, Charles Clermont-Ganneau (1846-1923), a French scholar, had a paper squeeze made of the inscription. Reacting to the attention the Europeans were giving their artifact, local people heated the stele in a fire and then smashed it into pieces with cold water hoping to find treasure inside. A third of the stele was permanently destroyed. In 1870, the remains were restored by the Louvre Museum in Paris.

The annals of Mesha mention Omri of Israel (886-875 BCE), the fighting of a holy war (Hebrew: herem), and other parallels to the book of Joshua (Josh 6:17-21) and the books of Samuel-Kings (1 Kgs 16:23-4; 2 Kgs 3:4).

Ivory furniture decoration showing a sphinx from Samaria, at the time of king Omri.

(Josh 6:24; 8:1–2, 18, 24–7; 10:42; 1 Sam 23:4; 2 Sam 8:2)

I am Mesha, ruler of Moab from Dibon. My father was the ruler of Moab for thirty years, and I became king after him. . . .

Omri, ruler of Israel, invaded Moab year after year because Chemosh, the divine patron of Moab, was angry with his people. When the son of Omri succeeded him during my reign, he bragged: "I too will invade Moab." However, I defeated the son of Omri and drove Israel out of our land forever. Omri and his son ruled the Madaba plains for forty years, but Chemosh dwells there in my time. I built the city of Baal-Meon with its reservoir, and the city of Qaryaten.

Long ago the tribe of Gad invaded Ataroth, but I defeated them and captured the city of Ataroth which the ruler of Israel had fortified. I sacrificed all of the people of Ataroth to Chemosh. I brought the altar of Israel (Moabite: *dwd*) from the sanctuary of Ataroth and mounted it before Chemosh in the sanctuary of Kerioth. Finally, I settled the tribes of Sharon and Maharith in the land which I had taken from Israel to claim it for Moab.

At that time, Chemosh said to me, "Go, take Nebo from Israel." So I deployed my soldiers at night and attacked Nebo from dawn until noon. I won a great victory and I sacrificed seven thousand men, women, and children from Nebo to Chemosh as I had vowed I would do. . . .

The king of Israel was invading Moab from Jahaz, which he had fortified. Chemosh, my divine patron, drove him out before me. I settled the households of two-hundred of my best soldiers in Jahaz to claim it for Dibon.

Egyptian painting of a fort defended from its parapets.
(Beni Hasan tomb, 19th century, B.C.E.)

I built Qarhoh with gates and towers, a palace and reservoirs. I also decreed: "Every household in Qarhoh is to have its own cistern." I had Israel's prisoners of war cut the beams for the royal buildings in Qarhoh. I built Aroer and a highway through the Arnon valley (Arabic: *wadi el-Mujib*). I also rebuilt the cities of Beth-bamoth and Bezer for fifty households from Dibon.

I reigned in peace over hundreds of villages which I had conquered and Chemosh dwelt there in my time. . . .

TELL DAN ANNALS
OF HAZAEL

In 1966, Avraham Biran took his Israeli team into the field at Tell Dan in northern Israel for the first time. Thirty seasons of work at the site have produced remarkable finds for understanding the world of the Bible between 1000 BCE, when David established a state in Israel, and 721 BCE, when Shalmaneser V of Assyria conquered more than half of the land ruled by David (2 Kgs 17:1-41; 18:1-12). In 1993,

Drawing of the Tell Dan Inscription. Lines 7 to 9 mention a Syrian victory against Jehoram, King of Israel, and Ahaziah of the House of David (9th century).

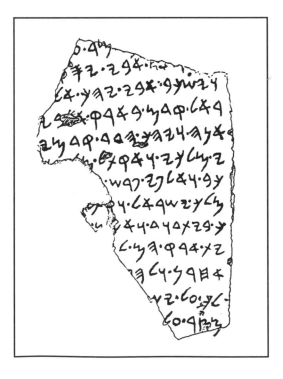

160

Biran's team recovered the annals of Hazael. They were inscribed in Aramaic on a stele that had been recycled as a paving stone. The first fragment is only eight and one-half inches wide, but originally it may have been twenty inches wide. Only thirteen lines are preserved. There are only three letters in the first three lines, and five letters in the last line. The longest line has only fourteen letters. One word is separated from the other with a dot. The stele is preserved today in the Israel Museum in Jerusalem. Two smaller fragments from the same inscription were recovered in 1994.

Hazael (842-800 BCE) was a ruler of Syria. His annals at Tell Dan celebrate a victory over Israel and Judah. These annals are only the fourth tradition outside the Bible to mention Israel. The others are the annals of Merneptah of Egypt (1224-1214 BCE), the annals of Mesha of Moab (830 BCE), and the annals of Shalmaneser III of Assyria (858-824 BCE). The annals of Hazael are the only tradition outside the Bible that mentions the "...house of David."

Parallels to the annals of Hazael appear in the annals of Jehu of Israel (844-815 BCE) in the books of Samuel-Kings (2 Kgs 8:25—10:36; 12:17-8).

. . . the father of my household, invaded Israel . . . before he slept with his ancestors. Then the king of Israel invaded the land of my father, and Hadad, my divine patron, made me king. With Hadad riding before me, I marched out of my land and destroyed seventy rulers with their corps of chariots and horsemen. I put [Jehoram], son of [Ahab] and ruler of Israel, and [Ahaz]iahu, son of [Jehoram] and ruler of the house of David, to death. I destroyed their cities and left their lands barren. . . . [When Jehu became king of] Israel, I laid siege to. . . .

KARATEPE ANNALS
OF AZITIWADA

Between 1945-47, the University of Istanbul recovered five inscriptions of the annals of Azitiwada (730-710 BCE) at Azatiwaqadiya in
Karatepe, Turkey. Two were written in Luwian hieroglyphics and
three in Phoenician, a West Semitic language. The only complete
inscription, which was carved across four adjoining columns and
one of the two stone lions flanking the gate, contains sixty-two lines.
These annals are the longest known inscriptions in Phoenician.

Azitiwada was appointed by Awariku (Assyrian: **Urriki**), the
king of Kue, to be governor of Adana. Kue and Adana today are
located in Cilicia, a southeastern region of Turkey. The annals
describe the steps that Azitiwada took to meet the needs of his people and to maintain good relations with other states. Its first person
style is similar to the annals of Mesha (840-820 BCE).

Titles, formulas like "...from sunrise to sunset," descriptions of
worship and trade, and the use of curses and blessings in the
annals of Azitiwada all have parallels in Solomon's prayer for wisdom (1 Kgs 3:1-15) and elsewhere in the Bible.

col i:1–3 (Isa 22:21; 45:6; Mal 1:11)

I am Azitiwada, the steward of Baal. I have been raised to my position of authority by my father, Awariku, king of Adana. With Baal's blessing I have become both father and mother of the Danunians in the plain
of Adana, extending their land from sunrise to sunset. . . .

*col i:3—col iii:2 (Gen 41:47–9; Judg 19:22; 1 Sam 1:21; 1 Kgs 3:1–15;
9:15–20; 2 Kgs 17:24; Ps 101:8)*

In my time, Adana enjoyed all the good things in life, full storehouses, and general prosperity. I filled the temple storehouses of Pa'ar,

A mother nursing her son, perhaps the queen and crown prince (from Karatepe in southern Turkey).

A Phoenician god standing on the back of a lion. He is holding a war club and a lion cub (from Amrith).

and greatly increased the supplies of arms and the size of the army at the command of Ba'al and the divine assembly.

I dealt harshly with traitors, expelling all troublemakers from the kingdom. I restored the household of Mupsh to power in Adana, ensured an orderly succession and maintained good diplomatic relations between Adana and its covenant partners. My deeds caused me to be held in high esteem by other rulers. My righteous and blameless actions were the outgrowth of my wisdom and my listening heart.

On all the frontiers of Adana, I built strong fortresses to guard against traitors who had never served the household of Mupsh. I, Azitiwada, placed all these traitors under my feet and Adana was at peace within the shelter of my fortresses.

I, Azitiwada, conquered the lands to the west, which no one before me had conquered. I subdued them and deported their populations to the eastern frontiers. I settled the Danunians in their place, and in my day the sun never set on Adana.

In those places which had been without peace, where men were afraid to leave their houses, in my day, with the help of Ba'al and the divine assembly, women spun wool in broad daylight.

Phoenician gate inscription with 21 lines of script by a Hittite sculptor.
(From Karatepe, 9th century, B.C.E.)

In all my days the storehouses were full, life was good, and the Danunians lived without care or fear. Ba'al and Resheph, divine patron of stags, commanded me to build this city and name it "Azitawadya." Its full storehouses, prosperity, law and order provide protection to the plains of Adana and for the household of Mupsh.

I established the worship of Ba'al Krntrys (Luwian: *Tarkhunza;* Latin: *Tarsus*) in Azitawadya. On their feast day every year, I offer an ox before the statues of all the members of the divine assembly. At the time of plowing and at the time of harvesting I sacrifice a sheep. . . .

col iii:4–11 (Prov 3:10)

May Ba'al Krntrys and the divine assembly of Azitawadya bless Azitiwada with many years of life, authority to rule, and strength beyond that of any king. May this city and the people who dwell here possess store-houses full of grain, and wine, oxen and livestock in abundance. May they have many children and in their strength of numbers become powerful. May they all serve Azitiwada and the house of Mupsh as Ba'al and the divine assembly have ordered. . . .

col iii:12—iv:1 (Gen 14:19; Josh 6:26; Ps 72:17)

If any monarch, prince or strong man removes the name of Aziti-wada from this gate or its statues and puts his own name on it, or if in renovating the city he tears down this gate made by Azitiwada and replaces it with a new gate containing his own name, whether with good or evil intent, may Ba'al the Cloud Rider, and El, the creator of the heavens and the earth, and every member of the divine assembly erase the name of that state and its ruler or strong man. May only the name of Azitiwada endure forever, like the names of the sun and the moon. . . .

ANNALS OF
SHALMANESER III

≋ *After 1250 BCE, when the Greek, Hittite and Egyptian empires col-
lapsed, there were no world powers for the next 350 years in Syria-
Palestine, and small states like Syria, Ammon, Moab, Edom, Israel,
Judah and Philistia began to appear. After 900 BCE, Ashurnasirpal II
(883–859 BCE) and Shalmaneser III (858–824 BCE), great kings of
Assyria, laid the foundations for a new age of empires.*

*In 1846 Austen Henry Layard (1817–1894) recovered a four-sided
obelisk of black limestone, six and one-half feet high from Nimrud
in what is today Iraq. It is preserved in the British Museum in London. There are five titled columns of cuneiform inscription. The
stepped pyramid on the top of the obelisk and about one-third of
its base are also inscribed. On the obelisk, Shalmaneser reports his
fifth western campaign in 841 BCE, which included Assyria's covenant with Israel. Assyria recognized Jehu as king of Israel (842–815
BCE). Jehu, in return, declared an armistice with Syria and abro-
gated Israel's covenant with Judah. The covenant is described, not
only in writing, but also in a relief that shows Jehu kneeling before
Shalmaneser as his client. Likewise, on a single, round-topped stone
stele or monolith, Shalmaneser describes his first six campaigns
into Syria-Palestine. There are one-hundred and two lines of cuneiform inscription. British archaeologists recovered this stele in 1861
at Kurkh, Turkey on the Tigris river. It is preserved today in the
British Museum (No 11884) in London. With his victory at Qarqar
on the Orontes river over the armies of twelve rulers, including
Hadad-ezer of Syria and Ahab of Israel, Shalmaneser established a
permanent Assyrian presence west of the Euphrates river.*

*Parallels to the annals of Shalmaneser III appear in the books
of Samuel-Kings (1 Kgs 16:29—22:40; 2 Kgs 9:1—10:33).*

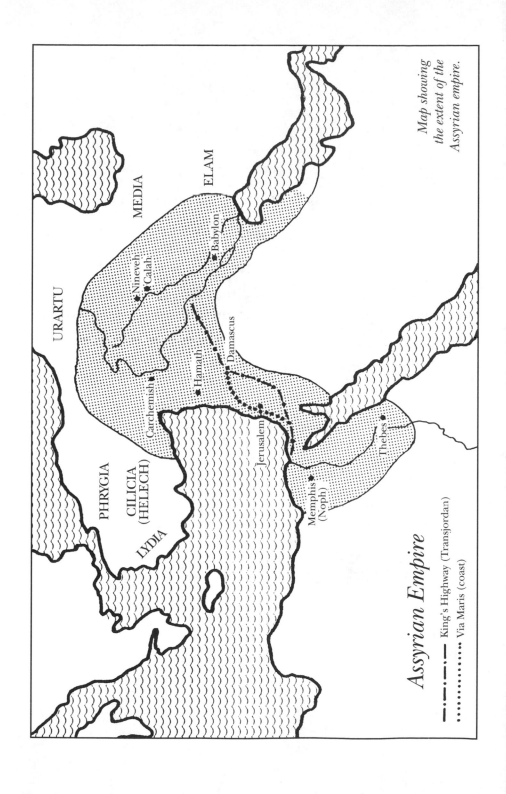

Assyrian Empire

— · — · — King's Highway (Transjordan)

· · · · · · · · Via Maris (coast)

*Map showing
the extent of the
Assyrian empire.*

URARTU

MEDIA

ELAM

PHRYGIA

CILICIA
(HELECH)

LYDIA

Nineveh
Calah

Babylon

Carchemish

Hamath

Damascus

Jerusalem

Memphis
(Noph)

Thebes

Kurkh stele (Monolith Inscription) ii:78–102 (Num 31:3–12; Josh 10:1–28; 11:1–12; 2 Sam 10:6–8; Ezek 37:1–2; Jer 7:33)

FOURTEENTH OF AIRU, YEAR SIX OF DAIN-ASSUR

After departing Nineveh, I crossed the Tigris river and marched to the towns of Giammu on the Balikh river. My terror-inspiring presence and the array of my weapons frightened the inhabitants so much that they killed Giammu, their leader.

I passed on to the towns of Sahlala and Til-sha-Turahi and installed the images of my divine patrons in their palaces. I performed a festival of celebration and then looted his palace treasury, sending the booty back to my capital at Ashur.

I crossed the flooding Euphrates river twice using goat-skin boats. I marched west of the Euphrates and camped at Ina-Ashur-utir-asbat on the Sagur river to collect tribute of gold, of silver, of copper and of copper vessels from Sanagara, the ruler of Carchemish; from Kundashpi, the ruler of Commagene; from Arame, the son of Guzi; from Lalli, the ruler of Melidea; from Haiani, the son of Gabari; from Kalparuda, the ruler of Hattina; and from Kalparuda, the ruler of Gurgum.

I marched west to Aleppo (Akkadian: Hamath). Afraid to fight, the people of Hamath surrendered (Akkadian: seized my feet) and paid tribute in gold and silver. I recognized Hamath as a new member of the empire by sacrificing to Adad, its divine patron.

I marched into the land of Irhuleni, the ruler of Hamath. I captured the cities of Adennu, Barga, and Argana, and plundered his palaces before setting them on fire.

I marched to Qarqar and laid siege to the city. Once it was captured,

Assyrian soldiers crossing a river by swimming or using inflated goat skins (palace of Sennacherib).

I set it on fire. Irhuleni, the ruler of Qarqar, mustered only 700 chariots, 700 cavalry and 10,000 soldiers, but his twelve covenant partners also fielded armies against me:

> Hadad-ezer, the ruler of Aram
> > 1,200 chariots
> > 1,200 cavalry
> > 20,000 soldiers
> Ahab, the ruler of Israel
> > 2,000 chariots
> > 10,000 soldiers
> Quea
> > 500 soldiers
> Musrea
> > 1,000 soldiers
> Irqanatea
> > 10 chariots
> > 10,000 soldiers
> Matinuba'il, the ruler of Arvad
> > 200 soldiers
> Usanata
> > 200 soldiers
> Adunu-ba'il, the ruler of Shian
> > 30 chariots
> > . . . soldiers
> Gindibu, the ruler of Arabia
> > 1,000 camels
> Ba'sa, son of Ruhubi, the ruler of Ammon
> > . . . soldiers

Jehu's attendants bring tribute of gold, silver, vessels, buckets and poles to King Shalmaneser III in 841 B.C.E. (from the Black Obelisk).

With the help of Ashur and Nergal, my divine patrons who go before me, I routed all these rulers, killing and wounding 14,000 soldiers. Like Adad, divine patron of the thunderstorm, I rained destruction upon them. Their corpses covered the battlefield, and their blood filled the valleys. The dead were too many to bury, and bodies formed a bridge across the Orontes river. I plundered their chariots and war horses.

YEAR EIGHTEEN

Black Obelisk, base lines 97–9

My sixteenth campaign west of the Euphrates took place eighteen years after I became the great king of Assyria. Hazael, king of Damascus, revolted against me. I attacked and defeated him, taking 1,121 chariots, 470 horses and a supply convoy.

YEAR EIGHTEEN

Assyrian Annals, fragmentary text from Year 18 (2 Kgs 10:34)

My sixteenth campaign west of the Euphrates took place eighteen years after I became the great king of Assyria. Hazael, king of Damascus, mustered a large army, and fortified Mt. Senir. I fought and defeated him, killing 16,000 of his soldiers. I took 1,121 chariots, 470 horses and a supply convoy. He ran from the battle to save himself, and I besieged

The "Black Obelisk" of Shalmaneser III showing King Jehu submitting himself to the Assyrian king as a vassal after the battle of Qarqar.

his capital city of Damascus. After cutting down his orchards, I marched as far as the mountains of Hauran. Along my line of march I destroyed every town, taking vast amounts of booty.

Eventually, I marched as far as the mountains of Ba'li-ra'si and erected a stele containing my royal image at the seashore. Having demonstrated my power, I accepted the tribute of people of Tyre and Sidon, and from Jehu, the son of Omri.

YEAR EIGHTEEN

Black Obelisk: over the relief of Jehu

Jehu, king of Israel, ransomed his life with silver, with gold bowls, vases, cups and pitchers, with tin, and with hard wood for scepters and spears. . . .

ANNALS OF TIGLATH-PILESER III

≋ *Between 1845 and 1851, on behalf of the British Museum, Austen Henry Layard excavated tell Nimrud, the ancient Assyrian city of Kalhu founded by Ashurnasirpal II (883–859 BCE), and expanded by Shalmaneser II (858–824 BCE), Tiglath-Pileser III (744–727 BCE) and Esarhaddon (680–699 BCE). The city was eventually destroyed in 612 BCE. The Nimrud annals of Tiglath-Pileser III were engraved on slabs in the Assyrian dialect of Akkadian using the cuneiform script.*

Tiglath-Pileser formally inaugurated a new age of empires in the world of the Bible. He completely reorganized Assyria's bureaucracy to gain political and economic control of the trade routes running from the Mediterranean coast inland to prevent any cut-off of Assyria's imports of metals, lumber and horses.

Parallels to the annals of Nimrud appear in the annals of Menahem, king of Israel, in the books of Samuel-Kings (2 Kgs 15:17–22).

YEAR

150–57

I, Tiglath-Pileser III, received tribute from:
    Kushtashpi of Commagene,
    Resin of Damascus,
    Menahem of Samaria,
    Hiram of Tyre,
    Sibittibi'li of Byblos,
    Urikki of Qu'e,
    Pisiris of Carchemish,
    I'nil of Hamath,
    Panammu of Sam'al,

*King Tiglath-Pileser III
(745–728 B.C.E.).*

Tarhulara of Gurgum,
Sulumal of Militene,
Dadilu of Kaska,
Uasurme of Tabal,
Ushitti of Tuna,
Urballa of Tuhana,
Tuhamme of Ishtunda,
Urimme of Hubishna,
and Zabibe, the queen of Arabia,

. . . which included gold, silver, tin, iron, elephant-hides, ivory, linen garments embroidered with different colors, blue wool, purple wool, ebony, boxwood, luxury items like . . . wild birds mounted with their wings extended and tinted blue, as well as horses, mules, large cattle, small cattle and camels, some already bred.

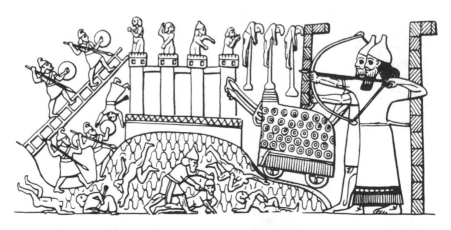

*Troops of Tiglath-Pileser III attack an unnamed town with archers, spearmen
and battering rams. Enemy victims are shown impaled or beheaded
(wall relief from his royal palace).*

ANNALS OF SARGON II

In 713 BCE, Sargon II (722–705 BCE) of Assyria founded a new city called the "...mountain of Sargon (Akkadian: **Dur-Sharrukin**; Arabic: **Khorsabad**)." When he died, his successor, Sennacherib, moved the capital back to Nineveh. Between 1842–44, Sargon's capital was excavated by Paul Emile Botta (1802–70) and Eugene Napoleon Flandin (1809–76) for the Louvre Museum in Paris. The annals of Sargon were among the inscriptions in the Assyrian dialect of Akkadian using cuneiform, which were carved into the reliefs on Sargon's palace walls and onto the thresholds of public buildings. The accounts in these official annals are repeated in the Khorsabad Display Inscription.

A covenant partner of Assyria, which was unable to meet its quotas, lost its self-determination and became an Assyrian vassal or colony. In a colony, native officials retained their titles and offices, but Assyrian personnel reviewed all domestic policies to guarantee the colony would meet the empire's military budget. Only states with healthy economies, efficient governments and popular rulers managed to maintain their self determination. Assyria's budget requirements increased continually and few states could meet its expectations and avoid a revolt. Depositions and revolutions were frequent. Any reticence or refusal on the part of local officials left an Assyrian colony subject to outright foreclosure. Assyria would deport all government personnel, redistribute the colony's population in developing regions of the empire and assign the colony a military governor, incorporating it completely into the empire as a province.

The annals of Sargon II chronicle the days when Israel went from the status of an Assyrian ally in 738 BCE, to an Assyrian colony in 732 BCE and finally to an Assyrian province in 721 BCE. Shalmaneser V (727–722 BCE) reduced the Israel of Hoshea from the status of a covenant partner of Assyria to its colony. Sargon, who called himself "...the conqueror of Samaria," converted Israel into *an Assyrian province after Hoshea defaulted on his tax payments. It took Assyria more than three years to win its war against "...the land of Omri (Akkadian: bit hu-um-ri-ia)," and to deport its people from the capital city of Samaria to faraway places like "...Halah... the Habor, the river of Gozan, and the cities of the Medes (2 Kgs 17:6)." Others were deported to nearby rural sections of Israel itself, and it is these people who become known in the New Testament as "Samaritans." Parallels to the annals of Sargon II appear in the annals of Hoshea in the books of Samuel–Kings (2 Kgs 17:3–6).*

FIRST YEAR

Assyrian Annals 10–27

The ruler of Samaria, in conspiracy with another king, defaulted on his taxes and declared Samaria's independence from Assyria. With the strength given me by the divine assembly, I conquered Samaria and its covenant partner, and took 27,290 prisoners of war along with their chariots. I conscripted enough prisoners to outfit fifty teams of chariots. I rebuilt Samaria, bigger and better than before. I repopulated it with people from other states which I had conquered, and I appointed one of my officials over them, and made them Assyrian citizens.

SECOND YEAR

Khorsabad, Display Inscriptions 33–7

In the second year of my reign, Ilubi'di, a Hittite conspirator and an imposter to the throne of Hamath in Syria, formed an alliance with Arvad, Simirra, Damascus and Samaria, and declared their independence from Assyria. Together they raised an army and attacked me. At the command of Assur, my divine patron, I, Sargon II, mustered an army and

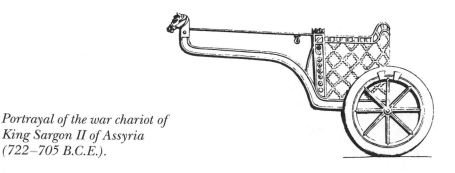

Portrayal of the war chariot of King Sargon II of Assyria (722–705 B.C.E.).

Troops of King Sargon II attack the city of Gaza in Palestine.
The city is shown on a mound with an Assyrian siege ramp and
battering rams to break through the gate (wall relief from his palace).

laid siege to Qarqar, the city of Ilubi'di. After I burned Qarqar to the
ground and skinned Ilubi'di alive, the people of Arvad, Simirra, Damascus and Samaria assassinated their rulers to restore peace and har-
mony once again.

SEVENTH YEAR

Assyrian Annals 120–25

Having been given a favorable omen by Ashur, my divine patron, I
campaigned against the Tamud, Ibadidi, Marsimanu, and Haiapa, the
Arab tribes who inhabit the desert and who have never submitted to the
word of any official or paid tribute to any king. Those that survived were
deported and settled in Samaria.

I then received tribute from the rulers of the desert coastal tribes:
Pir'u, the king of Musru, Samsi, the queen of Arabi, and It'amra, the
Sabean. They sent me quantities of gold dust, precious stones, ivory, herbs
and spices, horses and camels.

ANNALS OF SENNACHERIB

Sennacherib, great king of Assyria (704-681 BCE), inscribed annals for eight military campaigns on a six-sided clay prism about fifteen inches high. They are written in the Assyrian dialect of the Akkadian language using the cuneiform script. R. Taylor recovered this prism in 1830 from Nineveh (Arabic: Nebi Yunus) in Iraq. The Taylor Prism is now at the British Museum in London.

As a result of moves toward political autonomy by Hezekiah of Judah after 715 BCE, Sennacherib sent an army into Judah in 701 BCE to put down the revolt. He laid siege to Jerusalem and devastated the surrounding countryside and nearby cities like Lachish.

Parallels to the annals of Sennacherib appear in the annals of Hezekiah in the books of Samuel-Kings (2 Kgs 18:1—20:21).

Judean prisoners being led away to exile after the defeat of a city by the Assyrians (701 B.C.E.).

King Sennacherib shown on his throne before the gates of Lachish. (Wall relief from his royal palace, 701 B.C.E.)

THIRD YEAR

Taylor Prism iii:20–40 (2 Kgs 19:14–6)

Because Hezekiah of Judah did not submit to my yoke, I laid siege to forty-six of his fortified cities, walled forts, and to the countless villages in their vicinity. I conquered them using earthen ramps and battering rams. These siege engines were supported by infantry who tunneled under the walls. I took 200,150 prisoners of war, young and old, male and female, from these places. I also plundered more horses, mules, donkeys, camels, large and small cattle than we could count. I imprisoned Hezekiah in Jerusalem like a bird in a cage. I erected siege works to prevent anyone escaping through the city gates. The cities in Judah which I captured I gave to Mitinti, ruler of Ashdod, and to Padi, ruler of Ekron, and to Sillibel, ruler of Gaza. Thus I reduced the land of Hezekiah in this campaign, and I also increased Hezekiah's annual tribute payments.

Hezekiah, who was overwhelmed by my terror-inspiring splendor, was deserted by his elite troops, which he had brought into Jerusalem. He was forced to send me four-hundred twenty pounds (Akkadian: thirty talents) of gold, eleven-thousand two-hundred pounds (Akkadian: eight-hundred talents) of silver, precious stones, couches and chairs inlaid with ivory, elephant hides, ebony wood, box wood, and all kinds of valuable treasures, his daughters, concubines, and male and female musicians. He sent his personal messenger to deliver this tribute and bow down to me.

Siloam Annals

⌦ *Hezekiah (715–687 BCE), king of Judah, commissioned the construction of a water tunnel to secure Jerusalem's water supply in the event of an Assyrian attack on the city. The Siloam annals were discovered in 1880 by children playing near the tunnel's entrance into the pool of Siloam in Jerusalem. The inscription is nineteen and one-half inches wide and twenty-six inches long and was cut into the face of the rock wall of the tunnel. It is written in Hebrew, using cursive or longhand script. The first half of the annals have been removed and are still missing; the rest is now in the Istanbul Museum, Turkey.*

The Siloam tunnel inscription from Jerusalem showing an enlargement of the archaic script in which Hezekiah's builders left a record of their water tunnel project.

180

It is unclear just how the engineers laid out the route the diggers were to follow. More than likely, they were simply enlarging a fault in the bedrock through which water was already seeping. The course of the tunnel today indicates that the two teams were about to dig past one another, before they made ninety degree turns and connected the two channels. The inscription describes these exciting moments. Water tunnels from the same period (1000–587 BCE) have also been found at Gezer, Hazor and Megiddo, demonstrating that they were a common feature of a royal city's defenses. The Siloam annals are a dedicatory inscription. They do not seem to be royal, but rather the workers' celebration of a job well done. What remains of the inscription mentions neither Hezekiah, nor Yahweh, and, despite the fine execution of the letters, the inscription does not fill the space prepared for it on the rock. These experts at digging tunnels seemingly were amateurs at carving inscriptions.

Parallels to the Siloam annals appear in the annals of Hezekiah in the books of Samuel-Kings (2 Kgs 18:1—20:21) and in the books of Nehemiah-Chronicles (2 Chr 29:1—32:33).

(2 Kgs 20:20; 2 Chr 32:30)

. . . this is the story of how these two tunnels were joined together. The two teams working in opposite directions were digging toward one another with picks. The workers began shouting to each other when they realized they were four and one-half feet apart. Then, the teams turned toward one another following the sounds of their picks until they cut through the remaining rock and joined the tunnels. Thus, the water was able to flow through this tunnel one-hundred fifty feet underground for some eighteen hundred feet from the Gihon spring outside the city wall to the Siloam reservoir.

ANNALS OF NEBUCHADNEZZAR

≋ *The annals of Nebuchadnezzar II of Babylon (605–562 BCE) contain summaries of military campaigns during his fourth through seventh years (601–598 BCE). During this time, Egypt and Babylon both claimed Syria-Palestine as their territory. Therefore, Nebuchadnezzar and his predecessors mounted yearly raids into the area as a way of maintaining their claim.*

The annals are inscribed in the Akkadian language in cuneiform script on baked clay tablets a little more than three inches high. The British Museum recovered the tablets from Babylon, about fifty-five miles south of Baghdad, Iraq, and began publishing them in 1887.

As was the case with many rulers of Mesopotamia, Nebuchadnezzar uses the title: "King of Akkad" as a way of tying his rule back into antiquity when Akkadians like Sargon I ruled. Nebuchadnezzar refers to the area where he and his army campaigned as "Hatti," a name originally given to Syria-Palestine by the Egyptians. By Nebuchadnezzar's time this name was used by scribes throughout the ancient Near East. His campaigns generally took place during December (Akkadian: kislimu) as in the books of Zechariah and Chronicles (Zech 7:1; Neh 1:1) or March (Akkadian: adar) as in the books of Ezra and Esther (Ezra 6:15; Esth 3:7).

Annal 5, BM 21946: 5–7 (2 Kgs 24:1–17; Jer 37:10)

YEAR 4

Nebuchadnezzar, the king of Akkad, marched his army uncontested into Hatti. In November (Akkadian: *kislimu*) he led his army toward Egypt. When pharaoh heard of this, he sent out his own army. In the resulting battle heavy losses were inflicted on both sides. The king of Akkad then returned with his army to Babylon.

Annal 5, BM 21946: 8

YEAR 5

Nebuchadnezzar, the king of Akkad, remained in his own land outfitting chariots and their horses.

Annal 5, BM 21946: 9–10

YEAR 6, NOVEMBER

Nebuchadnezzar, the king of Akkad, marched his army into Hatti. He raided the desert taking a great deal of plunder from the herds of the Arabs and the statues of their divine patrons. The king returned to his own land in February (Akkadian: *addaru*).

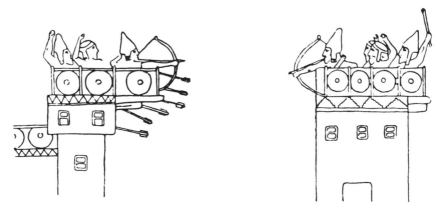

The defenders of Lachish fight off the Assyrian army.
Lachish was the second largest fortified city in Judah and
a prize for both Assyrian and Babylonian conquerors.

A Mushashu *dragon from the walls of Babylon at the time of*
Nebuchadnezzar. Made of glazed tiles.

Annal 5, BM 21946: 11–3 (2 Kgs 24:10, 13–7)

YEAR 7, NOVEMBER

In his seventh year, 598 BCE, Nebuchadnezzar put down a revolt by
Jehoiakim, king of Judah. The books of Samuel-Kings date the inva-
sion in the eighth year of his reign. Jehoiakim died during the siege
of Jerusalem and was succeeded by his son Jehoiachin. Nebuchad-
nezzar took Jehoiachin and his household back to Babylon as
hostages, and appointed Mattaniah as king of Judah. Mattaniah took
the throne name "Zedekiah."

Nebuchadnezzar, the king of Akkad, marched his army into Hatti.
He laid siege to the city of Judah. He captured the city on the second day
of February. He appointed a new king to his liking and carried away a
great amount of plunder from Judah to Babylon.

ARAD LETTERS

≋ From 1962-1967, Yohanan Aharoni directed an Israeli excavation of Arad (Hebrew: **Tell Arad**), which recovered some 200 ostraca or broken pieces of pottery that have writing or inscriptions on them in Hebrew and Aramaic. Some of the pieces of pottery are only 2.5 inches high. These Arad letters are preserved today in the Israel Museum in Jerusalem.

Most of the letters in Hebrew are military communiqués. Many authorize the commander of Arad to issue rations of grain, wine and oil to the troops under his command. On one curious ostracon, the name "Arad" is inscribed backward seven times.

The letters in Hebrew are from the Iron Age (1000–587 BCE) when fortresses like Arad, Ramoth-negeb (Hebrew: **horvat 'uza**) and Kinah (Arabic: **khirbet taiyib**) guarded the Edom highway like stage-coach stops and cavalry forts in the American west (2 Kgs 3:8). This east–west trade route connected the Coast Highway (Latin: **via maris**) in the west (Josh 19:8; 1 Sam 30:27) with the Royal Highway in the east. From Arad, the Edom Highway descends to the northern end of the Jebel Usdum mountains and from there down into the Arabah valley. Parallels appear in the books of Samuel-Kings, Ezra–Nehemiah and Jeremiah. For example, some letters refer to the households of priests like Pashhur and Meremoth mentioned in the Bible (Jer 20:1; Ezra 8:33).

ostracon 2

≋ Ostracon 2 is an order authorizing the commanding officer at Arad to issue rations to a unit of mercenaries under his command. It appears that a four-day ration for a unit of some seventy-five soldiers was three-hundred loaves of bread and eighty-five quarts of wine. Therefore, each soldier received about one loaf of bread per day (Jer 37:21) and about eight ounces of wine. New wine was recently

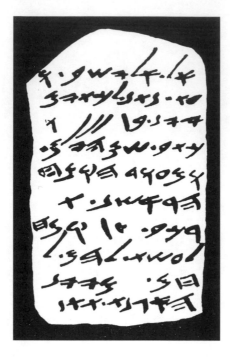

A potsherd of a certain Eliashib arranging trade shipments of oil and wine, found at Arad from c. 598 B.C.E.

fermented (Deut 32:14); old wine was stale or, at least, past the date when it was best to drink it (Ruth 2:14; Ps 69:21). The Kittim were mercenary soldiers from islands like Crete and Cyprus in the western Mediterranean.

To: Eliashib, commanding officer at Arad
From: . . . commanding officer at. . . .

Issue the Kittim 2 *bat* rations of wine and 300 loaves of bread for the next four days. Fill the *bat* ration jars with new wine. Deliver the rations tomorrow. Do not be late. Fill some of the jars with old wine, if some still remains.

ostracon 18

Ostracon 18 is written by a professional scribe in good biblical Hebrew using the ancient Hebrew script. An officer on assignment in Jerusalem is reporting to Eliashib in Arad. The report contains the earliest reference to the temple (Hebrew: beth YHWH) outside the Bible. The "sons of Keros" are mentioned in the list of temple servants in Ezra 2:44 and Neh 7:47.

Ivory decoration from a Canaanite palace at Megiddo showing the victorious general bringing prisoners and booty before the king on his throne, decorated with cherubim.

To: Eliashib, my commanding officer at Arad.
From . . . in Jerusalem

May Yahweh take good care of you.
Issue Shemaryahu one *lethech* ration of flour. Issue the Kerosite one *homer* ration of flour. I have carried out your orders. The person about whom you asked has sought sanctuary in the temple of Yahweh. . . .

ostracon 24

Arad was the headquarters for its sector of the Negeb. Ostracon 24 is an order to reinforce Ramoth-negeb, which is 6 miles southeast of Arad. Apparently, when Babylon invaded Judah from the north in 594 BCE, Edom invaded from the south (Ps 137:7-9; Lam 4:22). Whether or not the troops from Arad and Kinah, which is some 4 miles northeast of Arad, were successfully deployed to Ramoth-negeb is unclear. The destruction level at Arad where this communiqué was recovered indicates that Edom overran not only Ramoth-negeb, but Arad as well.

To . . . commanding officer at Arad
From . . . commanding officer at Jerusalem

. . . dispatch fifty soldiers from Arad and from Kinah . . . send them to Ramoth-negeb, under the command of Malkiyahu, the son of Qerab'ur, and he shall turn them over to Elisha, the son of Jeremiah, in Ramoth-negeb, before anything happens to the city. You are to carry out these orders of the king of Judah under penalty of death. This is my last warning: Get those soldiers to Elisha before Edom attacks.

LACHISH LETTERS

British archaeologists J.L. Starkey, Henry Wellcome and Charles Marston recovered twenty-one inscribed pieces of broken pottery or ostraca at Lachish (Hebrew: **Tell ed-Duweir**) in Israel between 1932–1938. Some of the pieces were about four inches high. The inscriptions were written in Hebrew using a longhand or cursive script with a reed pen and a black ink made from soot and gallnut juice. The letters were in the ruins of a guard room in the western gate of the city, where they were buried after Azekah and Lachish were destroyed by the Babylonian army of Nebuchadnezzar in 587 BCE. Azekah is eighteen miles southwest of Jerusalem, while Lachish is thirty miles' distant. The city of Lachish covered about thirty acres on the Wadi Ghafr. The ostraca are preserved today in the British Museum in London.

Four of the inscriptions are illegible and four are lists of names. One is an inscription on a jar. Twelve of the inscriptions are letters, five of which are written on pieces of pottery from the same jar. These letters reflect the breakdown in discipline in the face of Babylon's invasion. Jaush is a military commander. Hoshayahu is his

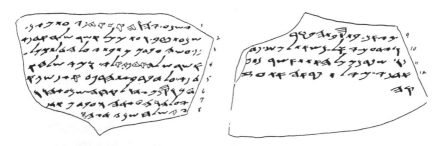

Front side (left) and back side (right) of a potsherd found at Lachish near the gate from the time of the Babylonian destruction of 598 B.C.E. called "letter #4."

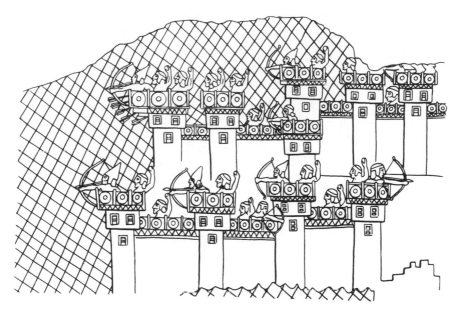

*Wall relief from the palace of Sennacherib, showing the defenders
of the Judean city of Lachish (701 B.C.E.).*

subordinate. Jaush is questioning whether or not Hoshayahu is, or
is not, cooperating with an unauthorized attempt by some members
of the Jerusalem government to solicit military assistance from Egypt.

The style of writing is similar to that in the books of Deuteronomy, Jeremiah and Samuel-Kings, but there are several stock phrases
as well as numerous misspellings.

Letter 3 (Jer 26:20–2)

To: Jaush, commanding officer in Jerusalem
From: Hoshayahu, commanding officer in Lachish, your servant

May Yahweh soon send my lord news of peace!

I have received your letter, but I cannot understand my commander's instruction: "If you did not understand my orders, have a scribe
read them to you!"

As Yahweh lives, I do not need a scribe to read your orders for me.
If one has come, I did not send for him. I always take immediate action
on those orders sent directly to me. I would never disobey a direct
order.

I have received the following intelligence report: "Coniah son of Elnathan, an army commander, has arrived on his way to Egypt and has requisitioned . . . men and supplies . . . from Hodavyahu son of Ahijah."

With regard to the letter of Tobiah, a royal official, which was sent to Shallum, son of Jaddua, by the prophet, saying "Beware!" I have already forwarded the prophecy to you.

Letter 4 (Jer 34:6–7)

To: Commanding officer in Jerusalem
From: Commanding officer in Lachish, your obedient servant

May Yahweh bless you with a good day.

I have posted your orders in writing. Following your orders to make a reconnaissance of Beth-haraphid, I discovered that it had been abandoned.

Semaiah has taken Semachiah into custody so that he can be transferred to Jerusalem for court-martial. I could not get him through the lines to Jerusalem today, but I will try again tomorrow morning.

This letter certifies to the commanding officer in Jerusalem that I remain on duty to carry out your orders. Judah's signal fire at Lachish still burns, even after the only other remaining signal fire at Azekah has gone out.

CHRONICLES,
EZRA,
NEHEMIAH

DECREE OF CYRUS

≋ Hormuzd Rassam (1826-1910) recovered a cylinder inscribed with a decree of Cyrus, the ruler of Persia (557-529 BCE), for the British Museum from Ashurbanipal's library at Nineveh. Cyrus had promulgated the decree shortly after his conquest of Babylon in 540 BCE. The inscription was written in the Akkadian language using cuneiform script on a cylinder about nine inches long. Few Persians understood Akkadian, but it was the official language in which all formal documents were published.

The decree indicts Nabonidus, whom Cyrus defeated, for failing to protect and provide for the land and people of Babylon. It then orders the repatriation of the hostages in Babylon, whom Nebuchadnezzar and Nabonidus had deported from the lands that they had conquered. Households from Judah had been deported in 597 BCE and again in 587-586 BCE following their failed revolts against Babylon (2 Kgs 24—5; Jer 34:1-7). The decree also provides royal subsidies to these peoples who were to rebuild their cities and the sanctuaries of their divine patrons (Ezra 1:1-4; 6:3-5).

Parallels to the decree of Cyrus appear in the books of Isaiah and Ezra. The book of Isaiah (Isa 45:1) acknowledges the decree by giving Cyrus the title of "Anointed" or "Messiah." He is the only non-Hebrew to be given such an honor. The temple in Jerusalem will not actually be rebuilt until ca. 515 BCE during the reign of Darius, the successor of Cyrus. The book of Ezra (Ezra 6:1-15) describes how Darius searched the royal archives for a decree of Cyrus, which may well have been a copy of this decree.

(1 Kgs 12:4; Isa 45:13; Ezek 10:18—9)

Nabonidus turned the worship of Marduk, ruler of the divine assembly in Babylon, into an abomination. . . . He also enslaved the people of Babylon to work for the state year round. . . .

The "Cyrus Cylinder," showing the inscription of King Cyrus the Great
written on a barrel-shaped clay cylinder surface.

Marduk, the ruler of the divine assembly, heard the people of
Babylon when they cried out and became angry. Therefore, he and the
other members of the divine assembly left the sanctuaries which had
been built for them in Babylon. Marduk . . . searched all the lands for a
righteous ruler to lead the akitu new year procession. He chose Cyrus,
the ruler of Anshan (Arabic: *tall-i Malyan*), and anointed him as the ruler
of all the earth. . . . Because Marduk . . . was pleased with Cyrus' good
deeds and upright heart, he ordered him to march against Babylon. They
walked together like friends, while the soldiers of Cyrus strolled along
without fear of attack. Marduk allowed Cyrus to enter Babylon without a
battle . . . and delivered Nabonidus, the king who would not lead the
akitu new year procession for Marduk, into the hands of Cyrus.

▧ *The elders and soldiers of Babylon surrender to Cyrus and his son,*
Cambyses, who resume the worship of all the members of the divine
assembly with sanctuaries in the city.

I entered Babylon as a friend of Marduk and took my seat in the
palace. Every day I offered sacrifice to Marduk, who made the people
love and obey me. Therefore, I ordered my soldiers not to loot the streets
of Babylon, nor to rape the women of Sumer and Akkad. I no longer
enslaved the people of Babylon to work for the state, and I helped them
to rebuild their houses which had fallen into ruin. Every ruler from the
sea above the earth to the sea below it, rulers who dwell in palaces in the
east and rulers who live in tents in the west came to Babylon to bring me
tribute and to kiss my feet.

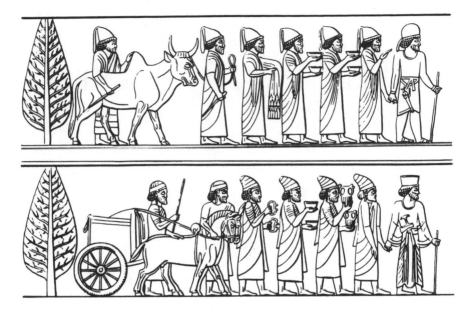

Babylonians and Persians bringing tribute to King Xerxes of Persia.
(From the royal palace of Persepolis.)

I returned the statues of the divine patrons of every land—Ashur, Susa, Agade, and Eshnunna, Zamban, Me-Turnu, Der and Gutia—to their own sanctuaries. When I found their sanctuaries in ruins, I rebuilt them. I also repatriated the people of these lands and rebuilt their houses.

Finally, with Marduk's permission, I allowed statues of the divine patrons of Sumer and Akkad, which Nabonidus had moved to Babylon, to be returned to their own sanctuaries . . . which I rebuilt.

May all the members of the divine assembly, whose statues I have returned to their sanctuaries, ask Bel and Nebo for a long life for me every day. May they remember me to Marduk, my divine patron, with the prayer: "Remember Cyrus and his son, Cambyses. They are the rulers who worship you by bringing peace to this land. They are the rulers who have filled your land with ducks and doves. . . . They are the rulers who have rebuilt the walls of your sanctuary.

ELEPHANTINE LETTERS

≋ Six papyrus letters belonging to Yedaniah son of Gemariah, the leader of a community from Judah on Elephantine Island on the southern border of Egypt, were discovered in 1907 by German archaeologists. They are currently housed in the Berlin Museum. The letters are written in Aramaic, the international language of the Persian empire, and date to the period between 420-407 BCE.

The Elephantine letters explain how to determine the date for Passover. They also describe the destruction of the Jewish temple on Elephantine by Egyptian soldiers. Curiously, at no point do these letters refer directly to traditions in the book of Deuteronomy that call for the celebration of Passover only in Jerusalem, and for the closing of all sanctuaries to Yahweh except the royal temple in Jerusalem.

The concerns of the community from Judah on Elephantine parallel some of the problems faced in Jerusalem and Judah under the Persians in the books of Ezra, Nehemiah and Chronicles. It is possible that the Hananiah mentioned in these letters as a senior Persian administrator in Egypt is the same as Hanani, the brother of Nehemiah (Neh 1:2; 7:2).

Text 30, AP 21, St. Mus. P. 13464, restored (Exod 12:15; Lev 23:5–8; Deut 16:3–4, 8)

YEAR FIVE OF DARIUS
419 BCE

≋ *Text 30 is fragmentary, but can be restored based on biblical parallels. The letter is not teaching the Jews in Egypt how to celebrate Passover for the first time, but rather how to date their celebration more accurately (Ezra 6:20).*

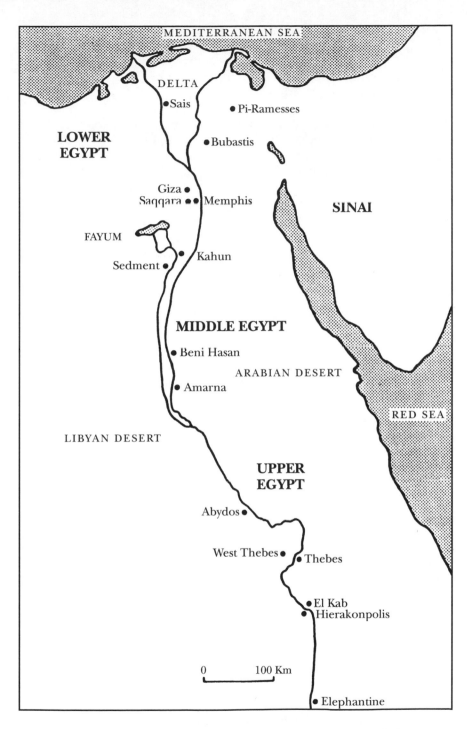

Map of Egypt, showing the major ancient sites, including Sais, Memphis, Amarna, Thebes and Elephantine.

To: The household of Yedaniah and the soldiers of Judah on Elephantine
From: Hananiah, your brother

May Elohim always bless you, my brothers from Judah.
. . . Darius the king sent this message to Arshama, the governor: . . .
begin the celebration of Passover on the fourteenth of March (Aramaic:
Nisan) at sunset. You shall celebrate the Feast of Unleavened Bread from
the fifteenth to the twenty-first day of March. You shall eat unleavened
bread for seven days.
. . . do not work on the fifteenth or the twenty-first of March. Do not
drink any wine or beer. Do not eat or keep any leavened bread in your
house from sunset on the fourteenth of March until sunset on the twenty-
first of March. . . .

*Text 34, AP 30/31; Berlin, St. Mus. P. 13495/ Cairo P. 3428 (Num 23:11;
1 Kgs 13:2–3, 21:23–4, 27; Ezra 8:23; Neh 2:5; 4:1; 9:1; Ps 137:7–9)*

TWENTIETH OF MARSHESHWAN, YEAR SEVENTEEN OF DARIUS NOVEMBER 25, 407 BCE

≋ *Text 34 describes the destruction of the temple on Elephantine by
the priests of Khnum and Vidranga the governor. Syene, the city of
Aswan today, is the larger settlement on the banks of the Nile river
around Elephantine Island.*

To: Our Lord Bagavahiah, governor of Judah
From: Yedaniah and the priests on Elephantine

May Yahweh, creator of the heavens, bless our lord forever, and grant
you favor with King Darius a thousand times greater than now. May you
have a long, healthy and happy life!
. . . during the month of June (Aramaic: Tammuz) in 404 BCE (Aramaic: year fourteen of Darius), when Arshama, the Persian governor
(Aramaic: satrap) of Egypt, was out of the country, the priests of Khnum
. . . issued an ultimatum: "The temple of Yahweh (Aramaic: *YHW*) on
Elephantine must be destroyed!" So, Vidranga, the governor of Elephantine, sent a letter to his son, Nafaina, the commander of Syene,
ordering him to destroy the temple. Nafaina responded by leading his
soldiers to Elephantine with weapons and axes.
The soldiers forced their way into the temple and completely
destroyed it. They smashed its stone pillars, wrecking its five stone gate-
ways, and burning the doors in their bronze pivots, the roof and all of

One possible model of the Temple of Solomon, showing the two pillars of Jachin and Boaz, the main doorway on the East, and the side chambers.

the fixtures. They looted the temple, taking the gold and silver basins and everything else of value.

Afterward, we and our households put on sackcloth, fasted, and prayed to Yahweh, creator of the heavens: ". . . may Vidranga be eaten by dogs, may all his property be destroyed, may all those who plotted evil against the temple be killed, and may we live to see it happen!"

It has now been three years since we sent this news to you, to Yehohanan the high priest, to the other priests in Jerusalem, to Avastana brother of Anani, and to the other officials of Judah (Aramaic: *Yehuda*). We have received no reply.

So we have continued to wear sackcloth and fast since June, 404 BCE. For three years, we have not had intercourse with our wives, nor have we anointed ourselves with oil or drunk wine. We have not offered grain or animals in the temple.

If it please our lord, since we have not been allowed to rebuild this temple, may consideration be given to its rebuilding. Consider the faithfulness of your servants and friends in Egypt. May a letter be sent from your hand which commissions the rebuilding of the temple of Yahweh on Elephantine. If you agree to do this, then offerings of incense and animals will be brought in your name to the altar of Yahweh. We and our entire households will pray constantly for you. If you do this, it will be a truly righteous action before Yahweh, worth more than one thousand silver and gold talents of offerings and sacrifices.

The details of these events have also been sent in a letter to Delaiah and Shelemiah, sons of Sanballat (Aramaic: *Sin-uballit*), governor of Samaria. Note that Arshama was unaware of these actions taken against us.

Text 35, AP 32, Berlin, St. Mus. P. 13497 (Ezra 6:1–5)

407 BCE

≋ *Text 35 contains a memorandum that appears to establish an agreement on the part of Bagavahia of Jerusalem and Delaiah of Samaria for the rebuilding of the Elephantine temple. Presumably, Arshama, the Persian governor of Egypt, has also confirmed this. What is interesting is that animal sacrifices are not mentioned, possibly as a way of minimizing the importance of the Elephantine temple in relation to the temple in Jerusalem.*

To: Arshama, governor of Egypt . . .
From:

The temple of Yahweh, creator of the heavens, was built prior to the time of Cambyses on Elephantine and was subsequently destroyed in year fourteen of Darius by the criminal Vidranga.
Let it be rebuilt on its original site. Let offerings of meal and incense be offered on its altar as they were in the past.

Text 36, AP 33, Cairo P. 3430 – J. 43467

407 BCE

≋ *Text 36 notes the prohibition of animal sacrifices. There is no clear evidence that the Elephantine temple was in fact rebuilt. Records from the military colony there end after 399 BCE and no archaeological remains have come to light. This draft copy contains no addressee.*

To:
From: Yedaniah son of Gemariah, Mauzi son of Natan, Shemaiah son
    of Haggai, Hoshea son of Yatom, Hoshea son of Nattum, who are
    all legal residents of Syene and own land on Elephantine Island.

If our lord will grant permission for the temple of Yahweh, our divine patron, to be rebuilt on Elephantine, then we agree not to sacrifice sheep, oxen, or goats, but only incense and grain. If our lord will issue this decree, then we will make a donation to our lord's household of . . . silver, and one-thousand bushels (Aramaic: *artabe*) of barley.

JOB,
ECCLESIASTES

DECLARATIONS OF INNOCENCE

Like the Pyramid Texts and the Coffin Texts, the Book of the Dead or the Book of the Coming Forth by Day was regularly carved or painted inside pyramids and tombs in Egypt from as early as 2500 BCE. The Book of the Dead did not reach its final form until 500 BCE. The entire book has not been found on any one scroll. From 1500-1530 BCE mass-produced excerpts from the Book of the Dead illustrated on papyrus were readily available to households that could afford them. Copies of the Book of the Dead are preserved today in the British Museum (Papyrus of Nu, #10477) in London and the Egyptian Museum in Cairo.

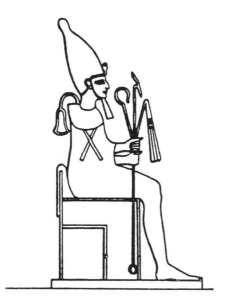

The Egyptian god Osiris wrapped as a mummy to show his rule over the land of the dead.

Declarations of innocence or negative confessions were perhaps the most popular excerpts from the Book of the Dead. They consist of at least one-hundred and ninety-two chapters of varying lengths. Each is designed to bring about the resurrection of the dead and assure a blessed afterlife. There are also descriptions of the under-world (Egyptian: duat), the gates, the caverns, the day, the night, and a litany to Ra.

Parallels to the declarations of innocence are found in the book of Job (Job 31).

Chapter 125

When you reach the Hall of Two Truths, confess your sins and say:

I have not sinned against my neighbors.
   I have not mistreated cattle.
I have not committed perjury in the temple.
   I have not sought restricted knowledge.
I have not done evil.
   I have not repeatedly made slaves work overtime.

Preparation of the mummy and bringing of offerings to the dead person, from the papyrus, The Book of the Dead.

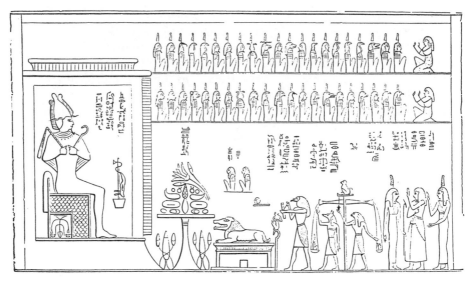

The "Judgment Hall of Osiris," from an Egyptian tomb painting showing various minor deities of the land of the dead before Osiris.

My name has not been reported to Amon-Ra.
  I have not blasphemed.
I have not deprived the poor of their property.
  I have not done anything which the divine assembly prohibits.
I have not given false witness against slaves to their masters.
  I have not caused pain to others.
I have not starved the hungry.
  I have not caused others to weep.
I have not killed.
  I have not commanded to kill.
I have not failed to make offerings to the divine assembly.
  I have not eaten the bread of the divine assembly.
I have not stolen the food offerings of the dead.
  I have not sexually abused boys.
I have not masturbated.
  I have not cut the bushel measure.
I have not moved boundary markers of another's fields.
  I have not used false weights for scales.
I have not taken the milk from the mouths of children.
  I have not deprived herds of their pastures.

I have not trapped the birds of the divine assembly.
    I have not diverted irrigation water into my fields at the wrong time.
I have not built a dam across a river to irrigate my fields.
    I have not doused a cooking fire when it was needed.
I have not been late making meat offerings to the divine assembly.
    I have not offered less than my best cattle to the divine assembly.
I have not failed to step aside for a procession of the divine assembly.
    I solemnly declare that I am innocent!

Declaration of Innocence before 42 members of the divine assembly

I have done nothing evil.
    I have not robbed.
I have not coveted.
    I have not stolen.
I have not murdered.
    I have not cut the grain ration.
I have not cheated.
    I have not stolen a sacrifice of the divine assembly.
I have not committed perjury.
    I have not stolen bread.
I have not sulked.
    I have not trespassed.
I have not slain the cattle of the divine assembly.
    I have not committed extortion.
I have not stolen the bread ration.
    I have not gossiped.
I have not allowed my mouth to betray me.
    I have not contended with another over property rights.
I have not committed adultery.
    I have not defiled myself.
I have not instilled fear in another.
    I have not trespassed.
I have not been intemperate.
    I have not been blind to truth.
I have not been quarrelsome.
    I have not turned a blind eye to justice.
I have not sexually abused a young boy.
    I have not been abusive of another.
I have not been too hasty.
    I have not defaced an image which belonged to the divine assembly.

I have not said too much.
  I have not committed treason.
I have not bathed in water reserved for drinking.
  I have not raised my voice.
I have not cursed the divine assembly.
  I have not been boastful.
I have not been arrogant.
  I have not desired more than I possess.
I have not cursed the divine patron of my city. . . .

A Sufferer and a
Soul in Egypt

A Sufferer and a Soul is a dispute over suicide composed during the Middle Kingdom in ancient Egypt between 2050-1800 BCE. It was written on papyrus sheets, the tops of which were already destroyed when archaeologists recovered them shortly before 1900. They are now preserved in the Berlin Museum as Papyrus Berlin 3024.

During the first intermediate period between 2258-2050 BCE, the social and political and economic structures of Egypt came apart. Consequently, teachers began to reevaluate Egypt's world view as well. A sufferer and a soul file a lawsuit against Egypt for its views on life and death. At the trial, the sufferer is the attorney for death and ka, the soul, is the attorney for life. The sufferer proposes committing suicide as an antidote to pain and failure. The soul argues that suicides are not eligible for the appropriate funeral services, which disqualifies the dead from the pleasures of the afterlife, and their survivors of any public support. The soul argues that funerals

Picture of an Egyptian funeral procession on ships across the Nile. Mourners and the internal organs of the deceased ride in the first boat while the body of the deceased is in the second boat. (Beni Hasan, 19th century, B.C.E.)

are a waste of time for rich and poor alike. As an alternative to sui-cide, the soul proposes that the sufferer just stop conforming to society's expectations and start enjoying life. The soul closes its counter-argument with two parables to which the sufferer responds with four laments. The first lament equates the soul's advice with a series of putrid metaphors, the second lists all the reasons why death is preferable to life when things are bad, the third describes death as a friend who will free suffering human beings from their painful lives and the fourth promises that all those who die will live happily ever after with their divine patrons. The first lines in each stanza of each lament are the same.

A Sufferer and a Soul evaluates various responses to the phe-nomenon of **Weltschmerz** *in people who conform to all of society's expectations, but who get sick of living when their efforts get them nowhere. Teachers in Mesopotamia and in ancient Israel used similar trial genres in their works such as the books of Ecclesiastes and Job. These traditions do not present solutions to suffering; they simply study it.*

1–39 (Job 3:17–9)

Hear me out, my soul.

My life now is more than I can bear,
  Even you, my own soul, cannot understand me.
My life now is more terrible than anyone can imagine.
  I am alone.
So, come with me, my soul, to the grave.
  Be my companion in death. . . .
If you cannot take away the misery of living,
  Do not withhold the mercy of dying from me.

Open the door of death for me.
  Is that too much to ask?
Life is only a transition.
  Even trees fall.
Crush out this evil life.
  Put an end to my misery.
Let Thoth, the divine judge, hear my case,
  Let Khonsu, guardian of pharaohs, protect me.
Let Ra, the divine boatman, judge me,
  Let Isis . . . defend me.

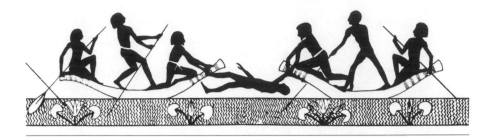

*Egyptians in boats on the Nile recover the body of a drowned man.
(Beni Hasan, 19th century, B.C.E.)*

Listen, my human friend—

It is so foolish for an ordinary human like you
   To want the funeral of a pharaoh.

lines 40–59

But, my soul—

I will not die without arranging a proper funeral.
   Only when death is a thief are funerals unprovided.
If you help me,
   I can rest in peace in the land of the dead.
I will take you with me to the grave,
   I will care for your tomb like your child.
I will shade you from the heat of the sun,
   I will make wandering souls envious of you. . . .
If you continue to oppose my death,
   You will never find rest in the land of the dead.
Trust me, my soul, my companion,
   My heir will carry out my last wishes.
My heir will stand beside my tomb on the day of burial,
   My heir will carry my body to its grave.

lines 60–89 (Eccl 3:12)

Now listen, my human friend—

There is no such thing as a happy funeral,
   Funerals always make people cry.

You just carry the body out of the house,
    You bury it on a sterile and sunless hillside.
Even granite chapels and pyramids decay,
    Monuments are forgotten as soon as the builders are gone.
They are pitiful as paupers' graves on the banks of the Nile,
    They are no different than burials without funerals.
They have only the Nile as a pallbearer,
    The sun as an embalmer, the fish as mourners.
So, listen to me,
    Take my advice.
Enjoy living.
    Stop worrying.

You have heard the parable about death. . . .
Once, a man plowed a field,
    Loaded the harvest on a barge, and towed it to market.
At sunset, a terrible storm came up.
    The man, safe in town, survived,
But his wife and children at home perished,
    Lost when their houseboat capsized in the Lake of the Crocodiles.
The man sat down and mourned: "Should I weep for a wife, buried
        without a funeral,
    And thus who cannot be raised to a new life?
Or should I weep for a child,
    Buried before it had even one life to live?"

You also know the parable about the stubborn man. . . .
Once a man ordered his wife to serve all her food at noon,
    But she refused: "This food is for our supper."
The man stormed out of the house,
    Arguing with himself as he went back to work.
When the man came home,
    He was still furious.
Why wouldn't he listen to his wife's advice,
    Why couldn't anyone in the household reason with him?

lines 90–140 (Prov 5:5; Jer 9:4–5; Am 5:14–5; Sir 24:15)

My soul, do you really want me to go on living?
    When my life smells worse than . . .
        . . . bird drop on a hot day,
        . . . rotten fish in the full sun,

. . . the floor of a duck coop,
. . . the sweat of fishermen,
. . . a stagnant fish pond,
. . . the breath of a crocodile?

Do you really want me to go on living?
   When my reputation is worse than someone . . .
    . . . accusing a faithful woman of adultery,
    . . . calling a legitimate child a bastard,
    . . . plotting to overthrow the government?

Can't you see?
   Everyone is a thief,
   There is no love among neighbors.
Can't you see?
   Hearts are covetous,
   People take what belongs to their neighbors.
Can't you see?
   The just have perished,
   Fools are everywhere.
Can't you see?
   Everyone chooses evil,
   Everyone rejects good.
Can't you see?
   Crimes outrage no one,
   Sins make everyone laugh.

Death stands before me today,
   Like health to the sick,
   Like freedom to the prisoner.
Death stands before me today,
   Like the smell of myrrh,
   Like a canopy on a windy day.
Death stands before me today,
   Like the perfume of the lotus,
   Like sitting in the land of drunkenness.
Death stands before me today,
   Like a well-beaten path,
   Like a soldier returning home from war.
Death stands before me today,
   Like clear skies after a rain,
   Like a treasure hidden in a field.

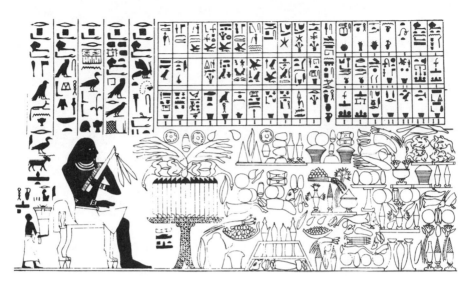

Scene from the tomb of a nobleman, with the deceased seated before tables of rich food for his time in the afterlife. (Beni Hasan, 19th century, B.C.E.)

Death stands before me today,
   Like home to the traveler,
   Like his native land to an exile.

Surely, whoever goes to the land of the dead
   Will live with the divine assembly,
   Will judge the sins of the wicked.
Surely, whoever goes to the land of the dead
   Will ride in the Barque of the Sun,
   Will collect gifts offered at temples.
Surely, whoever goes to the land of the dead
   Will be wise,
   Will have a hearing before Ra the creator.

lines 150–60 (Ps 94:19)

My human friend—

Throw your cares on the fire with your offerings,
   Get on with your life.

Stay with me here,
   Stop thinking about dying.
When it is time for you to die,
   When your body returns to the earth,
Then I will travel with you,
   Then we shall live together forever.

A Farmer and the
Courts in Egypt

🏳 *A Farmer and the Courts is part of the Berlin papyrus (#3023, 3025)
recovered by German archaeologists before 1900. It contains the
protests of an eloquent peasant who argues for his rights in the
courts of Egypt during the first intermediate period (2258-2052 BCE).
Narrative sections of prose introduce nine exchanges, which are composed in poetry, between the farmer and various judges. The teachers
who composed A Farmer and the Courts during the Middle Kingdom
(2134-1786 BCE) clearly felt that the events took place in a time of
unrest caused by political and social instability in Egypt.*

 *Parallels to A Farmer and the Courts appear in more than one
tradition in ancient Israel. The books of Judges and Ruth also reflect
the prejudice of a later period that earlier times were lawless. The
prophets champion human rights for the poor in much the same
language as the farmer. The book of Job follows a structure similar
to A Farmer and the Courts. In both, the petitioner is forced to
make one plea after another, seemingly without hope of relief, until
suddenly it is granted and his goods are restored. Finally, both the
Wisdom of Solomon and A Farmer and the Courts stress that while
individual human beings may die, the justice they do (Wis 8:13) and
their good names last forever (Wis 1:15).*

R:1–50 (1 Kgs 21:1–14)

Once there was a farmer named Khun-Anup, who lived in the Field
of Salt district near Thebes. One day he said to Marye, his wife: "I am
going down to the city for food. Go into the barn and see how much grain
is left from last year's harvest." After determining that there were twenty-
six measures of barley, the farmer took six with him to trade and left the
rest to feed his household.

Agricultural scenes from ancient Egypt, showing the picking and crushing of grapes (upper), and fishing and bathing cattle (lower). From Beni Hasan.

The farmer loaded the asses with salt, reeds, leopard skins, wolf hides, doves and other goods from his district to trade. Then he set out for the city. He traveled south toward Herakleopolis through Per-fefi, north of Medenit. Tut-nakht, son of Isri, who was an official of the chief steward Rensi, the son of Meru, was standing on the bank of the canal and saw the farmer coming.

As he watched the farmer approach, Tut-Nakht said to himself: "I think I have a scheme I can use to steal this farmer's goods."

At one point the public path along the embankment of the canal in front of Tut-nakht's house was no wider than a loincloth. One side of the path was flooded with water, and the other side was overgrown with barley from Tut-nakht's field. Tut-nakht told one of his slaves: "Get me some clothes from my house!" When the slave brought them, Tut-nakht laid the clothes down over the water.

B1:1–190 (Exod 20:16; Deut 10:18; 2 Sam 15:4; 2 Chron 19:7; Isa 6:10; Amos 5:14; 8:5; Mic 6:11–2; Zech 8:16; Job 20:20; 24:12; Ps 22:22–6; 25:17; Prov 15:27; Matt 7:12)

Just then, the farmer came down the path. Tut-nakht shouted to him: "Be careful, you farmer! You are about to step on my garments."

The farmer answered: "I am being careful! I do not wish to offend you, but your garments are right in my way. I cannot climb the steep embankment along the canal on one side of them, nor do I want to trample the grain in your field on the other. Please give me permission to pass."

As he stood there talking, one of the asses bit off a stalk of barley. Then Tut-nakht said: "Now I am going to confiscate your ass for eating my grain. I will sentence it to the threshing floor for this offense."

But the farmer pleaded: "My intentions are good. Only one stalk has been damaged. If you do not let me pay for the damage done and buy back my donkey, I will appeal to Rensi, the son of Meru, who is the chief steward and governor of this district. Is it likely that he will allow me to be robbed in his own district?"

Tut-nakht answered. "Why do the poor always want to speak to masters? You are speaking to me, not to the chief steward!" Then he took a stick and beat the farmer and confiscated his asses.

The farmer protested his painful sentence and the injustice done to him.

Tut-nakht tried to silence him in the name of Osiris, the divine patron of silence.

The farmer protested the attempt to silence him and swore by Osiris that he would not keep quiet until his property was returned.

For ten days, the farmer appealed to Tut-nakht without results. So, he went to Herakleopolis to appeal to Rensi, the son of Meru, who was the chief steward. As he was rushing off to board his barge, the official asked the farmer to file his protest with a lower court, which finally took his statement.

Eventually, Rensi and his council considered the case and decided that Tut-nakht was guilty only of harassing a farmer who no longer worked for him and should be sentenced only to return the farmer's goods. However, Rensi did not announce the verdict. So the farmer went to see about his appeal in person.

"You are the chief steward,
    You are my lord.
You are my last hope,
    You are my only judge.

When you sail the Lake of Justice,
    Fairness fills your sail.
You father the orphan,
    You husband the widow.
You brother the divorced,
    You mother the motherless.
I will extol your name throughout the land,
    I will proclaim you a just judge.

". . . a ruler without greed,
    . . . a great man without fault,
. . . a destroyer of lies,
    . . . a just judge, who hears the cry of the poor.
Hear me when I speak,
    Give me justice.
Relieve me of this burden of poverty,
    . . . the care which weighs me down."

The farmer appealed to Rensi in the name of Neb-kau-Ra, pharaoh of Upper and Lower Egypt.

So, Rensi went to the pharaoh and said: "My lord, I am hearing the case of a truly eloquent farmer. His goods have been stolen by a man in my service and he has come to me for justice."

The pharaoh said: "I am ordering you to keep this man waiting without giving him any reply. Just keep him talking. You must write down each of his speeches and send them to me. Furthermore, without letting this farmer know, I want you to provide for his wife and children as well as for his own needs."

Each day, a friend of the chief steward delivered ten loaves of bread and two jars of beer to the farmer. Rensi also ordered the governor of the Field of Salt district to deliver three measures of grain to the farmer's wife every day.

The second time that the farmer comes to see about his appeal, the chief steward asks him whether these goods were really worth going to prison over.

Spearing a crocodile in the Nile.

*Servants transport abundant food and goods to the tomb of
the deceased for the afterlife (from Beni Hasan).*

The farmer replies.

"Those who distribute the grain put more in their own ration.
    Those authorized to give full measures short their people.
Lawmakers approve of robbery
    —who is left to punish the wrongdoer?
    The Inspector condones corruption.
One is publicly criminal,
    The other tolerates injustice.
    Do not learn from such as these.
Punishment lasts for a moment,
    Injustice goes on forever.
Good example is remembered forever.
    Follow this teaching:
'Do unto others,
    As you would have others do unto you.'
Thank others for their work,
    Parry blows before they strike,
    Give jobs to the most qualified.
. . . make your shoreline a shelter,
    Clear out the crocodiles which infest your landing.
Speak the truth,
    Do not twist your tongue.
Do not perjure yourself,
    Do not bear false witness in court.

*The god Thoth with
the head of an ibis.*

Do not accept bribes,
  Do not graze on lies. . . ."

  The third time, the farmer said:

"Do justice,
  And live.
Carry out sentences on convicts,
  And fulfill your duty beyond all others.
Does the hand-scale lie?
  Is the stand-scale tilted?
  Is Thoth, divine patron of the scales, looking the other way?
Do not be tempted by corruption . . .
  Do not return evil for good,
  Do not substitute lesser for better goods. . . .
Do not steal,
  Do not make deals with thieves.
  Greed is blind.
Close your eyes to violence,
  And no one will punish criminals.
Ferry only those who can pay,
  And you become an honest man gone bad,
  . . . a shopkeeper who gives no credit to the poor."

When the farmer made this appeal before the chief steward at the gate court, Rensi had two guards arrest him and flog him.

Nonetheless, the farmer said:

"The son of Meru continues to do evil.
　He sees, but does not see,
He hears, but does not hear,
　He ignores what he is told. . . ."

The farmer eventually makes nine appeals to Rensi. In each appeal, the farmer recites all the wrongs done to him, describes Egypt as a world turned upside-down where lawgivers become lawbreakers, and appeals to Rensi and others in authority to take their responsibilities seriously and give him justice. In one final burst of frustration, the farmer decides that his only hope for justice will be in the afterlife where Anubis is the divine judge (Job 10:20–2; 14:7–14).

B2:114–35 (Job 5:26; 7:1–10)

"Since you will not grant my appeal,
　I will take it before Anubis himself."

Then, Rensi, the son of Meru and the chief steward, sent two guards to arrest the farmer. The farmer was frightened, thinking he was about to be sentenced to death.

Scenes of daily life and work in Egypt. (Beni Hasan, 19th century, B.C.E.)

"Death long-desired arrives like water for the thirsty
. . . like the first drop of milk on a baby's tongue."

▰ *Rensi reassures the farmer that no harm will come to him. Then he orders the transcripts of the farmer's appeals, which he had sent to pharaoh Neb-kau-Ra, to be read aloud and the pharaoh's judgment to be announced. Tut-nakht is summoned to the court and given an inventory of all the property that he is ordered to return to the farmer.*

A Sufferer and a
Friend in Babylon

A Sufferer and a Friend is a theodicy or dialogue about human misery. This version of the tradition developed in Babylon about 1000 BCE. It was written in cuneiform script, with the oldest copies coming from the Assyrian library at Nineveh of Ashurbanipal (668-626 BCE) and the most recent fragments possibly dating to the 5th century BCE Persian period. Archaeologists have reconstructed twenty-seven stanzas with eleven lines each of a sufferer and a friend from tablets that Austen Henry Layard (1817-94) recovered from tell Nimrud in 1845. They are preserved today in the British Museum in London.

A Sufferer and a Friend is an acrostic poem. The first letters in each couplet spell out "I am Saggilk-kinam-ubbib, priest, cantor, servant of the divine assembly and of the great king."

A Sufferer and a Friend is similar to the book of Job. Both are conversations, dialogues or arguments. It is also similar to the book of Ecclesiastes. Both argue that a world filled with suffering and evil proves that the divine assembly cannot be just.

lines 1–20 (Deut 6:24; 1 Sam 12:24; Ps 34:9; Mic 6:8)

The Sufferer

Come, my wise friend,
   Let me speak candidly with you.
Where can one find a teacher of your abilities?
   Where is there a scholar of your wisdom?
   Where is the counselor who will hear my grief?
I am without resources,
   I am lost in the depths of despair.

*A terra-cotta figurine
(a god?) of the
Phoenician type
(found at Ayia Irini).*

When I was a child, fate took my father from me,
  The mother who bore me went to the land of no return.
  My parents left me an orphan.

The Friend

Your story is too sad, my friend.
  Do not continue to dwell on these evils.
You have blinded yourself to common sense.
  Frowns have scarred your face.
Parents die,
  They cross the river.
If anyone could choose . . .
  Who would not choose to be rich?
The one who is faithful to his divine patron will be protected,
  The one who humbly fears his goddess will prosper.

lines 67–77 (Jer 12:1; Job 21:7–16)

The Sufferer

Your thoughts soothe like the north wind,
    They bring relief.
My friend, theoretically your advice is sound.
    Practically, the opposite is true.
Those who forget their divine patrons prosper.
    Those who pray constantly are homeless and destitute.
As a young man, I did the will of my divine patrons,
    I prayed and I fasted.
Prayer and fasting got me nowhere.
    The divine assembly decreed poverty for me, not wealth.
Cripples and fools outran me.
    Sinners prospered. I failed.

lines 235–42 (Job 8:5–7; 18:5–21)

The Friend

Sinners will lose the position you covet.
    Soon they will vanish.
Sinners will lose the wealth amassed without the help of their divine
        patrons.
    Their riches will become the prey of thieves.
If you do not do the will of your divine patrons,
    What hope is there for success?
Those who submit to the yoke of their divine patrons will never go
        hungry.
    They will eat even when food is scarce.
Seek the soothing wind of the divine assembly,
    And a year's losses will be restored in a moment.

lines 243–53 (Gen 25:27; Eccl 3:16)

The Sufferer

I have searched the world for order,
    But everything is upside down.

    The divine assembly is powerless.

The father tows his boat through the canal,
   While his son lies idly in bed.
The elder son struts about like a lion,
   While the younger son must be content as a teamster.
The elder son walks the street without concern,
   While the younger son gives food to the poor.
What good has it done me to bow down to the divine assembly,
   When now I bow before the dregs of society, who treat me with
      contempt?

lines 254–64 (Job 11:7; 15:2–4)

The Friend

You are wise and knowledgeable.
   Do not harden your heart.
   Do not falsely accuse your divine patrons.
The mind of the divine assembly is as unfathomable as the heavens,
   The way of your divine patrons is beyond human understanding. . . .
A cow's first calf may be a runt,
   While the second may be big and healthy.
A first child may be born a weakling,
   While the second may become a valiant warrior.
Though one may witness the will of one's divine patrons,
   No one can understand it.

lines 265–75 (Job 21:2; Jer 5:12; Amos 2:7; 5:10)

The Sufferer

Listen, my friend, to my words,
   Hear my irrefutable arguments.
People praise the powerful who kill,
   While they persecute the powerless, who are innocent.
People listen to the wicked, who despise their divine patrons,
   While they ignore the honest, who obey them.
People fill the storehouse of the wicked with gold,
   While they steal a beggar's bowl.
People lend a helping hand to the powerful . . .
   While they trample the needy underfoot.
Poor as I am, I am still oppressed,
   Despite my insignificance, I am persecuted by the self-important.

*Old Babylonian plaque
showing seven demons in
the upper register, and
Lamashtu, a feared female
demon, in the lower.*

lines 276–86 (Job 15:5; Amos 2:8)

The Friend

When Enlil, ruler of the divine assembly, created humans,
    When Ea the glorious pinched them from the clay . . .
When Mami, mother and queen, shaped them,
    The divine assembly endowed humans with twisted speech.
Their divine patrons empowered humans to lie,
    They gave them permission to speak falsely.
So people flatter the rich like royalty,
    Talk to them as if they were divine.
People treat the poor like thieves,
    Slander them like criminals.
People plot to kill the poor,
    Impose fines on them because they are powerless.
People terrorize the poor to death,
    Snuff out their lives like a flame.

lines 287–97 (Ps 28:9; 31:9; 69:17)

The Sufferer

You have been kind, my friend.
    Now look at how much I suffer.

Marduk (on the right), Adad, and other gods on a Babylonian cylinder seal.

Help me in my distress.
   Understand my suffering.
I am the humble slave of my divine patrons,
   Yet they do not help me.
I walk, without complaint, through the city square,
   I whisper, I do not cry out.
I keep my eyes down,
   I look only at the earth.
I do not join others at worship,
   I do not even stand with slaves.
May my divine patrons, who abandoned me,
   Now have mercy on me.
May the divine assembly, who abandoned me,
   Now have mercy on me.
May Shamash, the good shepherd,
   Once again shepherd his people as he should.

PSALMS,
LAMENTATIONS

LAMENTS FOR UR

⚏ *The Laments for Ur have been pieced together from over twenty separate clay tablets excavated at Nippur about ninety miles southeast of Baghdad in Iraq today. The Nippur excavations began in 1888. It was the first American dig in the ancient Near East. John P. Peters, Herman V. Hilprecht, and John H. Haynes served as directors of the project for the University of Pennsylvania. Over 30,000 cuneiform tablets were recovered from Nippur. The Laments for Ur were composed between 2000–1500 BCE. They are written in the Sumerian language. Sumerian, Hurrian and Eblaite are written in cuneiform, but are neither Indo-European nor Semitic languages. These tablets are preserved today in the University of Pennsylvania Museum in Philadelphia.*

*Ur (Arabic: **tell al-Muqayyar**) was pioneered by Ubaid peoples*

Sumerian Votive Tablets from Nippur showing naked priests and other personnel worshipping seated gods.

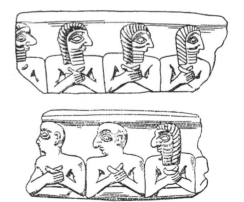

Typical Sumerian worshippers pictured on a fragment of a bas relief found at Lagash.

about 5000 BCE and developed into a major port city by the Sumerians after 3500 BC in order to link Mesopotamia with the Persian
Gulf and the Indus Valley. Although Ur was occupied until the conquest of Alexander in 333 BCE, the laments for Ur mourn the conquest of Ur III in 2004 BCE by Kindattu, ruler of Elam in south-
western Iran today. The eleven laments contain four hundred and
thirty-six lines. Each lament has a colophon or title (Sumerian:
KI.RU.GU). They also use antiphons or refrains. Most traditions celebrate monarchs. These laments, however, admit that even the greatest monarchs can die without honor, and even the most powerful
states fall. In the ancient Near East, rebuilding a temple in ruins was
a dangerous undertaking. Laments like those for Ur were sung at
critical stages of the construction to remind the divine assembly that
the builders who were restoring the temple were not the invaders
who had originally destroyed it.

   Laments for Jerusalem, which was destroyed by the Babylonians
in 587 BCE, are found in the books of Lamentations, Jeremiah, Ezekiel
and Psalms (Ps 137). They are parallels to these Laments for Ur.

FIRST LAMENT

≋ꞇ *The first lament is a litany naming Enlil, Ninlil, Inanna, Sin, Ningal, Enki and all the other members of the divine assembly who
abandoned Ur, Kesh, Isin, Uruk, Eridu, Ummah, Lagash and all the
other cities that were destroyed. Each stanza follows the same form.*

1+37 (Lam 2:9)

The ox has fled the barn,
   Wind blows through the gate of his stall.
Enlil, ruler of all the earth, has fled his temple,
   Wind blows through the gate of the city.
Enlil has fled Nippur,
   Wind blows through the gate of the city. . . .
   Wind moans pitifully through its doors.

SECOND LAMENT

≋ꞇ *The second lament is also a litany in which the members of the
divine assembly order their sanctuaries to mourn for Ur. As in the
first, the form of each stanza is the same.*

62

Put the temple at Eridu in mourning,
  Until the divine patron of Eridu can weep no more for Ur.

THIRD LAMENT

In the third lament, Ningal mourns the destruction of Ur in the ruins of the temple of Nanna (Sin), her husband. She uses the phrase "...the day of the storm" in the same way that the Bible uses the phrase "...the day of the Lord (Amos 5:18-20)" or "... on that day (Isa 24:21; 26:1; Zech 13:1-4)." A woman mourning for her husband or a mother weeping for her child (Latin: mater dolorosa*) is a common motif in laments that were sung by women mourners (Sumerian: GALA; Akkadian:* kalu*).*

88–109 (Job 7:13–4)

I, Ningal, mourn the day of the storm,
  The day of the storm fated for me.
My burden, the cause of my tears,
  The day of the storm fated for me.
My burden, predestined for me, godmother of Ur,
  The cause of my tears.
I trembled as the day of the storm drew near,
  The day of the storm fated for me.
My burden, the cause of my tears,
  The merciless day of the storm fated for me.
I could not flee the cruel violence of that day,
  Its fury was greater than all the joys of my life.
I trembled as that night drew near,
  The night of tears fated for me.
I could not flee the cruel violence of that night.
  The storm's fury filled me with fear.
  The storm's destruction kept me from sleep.
That night, I could not go to bed,
  That night, I could not fall asleep.
Night after night, I could not go to bed,
  Night after night, I could not fall asleep.
The land of Ur is filled with sorrow,
  Sorrow fated for my land.

The Sumerian god Ningursu holding his conquered enemies in a net. The eagle on the net closure is a symbol of the god ("Stele of the Vultures," the Louvre).

Should I scream for the life of my calf,
    Cry out for its release?
    I could not save my land from its misery.
My land was in distress,
    Distress fated for my land.
Even if I could flap my wings like a bird,
    Even if I could fly to save my city,
Still my city would be destroyed,
    Still my city would be razed to its foundations,
    Still my Ur would be destroyed where it lays.

FOURTH LAMENT

In the fourth lament, Ningal, like the widow of Tekoa (2 Sam 14: 1-20), goes to the divine assembly and petitions Anu and Enlil to reverse their verdict to destroy Ur. They refuse.

157–64

"Spare my city from destruction," I, Ningal, asked.
    "Spare Ur from destruction," I begged.
    "Spare its people from death," I pleaded with Anu and Enlil.

Anu would not listen to me,
   Enlil would not sooth my distress,
   He would not decree: "Grant this petition!"
Instead, they ordered the city destroyed,
   They ordered Ur destroyed.
Its fate was sealed,
   Its people sentenced.

FIFTH LAMENT

≋ *The fifth lament describes the storm that Enlil unleashes to destroy*
   Ur. It uses metaphors like droughts, earthquakes, floods and fire
   storms to describe the invasion of Ur by Elam.

173–90 (Ps 57:1; Jer 49:36; Ezek 13:13)

Enlil prepares the storm. Let the people mourn.
   The winds bringing rain to the land, he withholds. Let the people
      mourn.
The good winds he stores in Sumer. Let the people mourn.
   He gives the burning winds their orders. Let the people mourn.
He puts Kingaluda in charge,
   He makes him keeper of the storm.
He prepares the storm of death. Let the people mourn.
   He prepares the burning winds. Let the people mourn.
Enlil and Gibil prepare the sirocco winds. Let the people mourn.
   The burning sirocco howls. Let the people mourn.
The storm of death sweeps the earth. Let the people mourn.
   The burning wind rushes unrestrained to the sea.
Great waves swallow the city's ships.
   Earthquakes rock the pillars of the earth. Let the people mourn.
Fire storms ignite and explode in the wind. Let the people mourn.
   Fires flank the path of the wind,
Searing as the desert heat,
   Scorching as the noon sun.
Dust shrouds the sun,
   Cuts off its life-giving light.

Sixth Lament

⊜ *The sixth lament describes the aftermath of the storm. Bodies are*
piled high in the gate and the walls and buildings of the city are
in ruins.

208–28 (Amos 4:3; Jer 9:21–2, 16:4; Lam 4:3–5; 2:21)

When the storm subsides, the city is in ruins.
   The temple of Nanna is in ruins. Let the people mourn.
When the storm subsides, bodies lay like broken pots,
   The dead are scattered everywhere. Let the people mourn.
The walls were breached,
   The main gates are blocked with corpses. Let the people mourn.
The main streets are choked with dead.
   Bodies fill the streets.
Where crowds once celebrated festivals bodies lay in every street,
      corpses piled on every road.
   In the squares where people danced, heaps of corpses lay.
The blood of the dead fills every crevice like molten metal in a
      worker's mold.
   The flesh of the dead, like lard left in the sun, melts from their
      bodies.
Warriors wounded by an axe lie bleeding.
   Warriors wounded by a lance go untended.
Soldiers lie in the dust,
   Fighters gasp like gazelles pierced by hunters' spears.
The elders of Ur were slaughtered. Let the people mourn.
   The wise of Ur were scattered. Let the people mourn.
Mothers abandoned their daughters. Let the people mourn.
   Fathers disowned their sons. Let the people mourn.
Women and children were abandoned,
   Their property is looted.

Seventh Lament

⊜ *In the seventh lament, Ningal mourns the destruction of Ur by cat-*
aloging every person, place and thing destroyed. After each entry,
the audience chants "Alas!" or "Woe!"

261+265+283, 292–95 (Amos 5:16; Isa 5:13; Jer 11:19)

All the buildings outside the walls are destroyed.
  Let the people say: "Alas!"

Ur, my innocent lamb, has been slaughtered.
  Its good shepherd is gone.

The daughters of Ur have been married to Shimashki and Susa.
  Let the people say: "Woe!"

Woe! The city and temple are destroyed.
  O, Nanna, the sanctuary of Ur is destroyed, its people dead.
Woe! I have no place to sit or stand.
  Woe! An unknown city stands in place of my city.

EIGHTH LAMENT

≋ *The eighth lament catalogs the disasters that have befallen Ur. Its divine patron, Ningal, no longer enjoys the offerings that Ur formerly made to her. After each disaster, the audience chants "With Ur gone, how can Ningal survive?" The lament concludes with a series of petitions seeking the rebuilding of Ur (Jer 30:8-9; 31:38-40).*

381–84 (Lam 3:31–3)

May Anu, ruler of the divine assembly, decree: "It is enough!"
  May Enlil, ruler of all the earth, grant Ningal a better fate.
May Anu rebuild Ur,
  May he restore the majesty of Ningal.
May Anu return your city to its former grandeur,
  May he make you, once again, its queen.

≋ *The conclusion of the laments for Ur repeats the petitions initiated in the fourth lament. They ask that Ur be spared from the storm or rebuilt after its destruction.*

HYMN TO NINKASI

⚏ *A hymn to Ninkasi is found on several clay tablets: AO 5385 in the Louvre in Paris, a Nippur tablet (Ni 5469) in the Archaeological Museum in Istanbul, and a text in the collection of cuneiform tablets in the Staatliche Museum in Berlin (VAT 6705).*

The hymn describes how Sumerians brewed beer. They baked a bread (Akkadian: bappir) *from barley or emmer wheat and sweetened with date honey. The dried bread was crumbled, and cooked with water and sprouted barley. This mash was spread on a large mat to cool. The mash was seasoned with date honey and fermented. Finally, it was filtered through a strainer into a storage jar. Unfiltered beer was drunk from a common bowl through long reeds or metal straws.*

Beer is mentioned frequently in the Bible (Deut 29:6, 1 Sam 1:15; Isa 29:9; 28:7; 24:9), and was offered to Yahweh as a sacrifice (Num 28:7; Deut 14:26). Wise rulers (Prov 31:4), Nazirites (Num 6:3; Judg 13:4-14) and priests, on days they were scheduled to enter the sanctuary (Lev 10:9), did not drink beer. The poor drank beer to forget their suffering (Prov 31:6). Fools, who drank too much beer, became drunks (Ps 69:12; Isa 5:11+22; 56:12), started fights (Prov 20:1) and became false prophets (Micah 2:11).

You, Ninkasi, were born at the source of the rivers,
   You were nursed by Ninhursag. . . .
She laid the foundations of your great city on the sacred lake,
   She finished its walls for you. . . .
Your father was Enki-Nudimmud,
   Your mother was Ninti, queen of the underworld. . . .

You, who soothe the mouth, knead the dough with a great paddle,
   You sweeten the bread bowl with dates.

Assyrian scene of noblemen banqueting.

You bake the bread in a great oven,
　　You stack the barley in piles to sprout. . . .

You, who slake thirst, dampen the piles of barley malt,
　　While your great dogs guard them from thieves. . . .
You ferment the bread and malt in a jar,
　　Waves of foam rise and fall. . . .

You, divine patron of brewers, spread the mash on great reed mats,
　　You cool the wort. . . .
You press the mash with both hands,
　　You filter the honey sweet brew. . . .

Your strainer, Ninkasi, makes sweet music,
　　As you skillfully drain the wort into a storage jar. . . .
When you serve the filtered beer from the jar,
　　It gushes out like the Tigris and Euphrates. . . .

EBLA ARCHIVES

During their 1974 season, Giovanni Pettinato and Paolo Matthiae from the University of Rome uncovered the royal archives of Ebla (*Arabic:* **tell Mardikh**) in Syria. These archives are preserved on clay tablets in the Eblaite language written in cuneiform script. The language of Ebla is Semitic. Semitic languages are divided into east

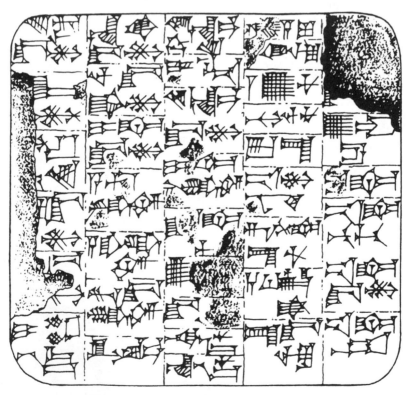

Copy of a tablet found at Ebla, written in cuneiform (front side).

Semitic and northwest Semitic languages. Akkadian is the only east Semitic language. The dominant northwest Semitic language is Aramaic. Eblaite may be a dialect of either Aramaic or Akkadian. The tablets are terra-cotta. Most are 6×6 inch squares. There are also round tablets from 1 inch to 4 inches in diameter, and rectangular tablets from 10×9 inches to 14×12 inches. They are preserved today in the Aleppo Museum in Syria.

Between 3000-2275 BCE, Ebla engaged in trade and war with states throughout the world of the Bible, including Ur, Mari, Byblos, Hazor, Megiddo, Gaza, and Jaffa. Until the discovery of Ebla's massive temples and palaces, scholars had assumed that Egypt and Mesopotamia were the only great cultures during the early Bronze period (3000-2000 BCE). Today, the thousands of tablets recovered at Ebla constitute the largest single find from the period. Eighty percent of the tablets found at Ebla are administrative. There are also word lists or dictionaries in which Eblaite nouns are translated into Sumerian and Akkadian. Some tablets contain letters, diplomatic records and a few hymns.

Initially, there was some excitement that the book of Genesis might have modeled the character of Abraham negotiating with Lot (Gen 13:5—14:24) on Ibrim, an official of Ebla, whose divine patron was Ya. "Abraham" and "Ibrium," "Ya" and "Yahweh" seemed identical. More careful study, however, showed there were more differences than similarities between these Ebla traditions and the Bible.

Hymn to the Creator of the Heavens and the Earth

Three exercise tablets contain almost the same text, which is translated here as a hymn celebrating the divine patron of Ebla as the creator of the heavens and the earth. The same text has also been translated as a list of Sumerian personal names beginning with LUGAL and two quotations. The hymn follows a pattern also found in the Enuma Elish stories from Babylon, a hymn to Ptah and a hymn to the Aton from Egypt as well as the creation of the heavens and the earth in the book of Genesis (Gen 1:1—2:4a).

TM. 75. G. 1682 (Gen 1:1—2:4a; Ps 104:5–9)

You are the creator of the heavens and the earth,
There was no earth until you created it.
There was no light until you created it.

There was no sun until you created it.
You alone rule over all creation.
You alone feed us.
You alone protect us. . . .
You alone never sleep.
You alone never die.
You alone deliver us from our enemies.
You alone give us peace.

BENEFITS

≋ *Part of the administrative pattern in the Eblaite palace was the issu-*
ing of rations of bread, wine, garments and tools to various officials,
visiting dignitaries and messengers.

TM.75.G.411

Issue king Ibbi-Sipis (2280–2250 BCE?) five *ninda* rations . . . and two
    ninda rations of bread.
Issue the queen two *ninda* rations of bread.
Issue royal officials two *ninda* rations of bread.
Issue the sons of royal officials three *ninda* rations of bread.
Issue Dubuhu-Hada four *ninda* rations of bread.
Issue Iptura two *ninda* rations of bread.
Issue sons of the king two *ninda* rations of bread.
Issue daughters of the king two *ninda* rations of bread.
Issue elders two *ninda* rations of bread . . . one axe, eight *ninda*
    rations. . . .
Issue ambassadors of foreign states four axes, ten *ninda* rations. . . .

A LETTER OF ENNA-DAGAN

≋ *Enna-Dagan was the commanding officer of the soldiers who con-*
quered Mari. The king of Ebla subsequently appointed him the gov-
ernor of Mari, although he labels himself as "king of Mari" at the
end of his letter. Phrases like "I inflicted heavy casualties" and the
repetitious manner of this military communiqué are typical of annal
writing not only at Mari, but also Assyria. Parallels to this type of
tradition may be found in the accounts of the wars of Israelite kings
in the books of Samuel-Kings.

TM.75.G.2367 (2 Sam 8:1–12; 1 Kgs 15:16–22)

From: Enna-Dagan, commanding officer at Mari
To: . . . king of Ebla

I laid siege to the cities of Aburu and Ilgi in the land of Belan. There, I defeated the king of Mari. In the land of Labanan I inflicted heavy casualties (Eblaite: heaped up corpses).

I laid siege to the cities of Tibalat and Ilwi. There, I defeated the king of Mari. In the land of Angai, I inflicted heavy casualties. . . .

I laid siege to the cities of Raeak, Irim, Asaltu and Badul. There, I defeated the king of Mari. Near the border of Nahal, I inflicted heavy casualties.

At Emar, Lalanium and a trade colony of Ebla, I defeated the soldiers of Mari, under the command of Istup-sar. At Emar and Lalanium, I inflicted heavy casualties.

I liberated Galalabi . . . and a trade colony.

At Zahiran, I defeated Iblul-Il, the king of Mari and Ashur. I inflicted extremely heavy casualties (Eblaite: seven heaps of corpses).

At Sada, Addali and Arisum in the land of Burman, I defeated Iblul-Il, the king of Mari, and their Sukurrim allies. I inflicted heavy casualties.

At Saran and Dammium, I defeated Iblul-Il, the king of Mari. Twice I inflicted heavy casualties.

Iblul-Il, the king of Mari, fled toward Nerad and took refuge in his fortress at Hasuwan. He sent the taxes which Mari owed Ebla to the city of Nema.

I defeated Emar, inflicting heavy casualties.

At Ganane, Nahal and Sada in the land of Gasur, I defeated Iblul-Il, the king of Mari. I inflicted extremely heavy casualties.

I, Enna-Dagan, now king of Mari, defeated Iblul-Il, the former king of Mari, for the second time at the city of Barama. At Aburu and Tibalat in the land of Belan, I inflicted heavy casualties.

STORIES OF
BA'AL AND ANAT

⧄ The stories of Ba'al and Anat are preserved on six broken clay tablets from Ugarit. They were written in the Ugaritic language in the
cuneiform script about 1400 BCE. The tablets were recovered along
with hundreds of others by a French team headed by Claude F.A.
Schaeffer (1898-1982), which dug at Ras Shamra, Syria between
1929-39 and after 1950. Hans Bauer (1878-1937) pioneered the translation of Ugaritic, an alphabetic language with thirty-two letters.

Much of the text of the stories of Ba'al and Anat is fragmentary. Therefore, it is impossible to tell the exact order of the stories.
They may have been told during a seasonal festival like the celebration of the new year when the people of Ugarit mourned the
death of Ba'al during the dry season that was ending and his resurrection to life during the rainy season that was just beginning (Ezek
8:14).

Parallels to the stories of Ba'al and Anat appear in the book of
Psalms and in the prophets.

I:ii, 1–42 (Exod 19:10; Judg 7:12; 2 Kgs 9:30; Isa 63:3–6; Cant 4:13–4;
Esth 2:9; Ps 16:9; 104:3; Rev 14:18–20; 19:13)

⧄ Anat celebrates the new year or the grape harvest with a battle in
which she wades in the blood of her enemies like farmers at Ugarit
waded in the juice of their grapes. Slaves arm Anat for battle with
cosmetics as if she were preparing to make love. The language and
motifs of war and sexual intercourse are interchangeable. Each is a
passionate activity that arouses all five senses.

Seven slaves rubbed the skin of Anat with cream,
  They tinted her hands and feet with henna.

Slaves scented the body of Anat with coriander perfume,
  They draped her in a purple robe.
Anat locked the doors of her sanctuary.
  She joined her warriors at the foot of the mountain.

Anat waged a fierce battle on the plain,
  She slaughtered the armies of two cities.
She vanquished soldiers from the seacoast in the west,
  She destroyed soldiers from the east.
Their heads lay like clods of soil under her feet,
  Their hands were matted like locusts in a swarm around her.
She strung their heads to make a necklace,
  She wove their hands to make a belt.
She waded up to her knees in warriors' blood,
  Up to her thighs in their guts.
With her spear she routed seasoned warriors,
  With her bow she turned back the veterans.

Anat went back to her sanctuary,
  The divine warrior returned to her palace.
The fierce battle on the plain was not enough for her,
  With the slaughter of two armies, she was not content.
So, she built bleachers for soldiers,
  Set up tables for warriors . . . thrones for heroes.
Once again, Anat could fight with vigor,
  Once again, she could slaughter every enemy in sight.
Anat's body trembled with gladness,
  Her heart filled with joy, she gloated with triumph,
Again, she waded knee-deep in warriors' blood,
  Up to her thighs in their guts.
Finally, these deadly games were enough for her,
  With the slaughter in her arena she was content.

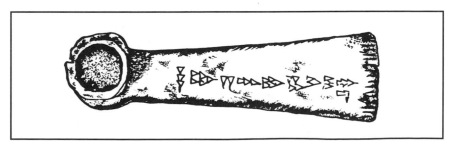

An axe head from Ugarit with a cuneiform inscription on it.

The warriors' blood was washed from her house,
   The oil of peace was poured from a bowl.
Anat the virgin warrior washed her hands,
   Anat the valiant widow cleaned her nails.
She washed the warriors' blood from her hands,
   . . . their guts from her nails.
She dismantled the bleachers,
   She put the tables aside, and took down the thrones.
She washed herself with dew from the sky,
   She anointed herself with oil from the earth,
She bathed with rain from the Rider of the Clouds
   With dew from the sky, and moisture from the stars.

I:iv, 47—v, 4 (1 Kgs 2:9; Isa 46:4; Jer 11:19)

▧ *Unlike the other members of the divine assembly, Ba'al does not have a sanctuary of his own (2 Sam 7:1-17; 1 Kgs 5:3-6; 1 Chr 17:1-14). He shares the house of El, his father, along with his sisters. When he complains about these arrangements, Anat intercedes with El for him.*

Ba'al appeals to Anat:

"I have no house like the other members of the divine assembly,
   No sanctuary like the other sons of Asherah.
I must stay on in the house of El, my father,
   I must lodge in the house of unmarried women,
With Asherah the sea,
   With Pidray the dew,
With Tallay the rain,
   With Arsay the springs."

Anat swears to Ba'al:

"El the bull will listen to me,
   I will make sure that he answers me.
I shall lead him like a lamb to slaughter,
   I shall cover his old grey head with blood, fill his old grey beard with
      guts . . .
If he does not give Ba'al a house like the other members of the divine
      assembly,
   If he does not give Ba'al a sanctuary like the other sons of Asherah."

The god Baal shown as god of the storm, with his lightning spear and thunder club.

I.v, 5–39 (Prov 9:1; Eccl 11:2; Job 36:26; 38:16; Ps 29:10; 95:3; 96:4; 97:9)

Anat stamped her foot and the earth trembled,
    She headed straight for El.
She journeyed to the source of the twin rivers,
    She journeyed to the fountain of the twin waters.
She walked right into El's royal compound,
    She burst into the tent of the king, the father of time. . . .

Then Anat the virgin spoke:

"El, how can you rejoice with your sons,
    How can you celebrate with your daughters?
How dare anyone in your palace be happy. . . .

I am going to smash your skull,
    Cover your old grey head with blood, and
    Fill your old grey beard with guts.
I am going to drive you from the seven chambers of wisdom,
    From the eight halls of judgement."

El spoke:

"My daughter, you are a warrior,
    No one else surpasses your ferocity.

Tell me, Anat, my virgin daughter,
  What do you want me to do?"

Anat the virgin warrior answered:

"El, your decrees are wise.
  Your wisdom endures forever.
  Happy the life which you command.
Ba'al the great is our leader,
  Ba'al is a deliverer beyond all others.
All of us must bear his chalice,
  All of us must hand him the cup."

El the bull cried out,
  El the king, who created him.
Asherah and her sons cried out,
  The godmother and her household:

"Ba'al has no house like the other members of the divine assembly.
  He has no sanctuary like the other sons of Asherah."

≋ *By this combination of threats and flattery, Anat convinces El that Ba'al must have his own sanctuary. El orders Kothar-wa-hasis, the divine craftsman, to build the house of Ba'al.*

III.i, 12–38 = KTU 1.2 I (1 Kgs 18:42; Ps 24:9)

≋ *Yam the sea and Nahar the river dispute Ba'al's right to a sanctuary of his own. Soon, a struggle begins between Ba'al, whose storms bring life-giving rain, and Yam and Nahar, whose waves and floods destroy life.*

Yam the sea sent messengers to the divine assembly,
  Nahar the river dispatched envoys to the holy ones. . . .
They departed at once,
  They did not delay.
They headed straight to the mountain of El,
  They went directly to the divine assembly.
The members of the divine assembly were eating,
  The holy ones were right in the middle of a meal.
Ba'al stood beside El.

When the divine assembly saw the messengers of Yam coming,
      When they caught sight of the envoys of Nahar on their way,
They put their heads on their knees,
      They buried their faces in the cushions on their couches.

Ba'al rebuked them:

"Why should you put your heads on your knees,
      Why should you bury your faces in the cushions on your couches?
Do not be afraid of the messengers of Yam,
      Do not fear the envoys of Nahar.
Lift your heads up off your knees,
      Raise your heads from the cushions on your couches.
I will speak to the messengers of Yam for you,
      I will deal with the envoys of Nahar."

The divine assembly lifted their heads from their knees,
      They raised their heads from the cushions on their couches.
When the messengers of Yam arrived,
      When the envoys of Nahar entered,
They did not bow before El,
      They did not prostrate before the divine assembly.

They addressed El the bull, father of Yam . . . :

"Hear the word of Yam, our lord.
      This is the decree of Nahar, our master:
El must extradite this prisoner,
      The divine assembly must stop protecting Ba'al.
Surrender Ba'al and his followers,
      I will take the son of Dagan into custody."

El the bull, the father of Yam, answered:

"Ba'al is the slave of Yam,
      The son of Dagan is the prisoner of Nahar.
The divine assembly turns Ba'al over to you as a gift,
      Accept him as a present from the holy ones."

≋   *Ba'al takes out his battle-ax and is about to kill the messengers when Asherah reminds him that they enjoy diplomatic immunity (Jer 26:16-19). Nonetheless, it seems that Yam does succeed in driving*

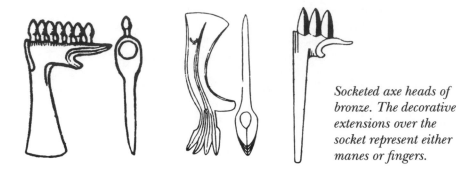

Socketed axe heads of bronze. The decorative extensions over the socket represent either manes or fingers.

Ba'al away from Mt. Zaphon. Then Yam tries to get El's permission to build a house of his own. Athataru, who oversees irrigation, argues that Yam should not have a house because he has no wife. Yam counters by demanding that El give him both a wife and a house. Finally, Kothar-wa-hasis convinces Ba'al to intervene.

III.iv,8–23 = KTU 1.2 IV (Judg 5:27; 2 Sam 7:13; Ps 68:4, 145:13; Rev 11:15)

Kothar-wa-hasis said:

"Listen to me, almighty Ba'al,
　　Hear me out, Rider of the Clouds,
Now is the time for you to strike,
　　Slay your enemies, and eliminate your rivals.
Now is the time to found an everlasting kingdom,
　　Establish your dominion throughout all generations."

Then, Kothar-wa-hasis forged a battle-ax.
　　He christened it "Chaser."
"Chase Yam away,
　　Chase Yam from his throne,
　　Chase Nahar from his seat of power.
Fly from the hand of Ba'al,
　　Fly like an eagle from his fingers.
Sever the shoulder of Yam the sea,
　　Cut off the arms of Nahar the river."
Yam, however, was too strong,
　　He did not fall.
Yam did not even waver,
　　He did not collapse.

So, Kothar-wa-hasis forged another battle-ax,
　　He christened it "Expeller."
"Expel Yam,
　　Expel him from his throne,
　　Expel Nahar from his seat of power.
Fly from the hand of Ba'al,
　　Fly like an eagle from his fingers.
Split the skull of Yam the sea,
　　Separate the eyes of Nahar the river.
Now Yam will fall,
　　Now Nahar will collapse on the earth."

〰　*Expeller helps Ba'al defeat, but not destroy, Yam. The fierce winter
　　storms along the Mediterranean coast can only temporarily be held
　　in check. Ba'al is proclaimed "Ruler of the Divine Assembly."*

*IV.vii, 50–2; V.i, 15–35; V.ii, 2–13 (Isa 5:14; Prov 1:12; Job 10:9; 42:2;
Eccl 3:20; Ps 42:1; 49:14; 132:7; 141:7; Hab 3:17)*

〰　*The house of Ba'al is constructed on the rain clouds. There is a
　　remarkable window in the clouds through which Ba'al's thundering
　　voice can be heard announcing the rain he sends to farms all over
　　the earth (1 Kgs 18:36–45). Nonetheless, life and fertility must con-
　　tinue to battle with death and infertility. Mot, who oversees the
　　land of the dead, sends searing sirocco winds to dry up the moisture
　　from the rains of Ba'al. Crops and orchards wither (Hos 13:15). Ba'al
　　dispatches two messengers to Mot to defend his right to rule the
　　land of the living.*

Ba'al proclaimed,

"I alone rule the divine assembly,
　　Who but I can feed the holy ones?
　　Who but I can feed the peoples of the earth . . . ?"

Mot, the son of El, responded,
　　Death answered Ba'al:
"My appetite is like that of a lion,
　　My energy is like the dolphins in the sea.
Death is a pool luring the wild oxen,
　　Death is a spring baiting herds of deer.

The dust of the grave devours its prey,
   Death eats whatever it wants with both hands. . . .
I will drink the moisture of Ba'al,
   My throat will swallow the son of El's rain.
   The mouth of the beloved of El will consume you. . . .
The lower lip of Mot stretches down to the earth,
   His upper lip reaches to the sky,
   He will lick the stars with his tongue.
Ba'al's rain will run off into Mot's mouth,
   His moisture will be swallowed by Mot's throat."

The olives shrivel,
   The earth's produce dies,
   The fruit of the trees drops off.
Almighty Ba'al becomes frightened,
   The Rider of the Clouds is terrified.
"Go. Tell Mot, the son of El,
   Deliver this message to the beloved of El.
Hear the word of Ba'al the Almighty,
   This the message of the greatest hero of all.
'Come to me, O Mot, son of El,
   I will be your slave forever.'"

⌇ *Ba'al dies when the moisture from the rain withdraws deep into the
earth and the growing season comes to an end. Ba'al's death is
mourned by the divine assembly, especially El and Anat. They put
dust in their hair and slash their bodies with knives (Jer 16:6; Ezek
27:30). Anat arranges a huge funeral and sacrifices hundreds of animals. As a childless widow, she petitions Asherah for a son to succeed Ba'al (Gen 38; Deut 25:5-10; Ruth 4). Asherah nominates two
candidates.*

VI.i, 48–65 (Ps 132:7)

Asherah said to El:
   "Make Yadi Yalhan king. . . ."

El kindly refused.
   El gently answered:
"Yadi Yalhan is too feeble to take Ba'al's place,
   He cannot wield the son of Dagan's spear."

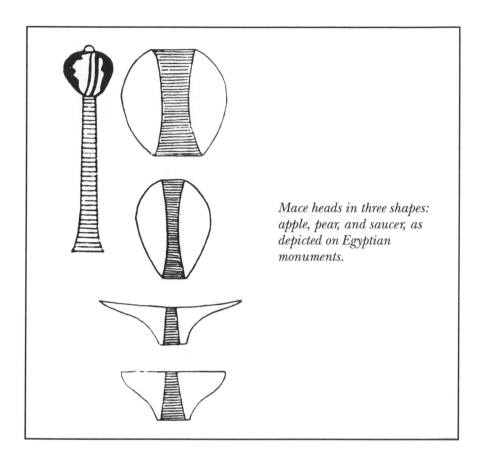

Mace heads in three shapes: apple, pear, and saucer, as depicted on Egyptian monuments.

Then Asherah said,
    The sea spoke:
"Make Athtar the awesome king.
    Let Athtar the awesome become king."
Athtar the awesome climbed Mt. Zaphon,
    He ascended the throne of Ba'al the almighty.
His feet did not even reach the footstool,
    His head did not even touch the headrest.
So Athtar the awesome resigned: "I cannot serve as king,
    I cannot dwell on the heights of Mt. Zaphon."
So Athtar the awesome descended,
    He stepped down from the throne of Ba'al the almighty.
Athtar became a ruler in the underworld,
    He became the overseer of the river of the dead.

VI.iii, 3–9 (Jer 11:5; Job 19:25; Ps 126:4)

🕮 *Anat hunts down Mot. Using a legal gesture, she grabs the hem of Mot's tunic (1 Sam 15:27) and demands that Ba'al be raised from the dead. Mot argues that Ba'al is no better than any other victim whom he harvests on his insatiable rounds of the earth. Anat seizes Mot, cuts him to pieces with her sword, and sows the pieces like seeds in a field. Then she goes back to El and asks him whether Ba'al is truly dead.*

"If Ba'al the almighty lives,
   If the most high, the ruler of the earth, breathes,
Then in a dream from El the kind and compassionate,
   Let me see Ba'al through the eyes of the creator of all.
Let the heavens rain olive oil,
   Let the dry stream beds flow with honey.
Then I will know that Ba'al the almighty lives,
   I will know that the most high lord of the earth breathes."

🕮 *El dreams and begins to laugh when he realizes that Ba'al is alive and that the crops will bloom again. El tells Anat to talk with Shapshu the sun, and ask her to look for Ba'al. Shapshu agrees, and begins by pouring wine into the dry furrows of the fields. Ba'al defeats both Yam and Mot to regain his title as ruler of the divine assembly. His return to life coincides with the coming of the rains that restore life and fertility to the land.*

VI.v, 9–24 (Ps 129:3; 132:18; Isa 26:14; Jer 15:7; 51:2)

In the seventh year, Mot, the son of El, spoke,
   He cried out to Ba'al the almighty:
"Because of you, Ba'al, I have lost face . . .
   Because of you . . .
I have been cut up with a sword,
   I have been burnt with fire.
I have been ground with a millstone,
   I have been winnowed with a sieve.
I have been scattered like seed in the fields,
   I have been sown in the sea.
Now give me one of your brothers to eat,
   Let us make peace.

*Ugaritic plaque with a
female fertility figure feeding
two male goats or stags.*

If you do not give me one of your brothers,
  I will make the dead devour the living."

Ba'al contrives to feed Mot his own brothers and thus wins the con-
test while still satisfying Mot's need to consume the living. In this
way, Ba'al emerges from the underworld while Mot eventually must
acknowledge that he cannot triumph over Ba'al.

VI.vi, 16–40 (Judg 16:3; 1 Sam 18:7; Ps 124:1–5; 125:3)

Mot plodded up Mt. Zaphon,
  He prostrated before Ba'al, lamenting:
"Mot was strong, but so was Ba'al.
  They gored each other like wild oxen.
Mot was strong, but so was Ba'al.
  They struck each other like serpents.
Mot was strong, but so was Ba'al.
  They kicked each other like stallions.
Mot was strong, but so was Ba'al. . . ."

Shapshu taunted Mot:
  "Listen to me, Mot, son of El.
You can never defeat Ba'al the almighty,
  El the bull, your father, cannot ignore you.

He will tear the doorposts out of your house,
    He will overthrow your throne,
    He will break your scepter in two."

Fear seized Mot, the son of El.
    The beloved of El trembled at the words of Shapshu.
Finally, Mot capitulated. . . . "Let Ba'al be enthroned as king,
    Let his majesty endure forever."

HYMN TO THE ATON

A hymn to the Aton was inscribed in Egyptian hieroglyphics on the wall of the tomb of Eye (or Apy), which pharaoh Akhenaton (1353-1335 BCE) built for Queen Nefertiti's father at Tell el-'Amarna. El-'Amarna stands on the east bank of the Nile just north of the massif of Jebel Abu Feda about one-hundred miles south of today's Cairo. The royal tombs were cut into the walls of a ravine about 4 miles from the city in the wadi Abu Hasah el-Bahri. The Egypt Exploration Fund excavated the site in 1891 and the German Orientgesellschaft continued the work from 1911-1914.

The hymn to the Aton contains some lines from older hymns celebrating the Aton or sun disc, and other members of Egypt's divine assembly like Ra as Har-of-the-horizon and Shu. Akhenaton emphasized the worship of the Aton and his son, the pharaoh. Technically, this world-view was not the monotheism of Judaism, Christianity and Islam today. By elevating Aton as the sole divine patron of Egypt, by changing his name from Amon-ophis IV to Akhenaton, and by moving the royal palace from Thebes to Amarna, Akhenaton attempted to federalize the government of Egypt. He wanted to increase the authority of the pharaoh, and decrease the authority of the priests and their divine patron, Amon-Ra. The reform succeeded only until the coronation of Tut'ankh-amon (1333-1323 BCE), when the priests once again resumed control.

The hymn celebrates the creator of Egypt shielded by the sun. From behind this solar screen, the warmth and light of the rays of Aton gently reach out to every corner of the land and bring Egypt to life. Close parallels to the hymn to the Aton appear in the book of Psalms. Interestingly, both Aton and Yahweh are celebrated for doing everything that good midwives do for mothers and their children. Both join a woman and a man, advise expectant mothers on proper nutrition, massage the agitated fetus during midterm traumas, clear the airway of the newborn, and supply everything else the newborn needs.

Akhenaton with his wife and daughters worshipping the sun disk, called the Aton, *who extends life-giving rays pictured as hands.*

Strophe 2–4 (Ps 104:20–3)

As you, Aton, rise over the horizon,
   Your beauty, Giver of Life, is made manifest.
You rise in the east,
   You fill the land with beauty.
Your glory shines high above the land,
   Your rays enrich the land you have created.
O Ra, you reach to the ends of the earth,
   You bestow them on Akhenaton, your beloved son.
Although you are far away,
   Your rays touch the earth.
Although you shine on every human face,
   No one sees you go.

When you set upon the western horizon,
   The earth lies in darkness and death.
Sleepers lie beneath their covers,
   Seeing no one around them.
Their pillows could vanish,
   They would not even notice.

The lion leaves his cave, the snake strikes,
    When darkness blankets the land.
The lands are quiet,
    Their creator rests on the horizon.
At daybreak, you rise again over the horizon,
    You shine as the Aton bringing day.
Your rays chase away the darkness,
    The two lands of Egypt rejoice.
Awake and erect,
    You raise them up.

Strophe 5–8 (Gen 7:11; 11:9; Ps 8:1; 104:11–4, 25–7; 139:13; Col 1:15–20)

Bathed and dressed,
    They raise their hands in praise.
The whole land goes to work. . . .

Cattle graze contented,
    Trees and plants turn green.
Birds fly to their nests,
    They spread their wings to praise your ka.
All things come to life
    When you have risen.
Ships and barges sail up and down,
    Canals open at your rising.
Fish swim the river,
    Your rays penetrate even dark waters.
O Lord, our Lord, how majestic is your name.
    You join a woman and a man,
You massage the fetus in its mother's womb,
    You soothe the crying child unborn.
You nurse the hungry infant in the womb,
    You breathe into its nostrils the first breath of life.
You open the newborn's mouth on the day of its birth
    You meet every human need. . . .

In Syria-Palestine, Ethiopia and Egypt,
    You assign each a place.
You allot to each both needs and food,
    You count out to each the days of life.
They have separate languages,
    And varied natures as well.

Their skins are different,
    For you have so distinguished the peoples.
You have made a Nile in the underworld,
    So it may be brought forth at your command
    To feed the people of the land.
Thus have you made them, wearying yourself.
    On their behalf, you are lord of all.
In this way the Aton of the day arises,
    Majestic in its greatness.

Strophe 10–1: Ps 104:10, 24

You also give life to all distant lands,
    For you have placed a Nile in the heavens,
So that rain may fall upon the sea and make waves
    Upon the mountains like those in the sea, irrigating their fields.
How efficient are your designs, O lord of all time,
    With a Nile in the heavens for the other lands and their creatures,
    With a Nile springing from the underworld for Egypt.

Your rays give sustenance to every field,
    Your rising brings them life and growth.
You have established the seasons
    To nurture all that you have made,
The winter to cool them and the heat
    So they may feel your touch.

You made the heavens in which to rise,
    That you might observe all things.
You alone are the Aton,
    Yet you alone rise,
You alone are the source of life.
    Appearing, glistening, departing and reappearing,
Your manifestations are numberless.
    You are the Aton, the source of life.
Every town, harbor, field, road and river sees your light,
    They feel your warmth.
You are the Aton,
    You are the light of the earth. . . .

Strophe 12–3: Ps 104:29–30

You are my desire,
   No one knows you except Akhenaton, your son.
You have revealed yourself to me,
   You have shown me your plans and your power.
Your hand made Egypt,
   You created it.
When you rise,
   The earth lives.
When you set,
   The earth dies.
You are life itself,
   All live through you.
Every eye sees clearly until you set,
   All work must wait until you rise again.
At your rising, every arm works for your pharaoh,
   At your creation, every foot sets off to work.
You raise up the people for the son of your body,
   For the pharaoh of Upper and Lower Egypt.
Akhenaton rules with the spirit of Ma'at, the divine patron of
      knowledge . . .
   Akhenaton and her royal highness, Nefertiti.

PROVERBS,
SIRACH,
WISDOM

TEACHINGS OF
PTAH-HOTEP

Ptah-Hotep taught during the Old Kingdom in Egypt (2575–2134 BCE). The teachings of Ptah-Hotep are preserved on papyrus sheets in hieratic or longhand Egyptian writing as well as on clay tablets in hieroglyphic Egyptian. They were recovered in Egypt around 1900 by archaeologists from France and are at the Bibliothèque Nationale in Paris.

In the ancient Near East, a teacher like Ptah-Hotep bore the title "Father" or "Mother" (Prov 1:8). A student was called "Child." Teachers taught students to observe, to judge and to act. They used the saying (Prov 1:17) to hand on their observations, and the analogy (Hebrew: masal) to hand on their judgments (Prov 9:17; 10:1). Analogies linked together form an essay, which is the most common genre in the teachings of Ptah-Hotep. Introductory and concluding essays, which offer students general encouragement to excel in life, sandwich essays that provide advice on specific careers and professions into which they will graduate. Students memorized the sayings and analogies of their teachers. Competent students, who could apply teachings and act accordingly, were "…like golden apples in silver settings" (Prov 25:11). The incompetent, who could not apply what they learned were like "…a proverb which hangs limp in the mouth of a fool like crippled legs" (Prov 26:7).

The teachings of Ptah-Hotep are widely echoed in the books of Proverbs, Ecclesiastes and Sirach. Wisdom traditions teach students how to avoid pride, get good advice (Prov 2:4), practice table manners (Prov 23:1; Sir 31:12), be reliable (Prov 25:13), make friends (Sir 6:7), and deal with women (Prov 6:24; Sir 9:1).

50–60 (Prov 2:1–5; 19:20)

My students, in all things, be intelligent, not arrogant,
  Be wise, not over-confident.
Seek advice from the powerless,
  As well as from the powerful.
No one ever reaches one's full potential,
  There is always more to learn.
Wisdom hides like emeralds,
  But it can always be uncovered . . .
. . . in a poor man,
  . . . in a young woman grinding grain.

85–95 (Prov 11:21; 17:13)

If you become a ruler, do what is right,
  Stay above reproach.
Be just in your decisions,
  Never ignoring the law.
Injustice brings punishment,
  Injustice brings all your work to nothing.
Injustice brings success for a moment,
  Justice brings success for two generations. . . .

120–42 (Prov 23:1–3)

If you work for someone else,
  Take what your master offers.
Do not look about with envy,
  Do not always hope for more.
Stand humbly until your master speaks to you,
  Speak only when spoken to.
Laugh when your master laughs,
  Try to please your master in everything.
But remember this,
  No one knows what is in another's heart.
When masters are at the table,
  They may seem to dispense favors as they see fit,
. . . to favor those who are useful,
  . . . to favor those who think as they do.
The *ka*-soul is guided by the divine assembly,
  Therefore, do not complain about their choices.

Egyptian scribes at work (from Beni Hasan).

147–60 (Prov 25:13; Sir 19:7, 10)

If you become a messenger for the powerful,
    Be completely reliable on every assignment.
Carry out your orders to the letter.
    Withhold nothing,
    Forget nothing,
    Forge nothing,
    Repeat nothing,
    Embellish nothing.
Do not make harsh language worse.
    Vulgarity turns the mighty into enemies.

175–85

If you work for the newly rich,
    Ignore their former lack of wealth and distinction.
Do not be prejudiced against them,
    Do not detest them for once being lower class.
Respect them for their accomplishments,
    Acknowledge them for their acquisition of land.
Land does not come of itself,
    Land must be earned.
It is their law for those who wish it.
    As for those who overstep, they are feared.
It is the divine assembly which determines the quality of people.
    The divine assembly defends us all, even when we sleep. . . .

265–76

If you become a judge,
    Listen patiently to the plaintiff's suit.

Give plaintiffs time to air their cases.
    Plaintiffs want petitions heard more than granted.
If you interrupt plaintiffs, and are rude to petitioners,
    People will complain: "Why does the judge do that?"
To grant every petition is unnecessary,
    To hear every petition calms passions, prevents violence.

278–96 (Prov 6:23–9; 7:24–7)

If you become the father of a household or are a houseguest,
    Stay away from the women of the house.
Keep your mind on business, your eyes off pretty faces.
    Foolish dreamers become casualties of unwise actions.
Escape love sickness and lust,
    And succeed in everything else you do.

318–23 (Prov 15:27)

If you inherit land, take only your own portion of the land,
    Do not covet the land of others.

Wall scene from the funerary temple (mastaba) *of Ptahhotep*
(5th dynasty; 2500 B.C.E.).

Those who respect the land of others earn respect,
    Those who defraud others lose their own land.
To covet even a small thing
    Is to transform the peaceful into warriors.

328–34 (Prov 12:4; 31:10–1 + 27–31)

If you become a landowner, establish a household,
    Be faithful to your wife.
Feed her, clothe her, make her happy,
    And she will provide you with an heir.
Do not sue her in court,
    But do not let her dominate you.
To judge a woman's moods
    Is to read a woman's eyes.
A wife who shares her husband's wealth
    Is a wife who is faithful to her husband.

429–31 (Eccl 6:2–3)

If you are promoted, be generous with the wealth the divine assembly
        gives you,
    Take care of your hometown now that you can.

565–74 (Hos 14:9; Prov 2:1–5; 19:20)

Finally, my students, remember, the wise follow their teachers' advice,
    Consequently, their projects do not fail.
The wise rise to positions of trust,
    Guided by their teachers' instruction.
The wise rise early to start to work,
    Fools rise early to worry about all there is to do.

TEACHINGS OF KHETY

≋ *More than six-hundred copies of the teachings of Khety have been recovered by archaeologists. Two copies by the same Nineteenth Dynasty scribe are preserved in the British Museum in London on the Papyrus Sallier II (art 10182) and on the Papyrus Anastasi VII (art 10222). Fragments of the text are found on the Papyrus Chester Beatty (art 10699), also in the British Museum. One Eighteenth Dynasty writing board contains fragments of the teachings of Khety and is preserved today in the Louvre Museum in Paris.*

The teachings of Khety are a satire that celebrates the work of scribes and makes fun of every other trade in Egypt. They developed during the Middle Kingdom (2040-1640 BCE), and were copied by scribes throughout the New Kingdom (1550-1070 BCE) to practice writing hieroglyphics.

Parallels to the teachings of Khety are found in the teachings of Ptah-hotep and of Amen-em-ope. The use of trades as a theme and the glorification of the scribal profession are also found in the book of Sirach (Sir 38:24—39:11). The importance of scribes and the esteem with which they were held are fairly common in the Bible (1 Chron 27:32; Ezra 7:6, 11; Matt 13:52) as is the attribution of skill and wisdom to professional scribes (1 Cor 1:20).

Khety gave his son Pepy this advice as they sat together in the cabin on the deck of a ship sailing south to the city where the pharaoh sat. He was en route to apprentice Pepy to the scribes who served the pharaoh.

"Learn to write, my son. I have seen how many other kinds of work destroy workers. Learning to write can save you from all this suffering. As it says in the book of Goals: 'Become a scribe, fulfilling others' needs, and you will never be poor.' No other profession may make this claim.

"I will make you see that writing is to be loved even more than your

*Egyptian scribes write on papyrus while holding palettes with
red and black ink. They carry reed pens behind their ears.
Scroll cases stand between them (c. 2400 B.C.E.).*

mother. It is clear that writing is better than any other work in all the land
of Egypt. Even as a young man, the scribe is treated with courtesy and
sent on important errands. Shortly into his career, he wears a robe of
office.

"I have never seen a sculptor or goldsmith serve as a messenger. But
I have seen them at work, at the mouths of their furnaces, with their
fingers resembling the scale-covered claws of a crocodile. Their sweat
reeks like the odor of rotten fish.

"The woodcutter is more wretched than a farmer. His field is the
forest, his hoe an axe. He works until dark. His arms ache with heavy
labor and he must still light his own fire.

"The jeweler works hard stones every day. To finish just one small
piece of jewelry is a full day's work. When he lies down at dusk, his back
aches and his thighs cramp.

"The barber shaves from dawn until dusk. He makes himself a slave
to the chins of the world. Like bees in search of flowers, barbers flit
from street to street in search of chins to shave. Only the persistent fill
their bellies.

"The arrow maker must sail north to the delta swamps in search of
arrow shafts. When his days are done, he has been bitten by gnats and
stung by sand flies until his body is a weakened shell.

"The potter is condemned to dwell in the clay while still among the
living. He is as filthy as a pig from wallowing in the mud. While firing his

pots, his clothes are caked with clay, his leather belt is rotting. Every breath he takes contains the fire of the kiln. He kneads the clay with his feet, and is exhausted by its weight. He clomps along the streets and tracks mud into every courtyard. . . .

"The gardener bears a yoke. His shoulders slump with age and there is a festering sore on his neck. In the morning he waters his vegetables, in the evening he tends his herbs, and at noon he works in his orchard. More than any other profession, the gardener works himself to death. . . .

"The weaver's life is worse than a woman's. With his feet tucked under him, he never breathes the fresh air. If he stops before the day's end, he is beaten with fifty lashes. He must bribe the doorkeeper with his food just to see the light of day. . . .

"The messenger treks into the wilderness, leaving his property to his heirs. Faced with the threat of lions and Asiatics, he can only be himself when in Egypt. When he returns to his door, he is exhausted by his journey. Whether his house be a tent or of mudbrick, his joy is never found there. . . .

"The fisherman's job is the worst of all. He toils by the river among the crocodiles. When his quota of fish is announced, he can only lament. His fear of the crocodiles blinds him, causes him to curse while others scorn.

Scene of workmen cutting down a tree (Old Kingdom).

*An early picture of an Egyptian scribe
(5th dynasty, c. 2500 B.C.E.).*

"If you know how to write, you will do better than any of these other workers. You will be your own boss. It is my responsibility to make this journey with you to the city where the pharaoh sits. Your time as an apprentice is no more than a day. Your work as a scribe will last for an eternity, longer than the mountains. The time will pass quickly, very quickly. . . ."

TEACHINGS OF
AMEN-EM-OPE

Shortly after 1900, archaeologists recovered two versions of the teachings or "...wise words" of Amen-em-ope. One version was written
in hieratic Egyptian longhand on papyrus sheets and is now in the
British Museum (#10474) in London. The other version is on a clay
tablet in Turin, Italy.

Amen-em-ope taught in Egypt between 1250–1000 BCE. The
teachings of Ptah-Hotep (3000–2000 BCE) and the teachings of Amen-
em-ope demonstrate the consistency of Egypt's world-view over the
2000 years separating one tradition from the other. Both contrast the
wise and the fool. The wise are soft-spoken or silent. Fools are hot-
tempered or hot-headed. The wise know when to talk and when to
listen. Fools let anger run or ruin their lives. There are, nonetheless,
striking differences between one tradition and the other. The teachings of Ptah-hotep promise material success. The teachings of Amen-
em-ope remind students that only the members of the divine
assembly are perfect, and that few of the wise have material success.

Like most of the peoples of Syria-Palestine, the Hebrews hated
Egypt as a house of slaves, but loved Egypt as a great teacher represented by Ptah-hotep and Amen-em-ope. The book of Proverbs
(Prov 22:17—24:22) preserves portions of the teachings of Amen-em-
ope and imitates its structure. Both have a general introduction followed by thirty chapters of surprisingly similar advice on specific
topics. "Have I not written for you thirty sayings of admonition and
knowledge, to show you what is right and true, that you may give
a true answer to those who sent you?" (Prov 22:20-1). The teachings
of James in the New Testament (James 3:1-18) are also indebted to
the teachings of Amen-em-ope.

CHAPTER ONE

iii:9–18 + iv:1 (Prov 22:17–8)

Listen to what I say,
　　Learn my words by heart.
Prosperity comes to those who keep my words in their hearts,
　　Poverty comes to those who discard them.
Enshrine my words in your souls,
　　Lock them away in your hearts.
When the words of fools blow like a storm,
　　The words of the wise will hold like an anchor.
Live your lives with my words in your heart,
　　And you will live your lives with success.
My words are a handbook for life on earth,
　　My words will bring your body to life.

CHAPTER TWO

iv:3–16 + v:1–8 (Prov 22:22; 25:21–2)

Do not steal from the poor,
　　Do not cheat the cripple.
Do not abuse the elderly,
　　Do not refuse to let the aged speak.
Do not conspire to defraud anyone yourself,
　　Do not encourage anyone else's fraud.
Do not sue those who wrong you,
　　Do not testify against them in court.

Scribes recording the bringing of gifts to a nobleman (from Beni Hasan).

Injustice can turn on fools quicker than
   . . . floods eroding the bank of a canal,
   . . . north winds bearing down on a boat,
   . . . storms forming,
   . . . thunderbolts cracking,
   . . . crocodiles striking.

Fools cry out,
   They shout to the divine assembly for help.
Let Thoth, divine patron of the moon, judge their crimes.
   You must steer the boat to rescue them.
Do not treat fools the way fools treat you.
   Pull the fool up out of high water.
Give the fool your hand.
   Leave the punishment of the fool to the divine assembly,
Feed fools until they are full,
   Give them your bread until they are ashamed.

CHAPTER THREE

v:9–10

Stop and think before you speak.
   It is a quality pleasing to the divine assembly.

CHAPTER FOUR

vi:1–12 (Ps 1; Jer 11:16; 17:5–8; Ezek 17:5)

Fools who talk publicly in the temple,
   Are like a tree planted indoors.
The tree blooms, but then withers.
   It is thrown into the ditch,
It floats far from home,
   It is burned as trash.

The wise who are reserved
   Are like a tree planted in a garden.
The tree flourishes, and doubles its yield. . . .
   Its fruit is sweet,
Its shade is pleasant,
   It will flourish in the garden forever.

CHAPTER SIX

vii:12–25 + viii:10–20 + ix:1–8 (Prov 15:16–7; 16:8; 17:1; 19:1+22; 22:28; 23:10; Hos 5:10)

Do not move a surveyor's stone to steal a field,
    Do not move the surveyor's line to take a farm.
Do not covet another's land,
    Do not poach on the widow's field.
To forge a claim to the public path through a field,
    Cries out to Thoth, divine patron of the moon, for justice.
Those who seize public lands,
    Are the enemies of the poor . . .
The enemies of public life,
    Are the destroyers of whatever they see.
Those who steal from the community,
    Are those whose warehouses will be robbed,
    Are those whose heirs will be defrauded of their inheritance.
Do not topple the markers on the boundaries of a field,
    Or your conscience will destroy you.
To please the pharaoh, our divine ruler,
    Observe the borders of your neighbors' fields.
To please the pharaoh, ruler of all,
    Maintain the borders of your own field.
Do not plow across the boundary furrow of your neighbors,
    And your neighbors will not plow across yours.
Plow only your own fields,
    Eat only bread from your own threshing-floor.
    There will always be enough.
Better a single bushel from your divine patron,
    Than five thousand stolen bushels.

Stolen grain does not make good bread in the bowl,
    Nor good feed in the barn,
    Nor good beer in the jar.
Stolen grain only spends the night in your granary.
    At dawn it vanishes.
Better is poverty from the hand of your divine patron
    Than wealth from a granary full of stolen grain.
Better is a single loaf and a happy heart
    Than all the riches in the world and sorrow.

CHAPTER SEVEN

ix:9—x:4 (Ps 39:6; 52:7; 62:10; Prov 21:6; 23:4–5; Eccl 5:10)

Do not spend tomorrow's riches,
 Today's wealth is all you own.
Do not set your heart on material goods,
 Time makes beggars of us all.
Do not work to lay up a surplus,
 Toil only for what you need.

Stolen goods only spend the night,
 At dawn they vanish.
Dawn reveals where stolen goods spent the night,
 But they have vanished.
At night, the earth opens its mouth
 And renders its verdict on stolen goods.
At night, the earth consumes stolen goods
 And absorbs them into the underworld.
At night, stolen goods dig a hole into the underworld.
 They fly away like geese into the sky.

CHAPTER NINE

xi:13–20 + xii:1 + xii:8–9 (Prov 14:7; 19:20; 22:24–5; 24:25)

Do not take counsel with fools,
 Do not seek their advice.
Do not speak back to superiors,
 Do not insult them.
Do not let superiors discuss their troubles with you,
 Do not give them free advice.
Seek advice from your peers,
 Do not ignore your equals.
More dangerous are the words of fools
 Than storm winds on open waters. . . .
Do not rush to embrace fools,
 Lest their advice drown you like a storm.

Workers slaughtering cattle for meat (from Beni Hasan).

CHAPTER ELEVEN

xii:10–4 + xiv:9–14 (Prov 23:8)

Do not covet the goods of the poor,
    Do not hunger for their bread.
The goods of the poor will stick in your throat,
    You cannot swallow them.

Those who perjure themselves to defraud the poor
    Lie only to steal from themselves.
Success obtained by fraud cannot last,
    The bad only spoils the good.
When you vomit a piece of bread too large to swallow,
    What you gained is lost. . . .

CHAPTER THIRTEEN

xv:20–7 + xvi:9–14 (Prov 14:5; 17:1; 22:26–7; Matt 18:27)

Do not cheat your neighbor with false ledgers,
    It is an abomination for the divine assembly.
Do not bear false witness
    And destroy your neighbor with your words.
Do not over-assess the property of your neighbor,
    And inflate what you are owed.
If a poor neighbor owes you a great debt,
    Forgive two-thirds, collect one-third.

Make honesty your guide to life,
    And you will sleep soundly, and wake happily.

Better to be praised for loving your neighbor
    Than loving your wealth.
Better is bread eaten with a contented heart
    Than wealth spent with sorrow. . . .

CHAPTER EIGHTEEN

xix:11–22 + xx:1–7 (Prov 16:9; 19:21; 20:9; 27:1; Matt 6:34; James 4:13–5)

Do not go to bed worrying,
    Wondering: "What will tomorrow bring?"
No one knows what tomorrow brings,
    The divine assembly is perfect, but humans fail.
Human words are one thing,
    Divine actions are another.
Do not say, "I am innocent,"
    And then file a lawsuit.
Judgment belongs to the divine assembly,
    Verdicts are sealed by divine decree.
Before the divine assembly, no one is perfect,
    Before the divine assembly, everyone has failings.
Those who always strive for perfection
    Can destroy it in a moment.

Control your temper, save your life.
    Do not steer your life with your tongue alone.
Make your tongue the rudder of your boat,
    But make Amon-Ra its pilot.

CHAPTER TWENTY

xx:8–9 + xxi:1–16 (Exod 23:8; Ps 15:5)

Do not bear false witness against your neighbor,
    Do not defame the righteous.
Do not court the favor of those dressed in white linen
    And ignore those in rags.
Do not take bribes from the powerful
    And oppress the poor for their sake.

Justice is the gift of the divine assembly,
    Given to whomever it wills. . . .

*Egyptian nobleman fishing in the papyrus marshes of the Nile
(Beni Hasan, 19th century, B.C.E.).*

Do not alter the decrees which the divine assembly has written,
  Do not do damage to the designs of the divine assembly.
Do not claim the power of the divine assembly,
  For you are subject to fate and fortune.

CHAPTER TWENTY-FIVE

*xxiv:9–20 (1 Sam 21:14; Job 10:8–9; 33:6; Ps 103:14; Isa 64:8;
Prov 17:5; 29:13; Eccl 3:1–10)*

Do not make fun of the blind,
  Do not tease the dwarf,
  Do not trip the lame.
Do not tease the insane,
  Do not lose patience with them when they are wrong.

Humans are clay and straw,
   The divine assembly is their sculptor.
Every day the divine assembly tears down,
   And every day it builds up.
The divine assembly can make a time for thousands to be powerful,
   And a time for thousands to be powerless.
Blessed are those who journey to the land of the dead.
   They will be safe in the hands of the divine assembly.

CHAPTER TWENTY-EIGHT

xxvi:9–14 (Ruth 2:2–9; 1 Kgs 17:12–6)

Do not arrest the widow gleaning your fields,
   Do not fail to be patient with her reply.
Give the stranger olive oil from your jar,
   And double the income of your household.
The divine assembly desires respect for the poor
   More than honor for the powerful.

CHAPTER THIRTY

xxvi:15–26 (Deut 6:4–8; Hos 14:9; Prov 22:20 + 29)

To study these thirty chapters
   Is to be educated and entertained.
They are the book of books,
   They give wisdom to the simple.
Blessed are those who teach them to the simple.
   They are pleasing to the divine assembly.
Fill your soul with these teachings,
   Put them in your heart.
Master these teachings,
   Hand them on to others.
The skilled scribe
   Will become a client of the pharaoh.

TEACHINGS OF AHIQAR

🔖 *Ahiqar (Aramaic: 'hyqr) introduces himself as an advisor to Senna-cherib, who ruled Assyria from 704-681 BCE or to Esarhaddon who ruled from 680-669 BCE. In 1906, German archaeologists recovered an edition of his teachings on the island of Elephantine, which is today part of the city of Aswan in southern Egypt. This copy of Ahiqar's teachings was written in Aramaic about 500 BCE on eleven palimpsest or recycled sheets of papyrus. Before the teachings could be written on these sheets, the previous writing had to be erased. Today they are preserved in the Staatliche Museum in Berlin.*

Ahiqar never had a child who could be his heir, so he adopted Nadin and trained him to take over his job in the Assyrian court. Once Nadin got into office, however, he betrayed Ahiqar by accusing him of treason. Ahiqar was sentenced to death, but the executioner carried out the sentence on a substitute and Ahiqar went into hiding. Ahiqar subsequently recovered his honor by helping the great king of Assyria win an enormous wager with the pharaoh of Egypt, and by exposing Nadin as a fool.

Seven sheets of papyrus with a total of nine columns preserve masalim, *which are sayings, proverbs and adages like those found in the book of Proverbs. There are also fables, in which plants and animals taunt each other, like one in the book of Judges (Judg 9:8-15) and in the fables of Aesop. Four sheets of papyrus with a total of five columns preserve stories like those in the teachings of Joseph in the book of Genesis (Gen 37:2—50:26), in the teachings of Tobit (Tob 1:1—14:15), where Ahiqar appears as Tobit's nephew (Tob 1:21-2; 4QTobaramᵃ), and in the* Thousand and One Nights *in Arabic.*

vi:81 (Prov 13:24; 19:18)

Spare the rod,
  Spoil the child.

283

vi:88

Lions ambush stags, shed their blood, eat their meat,
   So it is when humans meet.

vi:92 (Prov 6:16–9)

Two kinds of people are a delight.
   A third pleases Shamash, the divine overseer:
   Those who share their wine,
   Those who follow good advice,
   Those who can keep secrets.

vii:98 (Prov 26:2; Eccl 10:20; Sir 27:16–9)

Above all else, control your tongue.
   Do not repeat what you have heard.
A human word is a bird;
   Once released, it can never be recaptured.

vii:99 (Eccl 5:2)

Choose words carefully to teach another.
   The word is mightier than the sword.

vii:100 (Ps 52:2; Wis 18:15–6; Heb 4:12)

Rulers are often soft-spoken,
   But their words are two-edged swords.

vii:101 + 104 (Eccl 6:10; Isa 10:15; 45:9)

Never challenge the words of a ruler.
   Can kindling conquer the flame?
   Can flesh conquer the knife?
   Can farmers conquer rulers?

vii:105 (Prov 25:15; Sir 28:17)

Gentle is the tongue of a ruler,
   But it can break a dragon's bones.

*An ivory decoration piece from the Syrian city of Arslan Tash,
with winged godlike creatures protecting a figurine.*

viii:111 (Sir 22:15; 29:4–5)

I have hauled sand, and carried salt,
  But nothing is heavier than debt.

viii:114 (Ps 8:2; Wis 10:21; Jer 1:6–9; Matt 21:16)

When the young speak mighty words which soar,
  Their words become prophecies.
  With divine help, they even make sense.

viii:118

Once there was a leopard who was hungry.
  Once there was a goat who was cold.

The leopard asked: "Would you like my coat,
    Would you like me to cover you?"
The goat answered: "What comfort is your coat?
    You only want my hide."

A leopard does not approach a gazelle
    Unless it is looking for blood.

viii:125 (Job 24:13–7)

In the eyes of the divine assembly, a woodcutter working in the dark
    Is like a thief burglarizing a house.

ix:126 (Ps 11:2; 64:2, 7)

Do not draw your bow or shoot an arrow at the innocent.
    Their divine patrons will come to their help, and turn your arrows
        back on you.

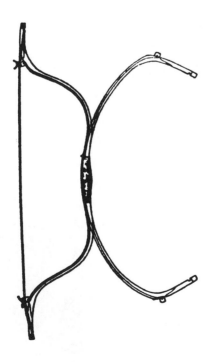

*A composition bow,
illustrating both
the strung and
unstrung states.*

ix:130 (Prov 6:1–5)

Do not borrow from the wicked.

When you borrow money,
    Work night and day to repay it.
Receiving a loan is sweet . . .
    Repaying a loan can cost all you possess.

ix:136 (Exod 20:17; Ps 131:1)

Do not be dissatisfied with your life.
    Do not covet honors which have been denied you.

ix:137 (Ps 62:10; Ezek 28:5; Lk 12:13–21; 1 Tim 6:10)

Amassing wealth corrupts the heart.

ix:138 (Exod 20:12; Prov 20:20; Sir 3:1–16)

Those who do not honor their parents' name
    Are cursed for their evil by Shamash, the divine judge.

x:142 (Sir 8:1)

Do not compete with those more powerful than you,
    Do not compete with those stronger than you.
    They will only add your power and strength to their own.

x:148

Do not be sweet enough to swallow,
    Do not be bitter enough to be spit out.

xi:165 (Judg 9:8–15; 2 Kgs 14:9)

A thorn bush asked a pomegranate tree:
    "Why so many thorns to protect so little fruit?"
The pomegranate tree said:
    "Why so many thorns to protect no fruit at all?"

*A cylinder seal portraying the god Shamash seated with a two-faced god
and a bird-man and lesser deities (British Museum).*

xi:171 (Exod 22:26–7)

If unscrupulous creditors take hold of your cloak, let them have it.
  Shamash, the divine judge, will take their garments, and give them
    all to you.

xiii:192 (Mt 25:14–30)

Guard your master's well carefully,
  Next time he may entrust you with his gold.

xiii:204 (Job 39:5–8)

Once someone said to a wild ass: "If you will let me ride you,
  I will let you live in my stable."
The ass replied: "Why don't you live in the stable,
  Then I will not have to let you ride me."

xiv:208 (Jer 13:23)

Do not send the bedouin to sea, nor the sailor into the desert.
  Everyone's work is unique.

TEACHINGS OF ANKHSHESHONQY

The teachings of Ankhsheshonqy developed around 200 BCE. They are written in demotic script, a cursive style of Egyptian writing. The damaged papyrus on which they are written consists of twenty-eight columns. It is preserved today in the British Museum in London (#10508).

Ankhsheshonqy was a priest of Ra sometime between 945 and 712 BCE. Like Ahiqar, he was charged with treason and sentenced to prison. He had tried to talk a friend out of assassinating the pharaoh. When the plot was discovered, he was indicted as an accomplice because he did not report his friend to the pharaoh. While in prison, Ankhsheshonqy wrote to his heir on broken pieces of pottery from jars in which his wine ration was delivered (4:18). Like the teachings of Ahiqar, the teachings of Ankhsheshonqy are intended for ordinary people, not royal officials.

Parallels to the teachings of Ankhsheshonqy appear in the books of Proverbs and Sirach.

7:4–5 (Prov 23:9; Sir 22:7)

Do not instruct a fool who will only hate you.
  Do not instruct anyone who will not listen to you.

7:18 (Prov 29:19)

A slave who is not beaten becomes disobedient.

7:24

Do not say everything you think.

8:12 (Prov 6:25–6)

Do not marry a woman whose husband is alive
　　Unless you want to make an enemy.

8:17—9:4 (1 Sam 2:12—4:22; Prov 14:3; 15:4; James 3:1–18)

Blessed is a city with a just ruler.
Blessed is a sanctuary with a wise priest.
Blessed is a field which is fertile.
Blessed is a silo which is full.
Blessed is a treasury which is well managed.
Blessed is a household managed by a wise woman.
Blessed is a man who thinks before he speaks.
Blessed is an army with a courageous commander.
Blessed is a village whose elders cannot be bribed.
Blessed is a craftsman with good tools.

9:5–9

Do not ignore a legal claim.
Do not ignore a possible cure.
Do not ignore the pharaoh's command.
Do not ignore the needs of livestock.
　　He who ignores important matters will pay with his life.

A snake used as a hieroglyphic character.

9:12–3

Do not live in the same house with your in-laws.
Do not live as a neighbor with your master.

10:6 (Prov 23:9; Sir 22:7)

Fools cannot tell teaching from insult.

11:8–10

Do not kill a snake and then leave its tail.
Do not hurl a spear you cannot aim.
   He who spits in the wind can expect to get wet.

11:11–4

Honor is based on one's household.
Honor is based on one's health.
Honor is based on an honest face.
Honor is based on what is done with one's hands.

11:19

Do not shame your son in front of his mother unless you want to
    shame his father.

12:6 (Matt 7:12)

Do not do evil to someone and thus encourage another to do evil to you.

13:2

A wise man seeks friends,
   A fool seeks enemies.

13:12

When you find your wife with a lover, it is time to look for a new bride.

14:9 (Luke 17:11–9)

A kindness acknowledged by only one in one hundred
   Is a kindness which has not perished.

14:14

Once bitten by a snake,
   Forever frightened by a rope.

16:9–12

Borrow money to expand a farm, to marry a wife, to celebrate your
     birthday.
   Do not borrow money to live an easy life.

18:11 (Deut 21:18–21)

The children of fools wander in the streets,
   The children of the wise are at their parents' sides.

18:19–20

Blessed are those who warm their houses to the rafters.
   Cursed are those who build houses and mortgage them.

19:10 (Eccl 11:1)

Do a good deed and throw it in the water.
   When it dries you will find it.

19:11–2 (Prov 26:17)

When two brothers quarrel,
   Do not come between them.
Anyone who comes between two brothers when they quarrel
   Becomes their enemy when they make peace.

A figure of a snake, also used as a hieroglyphic.

20:4

Begin by planting a sycamore,
    End by planting any tree.

20:13

Snakes which are fed do not strike.

20:22–5

Waste is a vacant house.
Waste is an unmarried woman.
Waste is an ass which only carries bricks.
Waste is a boat which only carries straw.

21:14

Husbands who are ashamed of their wives will have no children.

22:3

Do not start a fire you cannot extinguish.

22:19

Give one loaf to your laborer,
    Receive two loaves from the work of his shoulders.

23:6–7 (Prov 6:25–6)

A man who makes love to a married woman will be executed on her
threshold.

23:8 (Ps 37:16; Prov 16:8)

Better to dwell in your own house
    Than in someone else's mansion.

24:12

Yesterday's drunkenness does not slake today's thirst.

26:5–8

Life savers go to prison.
    Murderers go free.
Those who save go hungry.
    Inscrutable divine hands direct the fate of all.

26:14 (Prov 16:1, 9)

Divine plans are one thing.
    Human thoughts are another.

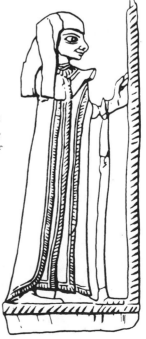

*A noble woman, from a
painting found at the
Canaanite city of
Megiddo.*

SONG OF SONGS

EGYPTIAN LOVE SONGS

Papyrus Harris 500 was recovered by British archaeologists at the beginning of the 20th century from the rooms that Ramses II (1290–1224 BCE) added to the Karnak temple near the city of Luxor in central Egypt today. The scroll, which is badly damaged in places, contained nineteen love songs divided into three separate groups. They are written in Egyptian hieroglyphics. The scroll is preserved today in the British Museum in London (P. British Museum 10060).

Erotica, like Egypt's love songs, teaches lovers how to make love and motivates them to make love well. In the world of the Bible, making love is a passionate work like farming, eating, fighting, learning and offering sacrifice. The language and imagery describing one is often used to describe another. Therefore, the lover sings "...feast on my breasts." Erotica teaches lovers how to arouse each of the five senses in order to create the passion necessary for making love. The songs are full of images of touching, tasting, smelling, hearing, and seeing.

Even though Egypt's love songs may be one thousand years older than those in the Song of Solomon, the parallels are unmistakable.

Her song:

I am still here with you,
   But your heart is no longer here with me.
Why have you stopped holding me?
   What have I done . . . ?
You no longer seek to caress my thighs. . . .

Would you leave me to get something to eat?
   Are you that much a slave to your belly?
Would you leave me to look for something to wear?
   Would you leave me holding the sheet?

*A deceased Egyptian woman enjoying a rich banquet in the afterlife,
attended by her children and attendants (Beni Hasan).*

If you are thinking about something to eat,
   Then feast on my breasts, make my milk flow for you.
Better a day in the embrace of a lover . . .
   Than thousands of days elsewhere. . . .

Her song:

Mix your body with mine . . .
   As honey mixes with water,
   As mandrake mixes with gum,
   As dough mixes with yeast . . .
Come to your lover,
   Like a horse charging onto the field of battle,
   Like a falcon swooping toward the marsh. . . .

His song: *(Cant 7:5, 13)*

My lover is a marsh,
   My lover is lush with growth. . . .
Her mouth is a lotus bud,
   Her breasts are mandrake blossoms.
Her arms are vines,
   Her eyes are shaded like berries.
Her head is a trap built from branches . . . and I am the goose.
   Her hair is the bait in the trap . . . to ensnare me.

Her song: *(Judg 15:1–8; Cant 4:10; 5:1)*

My cup is still not full from making love with you. . . .
    My little jackal, you intoxicate me.
I will not stop drinking your love,
    Even if they beat me with sticks into the marsh,
Even if they beat me north into Syria,
    Even if they flog me with palm branches south into Nubia,
Even if they scourge me with switches into the hills,
    Even if they whip me with rushes into the plains,
I will not take their advice,
    I will not abandon the one I desire.

His song: *(Gen 30:14–20; Cant 2:10–3; 7:13)*

I am sailing north with the current,
    Pulling the oar to the captain's command.
My bed is ready for a lover,
    I am headed for a holiday at Memphis.
I will pray to Ptah, the Lord of Truth,
    That a lover will sleep with me tonight.
The Nile makes me drunk with love.
    I see Ptah among the reeds,
    I see Sekhmet on the lotus leaves,
    I see Yadit sired in the lotus buds,
    I see Nefertem conceived in the lotus blossoms. . . .
The land reflects the joy of Hathor the Golden Goddess.
    Memphis is a jar of sweet mandrake wine,
    A gift for fair-faced Ptah.

Fishing in the Nile or one of its canals (Beni Hasan).

His song: *(2 Sam 13:4–6; Cant 2:5; 5:8)*

I will lie down inside my house,
   I will pretend to be sick.
Then my neighbors will come in to see,
   And my lover will come with them.
She will put physicians to shame,
   She knows how to cure my illness.

His song: *(Cant 5:2–6)*

The woman, whom I love, is the lady of a great house.
   You enter her house in the center.
The doors are wide open, the bolt is unfastened,
   Because she is angry with her lover. . . .

An Egyptian noble hunts birds in the Nile marshes and papyrus thickets.
(Beni Hasan tomb 3; 19th century, B.C.E.)

If she hired me to guard her door,
    At least when I made her angry,
I would get to hear her voice,
    Even as I tremble like a child.

Her song: *(Esth 2:12; Ruth 3:3)*

I am sailing north
    On the canal of pharaoh.
I turn into the canal of Pre,
    I will pitch my tent overlooking the canal.
I have raced without rest
    Since I first thought of the canal of Pre.
I can already see my lover . . .
    He is heading for the chamber of love. . . .
I will stand with you at the entrance to the canal of Ity,
    You will lead me to Heliopolis.
As wc walk . . . into the trees around the chamber of love . . .
    I gather branches, and weave them into a fan.
We will see if it works,
    We will see if it fans me on my way to the garden of love.
My breasts are smothered with fruit,
    My hair glistens with balm.
When I am with you . . .
    I am a noble woman filled with pleasure,
    I am the queen of Egypt.

ISAIAH, JEREMIAH, EZEKIEL, DANIEL, HOSEA, AMOS

STORIES OF
ISHTAR AND TAMMUZ

Austen Henry Layard (1817-94) excavated Nimrud in 1845 for the British Museum, locating both the palace of Sennacherib (704-681 BCE) and the library of Ashurbanipal (668-626 BCE) containing one of two important copies of the stories of Ishtar and Tammuz. The other, made during the Middle Bronze period (2000-1500 BCE), was found at Ashur at Koujunik, Iraq. No more than one-hundred fifty lines of these stories have survived. These were retellings of older stories in the Sumerian language in cuneiform script recovered at Nippur (Arabic: Nuffar). J.P. Peters, J.H. Haynes and H.V. Hilprecht directed the excavations at Nippur for the University of Pennsylvania between 1889-1900. These were the first major excavations in Mesopotamia under American auspices. Four-hundred and ten lines of the Sumerian stories are preserved on thirteen tablets. Some are preserved today at the Museum of the Ancient Orient in Istanbul, Turkey and some in the University of Pennsylvania Museum in Philadelphia.

From the beginning of the Bronze Age (3000-1250 BCE), Tammuz (Sumerian: Dumuzi) and Ishtar (Sumerian: Inanna; Akkadian: Astarte, Ashtartu, Ashtoreth) were celebrated as the divine patrons of herding, farming and childbearing. Ishtar and Tammuz were lovers separated by death, but reunited by love. In some of the traditions, it is Ishtar who descends into the land of the dead, and in others it is Tammuz. In both, the widowed partner faithfully pursues and rescues the other from the dead. The stories tell not only of two lovers, but also of the death of the earth during the long dry season, and its rebirth at the beginning of the wet season under the relentless labor of its farmers. They were told during a celebration (Akkadian: taklimtu) at the end of the long dry season during June and July (Akkadian: 27–29 Du'uzu), when Tammuz, like the crops, had withered and died. Like the last drops of moisture which the parched soil sucked deep into the earth, Tammuz was drawn by stages into the land of the dead. Ishtar, however, would not forsake him. Like the rain which moistens the soil at the end of the dry season so that farmers can plow and plant, the words and actions of Ishtar in the land of the dead bring Tammuz back to life. She raises him from the dead like the first leaves of the crops that sprout through the soil under a farmer's care at the beginning of the growing season.

Parallels to the stories of Ishtar and Tammuz appear in the books of Judges, Samuel-Kings and Ezekiel. At the end of the stories of how Jephthah delivers Israel from Ammon (Judg 11:1-40) there is a note that "...there arose a...custom that for four days every year the daughters of Israel would go out to lament the daughter of Jephthah..." (Judg 11:39-40). The reference may describe the way in which the Ishtar and Tammuz celebrations and stories were observed in early Israel. In a trial of Ahab and Jezebel (1 Kgs 16:29—22:40), tellers caricature the name of the queen of Israel (2 Kgs 9:37). Her parents would have named her: "Where is my lord?" or "Where is Tammuz (Hebrew: 'izebul)?," no doubt, because she was one of the first newborns at the end of the dry season, and her birth offered a promise of the renewal of life in the land. Nonetheless, throughout her trial, she is referred to as "shameless (Hebrew: i-zebul)" or as "excrement (Hebrew: zebel)." In a trial of Jerusalem (Ezek 8:1—11:25), Ezekiel indicts the women of the city for sitting at the north gate of the Temple and "...weeping for Tammuz" (Ezek 8:14). A similar indictment appears in the book of Jeremiah that refers to Ishtar as "...the queen of heaven" (Jer 7:18).

LOVE SONG

PAPS 107.6:23–45 (Judg 14:11–20; 16:4–22)

📖 *Ishtar and Tammuz, here as Inanna and Dumuzi, begin arguing with one another, which arouses their sexual passion. They describe their intercourse as if they are farming.*

Words of anger inspire words of passion.
  Quarrels arouse a desire for love.

A Sumerian grain-goddess, seated, presents grain to
a male vegetation god, perhaps Tammuz.

Her song:

Let the farmer who plows between the boundary stones in his field,
    Plow between these boundary stones.
Dumuzi plows between the boundary stones in his field,
    He is the farmer who plows between the boundary stones in his field.
    Let Amaushumgalanna plow between these boundary stones.
Let the plower who fills his cistern with rain from the roof
    Fill this cistern for her.
Let the plower who fills his cistern with rain off the walls
    Fill this cistern for her. . . .
Plow between these boundary stones,
    Plow between these boundary stones.
    Who else will plow this field for her . . . ?
Dumuzi was created for me,
    Amaushumgalanna was made for me,
    With a beard as dark and rich as lapis lazuli.
Dumuzi was created for me by Anu, my godfather,
    Amaushumgalanna was made for me,
    With a beard as dark and rich as lapis lazuli
With a beard as dark and rich as lapis lazuli
    With a beard as dark and rich as lapis lazuli. . . .

*The Sumerian story of Inanna's descent into the underworld is pri-
marily concerned with the conflict between Inanna, who rules the
heavens, and Ereshkigal, who rules the underworld. What is stressed
here is the attempted usurpation by Inanna and her complete fail-*

ure to overcome the power of death herself. However, the later Akka-dian story of Ishtar's descent, which is extant in Assyrian versions, uses some of the Inanna material and emphasizes the effect on nature and the mourning ritual for Tammuz.

ISHTAR'S DESCENT TO THE UNDERWORLD

Obverse Lines 1–20 (Judg 16:3; Job 17:13–6)

Ishtar resolved to travel to the Land of No Return,
　To the dark abode of Ereshkigal,
　To the house that none depart,
To the road to No Return,
　To the house in which no light may enter,
Where dust and clay are their meal,
　Where they dwell in darkness,

A nude statue of the goddess Ishtar from the early Babylonian period.

Where, like birds, their garments are exchanged for wings,
   Where dust covers every door and bolt.
When Ishtar reached the gate of the Land of No Return,
   She challenged the gatekeeper, saying:
"Open your gate so I may enter!
   If you fail to do this, I will smash the door,
I will shatter the bolt,
   I will uproot the doorpost, push aside the doors.
I will cause the dead to rise and consume like the living,
   The living will outnumber the dead!"

≋ *The gatekeeper announces Ishtar's coming to Ereshkigal and she is furious. However, she instructs the gatekeeper to allow Ishtar to pass.*

Lines 37–44

Unlock the gate for her,
   But make her adhere to the ancient law.
The gatekeeper opened the gate and bade her enter: "Come, my lady,
   So that the underworld may give you proper welcome.
Come, my lady,
   That rejoicing and celebration may begin in the palace."
At the opening of the first gate, he removed her crown.
   Ishtar asked, "Why have you removed my crown?"
   The gatekeeper replied: ". . . it is the law of Ereshkigal."

≋ *At each of the seven gates, the gatekeeper removes an item of Ishtar's clothing: earrings, necklaces, ornate breast plate, a belt containing birthstones that were suspended from her hips, bracelets from her arms and legs. Finally, Ishtar is as naked as the dead. When she passes the last gate, she confronts Ereshkigal.*

Lines 64–79

Ereshkigal was maddened by her presence.
   Ishtar rushed at her in a blind rage.
Ereshkigal commanded her vizier to inflict Ishtar with sixty diseases:
   Diseases of the eyes, sides, feet, intestines, head—her whole body!
Now that Ishtar has entered the underworld,
   The bull no longer mounts the cow,

The ass no longer copulates with the jenny,
   The man and the woman sleep apart. . . .

*With the earth devastated by the total lack of fertility, Ea formu-
lates a plan designed to restore Ishtar to the land of the living. He
creates Asushunamir to enchant Ereshkigal so that she will grant
him any request. When he asks for living water, Ereshkigal realizes
she has been tricked and she places a terrible curse on Asushunamir.
Then she uses Namtur, her vizier, to summon the divine elders
(Akkadian:* anunnaki*) as witness to her release of Ishtar for a price.*

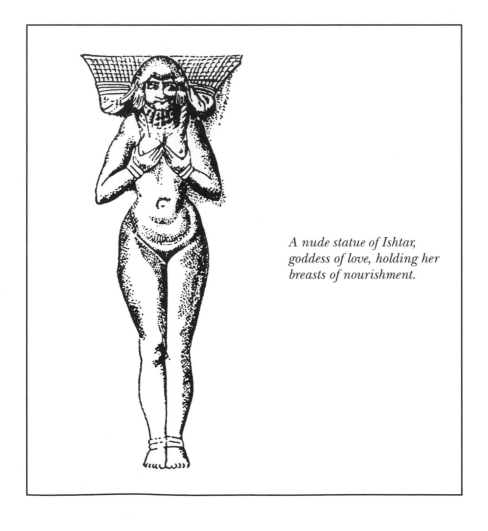

*A nude statue of Ishtar,
goddess of love, holding her
breasts of nourishment.*

Reverse Lines 31–4

Go, Namtur . . . assemble the anunnaki and seat them on golden
    thrones.
    Sprinkle the water of life on Ishtar and send her forth.

≋⟩ *Ishtar is escorted back through the gates of the underworld and is
given each of her garments in the reverse order from which they
were confiscated. However, she must find a substitute to take her
place in the underworld as the price of her return.*

Lines 46–50 (Ruth 3:3; Mk 16:1)

"She is to pay a ransom or be returned to me," decreed Ereshkigal.
    Take Tammuz, her husband,
Wash him and anoint him with oil,
    Clothe him in a purple garment
Allow him to play a flute of lapis lazuli,
    Let him find contentment with prostitutes.

≋⟩ *Ishtar returns, but Tammuz, the divine gardener, is permitted to
return to the earth only when it rains at the end of the dry season
and when mourners weep at the graves of the dead.*

Lines 56–8 (Ezek 8:14)

On the day when Tammuz comes up to me,
    When he greets me with joy,
With the playing of his lapis flute,
    With the sign of his carnelian ring,
When with him come the weeping men and women,
    Greeting me with cries of joy,
Then will the dead come up
    And smell the incense.

VISIONS OF NEFERTI

⧈ *The visions of Neferti begin with pharaoh Snefru (2680-2565 BCE) summoning Neferti to entertain him. Neferti announces the downfall of the Old Kingdom and the establishment of a new dynasty by Amen-em-het I (1991-1786 BCE), during whose reign the visions of Neferti were composed. They extol the accomplishments of Amen-em-het, and try to persuade him to extend his control eastward to prevent further invasions of Egypt from Syria-Palestine.*

There is one complete version of the visions of Neferti on papyrus in the Leningrad Museum (1116B). It was made during the 18th dynasty (1570-1305 BCE). Numerous other fragments have also been recovered since 1900.

The visions of Neferti, the books of Samuel-Kings (1 Kgs 13) and the book of Daniel (Dan 2—6) use the motif of entertaining a monarch with the prediction of his downfall. The motif of the slave who would be monarch in the visions of Neferti also appears in the stories of Hagar in the book of Genesis (Gen 16; 21).

10–4 (Dan 5:12)

"Your majesty, there is a priest in Bastet named Neferti. He is loyal, an accomplished scribe and a wealthy man." Snefru ordered: "Bring him to me."

Neferti prostrated before the pharaoh, who ordered: "Speak, Neferti. Entertain me with well chosen words and artful phrases."

15–9

Neferti asked: "Majesty, do you wish to hear what-has-happened or what-is-to-come?" Snefru answered: "Speak to me of what-is-to-come. Today has passed." Then he summoned a scribe to write down everything Neferti told him.

20–6 (Jer 16:6; Ezek 9:4; Dan 9:16–9)

"Stir yourself, my heart," Neferti prayed,
  "Cry for this land where you were born.
Do not commit evil by failing to speak.
  Those who could speak have been expelled,
  The powerful have been cast aside.
Do not be too weary to clear the facts,
  Rise to the task before you.
Officials no longer administer the land,
  What should be done is left undone.

"May Ra ordain a day of restoration,
  For Egypt is in chaos,
No order remains,
  No profit can be made.
No one cares about the pain in this land,
  No one sheds a tear for Egypt,
  No one cries out: 'What will be its fate?'
The sun is shrouded,
  The sun never shines,
The people cannot see,
  There is no life,
The sun is covered in clouds,
  Everyone is blind without it.
I can tell you what I see before me,
  I do not tell what will not be.

27–8 (2 Kgs 3:16)

"The canals are dry,
  They can be crossed on foot.
One searches for enough water to sail,
  The canals have turned into dry land.

Bird hunting with traps (Egyptian; Beni Hasan).

*Tomb painting showing dark-skinned Egyptian warriors fighting
lighter-skinned Asiatics (Beni Hasan, 19th century B.C.E.).*

Dry land replaces water,
    The canals have turned into dry land.
The south wind defeats the north wind,
    There is now just a single wind.

29–35 (Ezek 3:17; Joel 2:7)

"A strange bird will nest in the marsh,
    A strange bird will make its nest near the people.
The land is weak,
    Egypt cannot survive.
All good things perish,
    Fish-eating birds devour ponds of fish.
All good things perish,
    Egypt bows under the weight of invaders from Syria-Palestine.
Enemies arise in the east,
    Asia ravages Egypt.
Fortresses lack soldiers and supplies, no guard hears or sees the enemy
        of the night,
    The enemy who scales the walls with ladders,
The enemy who slips through the fortress gates,
    The enemy who ambushes the garrison in its sleep.
I alone stand watch through the night.

36–8

"Desert herds will drink from the Nile,
    Desert herders will settle on these shores without fear.
The land is unsettled, Egypt is without direction.
    As the saying goes: 'The mute leads the blind and the deaf.'

39–44 (Judg 21:25; Dan 11:14)

"I can describe it for you. . . .

"The land is in torment,
 What is happening should never happen.
Take up arms,
 The land is in turmoil.
Soldiers stockpile arrows,
 Soldiers eat blood, not bread,
 Soldiers laugh at the wounded.
No one weeps for the dying,
 No one mourns and fasts,

"Everyone looks after his own welfare.

"No one mourns for another,
 Every heart goes astray.
Everyone turns his back on murder,
 Everyone turns his back while one kills another.
Your own son is your enemy,
 Your own brother is your foe.
 Sons slay their own fathers.

45–71 (1 Kgs 13:2; Dan 11:2–4, 20–4; 12:1)

"Everyone says: 'I want.'
 All hope is lost.
Egypt is full of corruption.
 Laws are enacted, but ignored. . . .

*An Egyptian soldier trained to be
a stone slinger (Beni Hasan).*

The property of a citizen is seized,
    The property of a citizen is given to strangers.
I can show you landowners in need,
    I can show you strangers who prosper.
Those who do not work are paid,
    Workers are not.
Debts are only paid under threat,
    Sentences are imposed only at spear point.
Lips profess: 'You shall not kill,'
    Hearts burn with anger to destroy.
Egypt's land is scarce,
    Its rulers are many.
Egypt is poor,
    Its officials grow rich.
Egypt's harvest is small,
    Its taxes are great.
The sun withdraws from the earth,
    The sun shines, but there is no day.
No one knows the time,
    No one can see his shadow.

"The face of the sun does not dazzle the sight,
    No eyes fill with tears.
The light of the sun is like the light of the moon,
    The shape of the sun remains unchanged,
    The light of the sun still touches the face of the earth.

"I can show you a land in distress where the weak exercise power,
    I can show you a land where masters bow to their slaves.
    I can show you a society turned upside down. . . .
The hunted tracks the hunter,
    The living search for death.
Beggars are rich,
    The rich steal to survive.
The poor have bread,
    Slaves are set free.
Heliopolis has vanished,
    The birthplace of the divine assembly is no more.

"But a new pharaoh will come from the south,
    Amen-em-het the triumphant will be his name.
A slave's son will wear the white crown,
    A son of Nubia will wear the red crown.

He will unite the two lands of Egypt,
    He will have a firm grip on the oar,
    He will put a steady hand on the tiller.
Happy are those who will live in his time,
    Their names will last forever.
He will execute the conspirator,
    He will silence the traitor.
He will conquer Asia,
    He will burn Libya.
He will exile the revolutionary,
    He will imprison the spy.
The winged serpent will guard his brow,
    The *uraeus* serpent will protect him from rebels.
He will rebuild the fortresses,
    He will drive the invaders from Asia away.
They will humbly ask for water,
    They will humbly ask to allow their herds to drink.
Order will be restored to its rightful place,
    Chaos will be forced to flee.
    Happy are those who serve this pharaoh.

"The wise will pour out an offering for me
    When they see that what I have said has happened."

MARI LETTERS

⬚ *Mari (Arabic: tell hariri) was a state on the Euphrates in northern Syria. Along with other city states, it competed with Babylon for control of Mesopotamia until Hammurabi (1792-1750 BCE) conquered it in 1757 BCE. Artifacts recovered by a bedouin digging a grave in 1933 launched an ongoing French expedition directed first by André Parrot, and then Jean Margueron. Some 25,000 clay tablets, written in cuneiform, were recovered from the archives of Zimri-Lim, the last ruler of Mari. They are preserved today at the Louvre Museum in Paris and the Damascus Museum in Syria. Most of the tablets are about eight inches wide and ten inches high. Some are no larger than a postage stamp. Others are one to two feet high and one foot wide. There are economic records, diplomatic covenants and some thirty letters that mention prophets.*

At least three classes of male and female prophets advised Zimri-Lim. **Apilum** *prophets spoke for the divine assembly (A.2925/ A.2731).* **Assinu** *prophets were temple personnel (ARM 10.7).* **Muhhu** *prophets were ecstatics. The personal names of the prophets never appear in the letters, which could indicate that they were considered members of a sacred social class whose names could not be spoken (ARM 3.40).*

Until the Mari archives were recovered, the only parallels to the prophets of ancient Israel were in the memoirs of Wen-Amon from Egypt. The letters contain messenger formulas like "arise, go... and say to...." similar to those found in the Bible. Although prophets in both Mari and Israel confront their monarchs in times of crisis, there are differences between them. Mari prophets never seem to speak to the people of Mari as a whole. They also use divination to interpret omens more regularly than the prophets of Israel.

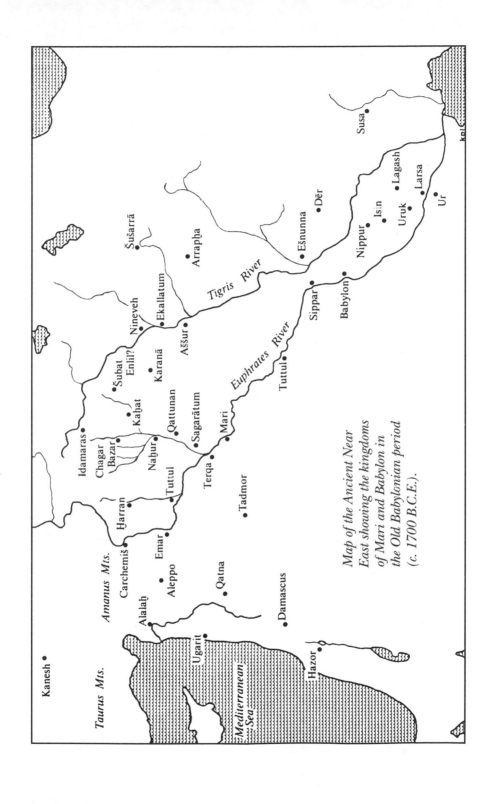

Map of the Ancient Near East showing the kingdoms of Mari and Babylon in the Old Babylonian period (c. 1700 B.C.E.).

A.2925/A.2731 (Hos 11:1–9; Amos 5:15; 1 Sam 12:14–5)

To: Zimri-Lim, king of Mari
From: Nur-Sin, official of Mari

Repeatedly I have written to the king about the gift of livestock which he promised to the sanctuary of Addu, his divine patron. Addu, the divine patron of Kallassu, is still waiting for this livestock which you promised him. . . .

An apilum prophet of Addu, divine patron of Halab, told me: "I am Addu, your divine patron. I am the divine patron of Halab . . . who helped you regain your father's throne. Have I ever asked too much of you? Hear the cry of your people when they suffer injustice. Give them justice. Do what I ask and what I have written. Obey my word. Protect the land. Defend the state. . . ."

Statue of the god Dagan, from the Sumerian period.

ARM 13.23:1–15

To: Zimri-Lim, ruler of Mari
From: Mukannisum, official of Mari

After I offered the sacrifice to Dagan for the king's health, an apilum prophet of Dagan in Tuttul stood up and told me: "Babylon, what do you think you are doing? I will bring you down like a bird with a net. . . . I will give you, your seven covenant partners and all their land to Zimri-Lim."

ARM 10.7 (1 Sam 10:6; 24:5; 2 Kgs 3:15)

To: Zimri-Lim, king of Mari
From: Shibtu, queen of Mari

My lord, the palace is in good order. On the third day of the festival, Shelibum, an assinu prophet, fell into ecstasy in the sanctuary of Annunitum, your divine patron. He told me: "You, Zimri-Lim, will

Reconstruction of a painting from the royal palace of Mari showing the "investiture of King Zimri Lim" (as king).

be tested by a revolt. Take precautions. Surround yourself only with officials you trust. Let only officials who are faithful guard you. Do not go out of the palace without an escort. I will hand these rebels over to you."

To confirm the words of Shelibum, I am sending the king a lock of her hair and a piece of the hem from her skirt.

ARM 3.40:1–23

To: Zimri-Lim, ruler of Mari
From: Kibri-Dagan, official of Mari

My lord, you continue to enjoy the favor of your divine patrons, Dagan and Ikrub-El. The province of Terqa is peaceful.

The same day that I dispatched this report to the king, a muhhutum prophet of Dagan, your divine patron, came and told me: "Dagan has sent me to you. Write to Zimri-Lim and remind the king to offer a funeral sacrifice for Yahdun-lim, your father."

Therefore, I have written my lord this message so that he may take appropriate action.

ARM 10.50 (Ezek 8)

To: Zimri-Lim, ruler of Mari
From: The Lady Adad-duri in Mari

My lord, never since the time of your father's house have I had such a dream. In my dream I entered the temple of Belet-ekallim, but the goddess was not there. Nor were the flanking statues which previously had stood before her. I searched but, in my dream during the night watch, I could only weep.

I also had another dream in which Dada, the priest of the goddess Ishtar-pishra, stood in the gate of Belet-ekallim while a voice continually cried out, "Turn back, O Dagan. Turn back, O Dagan."

Finally, a muhhutum prophet rose in the temple of Annunitum and said, "Zimri-Lim, do not go on campaign. Stay in Mari while I take responsibility."

Let my lord be cautious. I have sent the hem and lock of hair from this woman.

STORIES OF WEN-AMON

Archaeologists recovered the stories of Wen-Amon at el-Hibeh, Egypt around 1899. They were written on papyrus in hieroglyphics during the twenty-first dynasty (1070–945 BCE) at the end of the New Kingdom. Today the papyrus is preserved in the Moscow Museum in Russia.

Pharaohs and priests regularly sent messengers to the Lebanon mountains to harvest timber for architectural beams, for carving, and for constructing the hulls and masts of ships. The stories of Wen-Amon tell the story of one such messenger and the difficulties he faced. Wen-Amon travels at a time when Egypt is embroiled in a civil war. Herihor, priest of Thebes in southern Egypt, and Smendes, ruler of Tanis in northern Egypt, are both trying to overthrow pharaoh Ramses XI (1100–1070 BCE). The rulers of the Sea Peoples in Syria-Palestine and Cyprus take advantage of Egypt's weakness to drive hard bargains by bullying Wen-Amon. Wen-Amon is consumed with detail, and seems almost unaware of how much times have changed. He naively employs outdated techniques in his negotiations that are absolutely useless with rulers like Beder, Tjerker Ba'al, and Hatiba.

The stories of Wen-Amon do an excellent job of describing the international power vacuum in the ancient Near East during which Israel emerged. They also footnote some interesting manners and customs that appear in the Bible. The use of threats by Wen-Amon recalls those made by Rabshakeh, the messenger of the great king of Assyria, to the officials of Hezekiah in the books of Samuel–Kings (2 Kgs 18:13–37). Wen-Amon carries a statue of Amon, his divine patron, along with him and uses it just as Rachel uses the statues of the divine patrons (Hebrew: teraphim) of her household in the book of Genesis (Gen 31:19–35). Ecstatic prophets appear in Byblos to advise their monarchs just as they do in Israel. The cedars of Lebanon are sacred property just like the plunder from cities like

Jericho in the book of Joshua (Josh 6:17-21), and their misappropri-
ation demands the death penalty (Josh 7:10-26). Tjerker Ba'al harvests
the cedars of Lebanon for Wen-Amon, just as Hiram of Tyre does
for Solomon in the books of Samuel-Kings (1 Kgs 5:10-1). Tanetne
heals Wen-Amon by singing, just as David heals Saul by playing the
lyre (1 Sam 16:14-23).

i:100–50 (Gen 31:19; 2 Kgs 3:15)

I, Wen-Amon, priest at the gate of the temple of Amon, was dispatched to buy timber for the sacred boat of Amon-Ra, ruler of the divine
assembly. When I docked at Tanis, I presented my letters of introduction
from Amon-Ra to Smendes and his wife, Tanet Amon. They ordered them
read aloud and agreed to do as Amon-Ra had commanded. I remained
for the rest of that month in Tanis and then sailed in a ship under the
command of Mengebet.

When my ship docked at Dor, Beder, who was the ruler of the Tjerker,
welcomed me with fifty loaves of bread, a jar of wine and a side of ox.

While we lay in port, one of the ship's crew stole the sixteen ounces
of gold and the ninety-eight ounces of silver in bullion and vessels, which
I was supposed to use to pay for the timber.

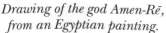

Drawing of the god Amen-Rē,
from an Egyptian painting.

An Egyptian musician playing a harp
(c. 1000 B.C.E.).

I went straight to Beder and reported: "I was robbed while at anchor in your harbor. As ruler of Dor it is your responsibility to investigate the crime and recover this gold and silver, which came from Amon-Ra, ruler of the divine assembly, lord of the two lands of Egypt, and from Smendes and Herihor and other Egyptian officials, and from you, Weret, Mekmer and Tjerker Ba'al, ruler of Byblos."

Beder replied: "Be careful whom you charge with a crime this serious. Do not bring your complaints to me. If the thief who boarded your ship and stole your gold and silver was my subject, I would reimburse you from my own treasury until the thief was apprehended. Since the thief was from your own ship's company, it is not my responsibility. Nevertheless, give me a few days and I will see if we can find him for you."

So I waited nine days in the harbor. Finally, I went back to Beder. "Since you cannot find my gold and silver, at least let my ship sail." He refused. "If you expect me to find your gold and silver, you must be patient and stay here where I can contact you." I decided I could wait no longer and so worked my way up the coast to Tyre on foot.

Eventually I left Tyre for Byblos, and its ruler Tjerker Ba'al. In the harbor at Byblos there was a Tjerker freighter from Dor. I confiscated one-hundred and one ounces of silver bullion from the ship's master and told him I would keep it until Beder recovered my gold and silver or apprehended the thief who stole it. In the tent which I had pitched on the harbor shore, I celebrated my strategy for replacing the gold and silver which I had lost. I hid my treasure in a statue of Amon, patron of travelers, which I had brought along to protect me on my journey.

As a reprisal for my actions, Tjerker Ba'al of Byblos ordered me out of his harbor. I responded: "How shall I go? Are you going to pay for a ship to take me back to Egypt?" I spent twenty-nine days camped at the harbor of Byblos and every day the harbor master sent the same message: "Get out of my harbor!"

One day, when Tjerker Ba'al was offering a sacrifice, a prophet went into a trance and became ecstatic. The prophet announced: "Summon this Egyptian messenger and his statue of Amon, patron of travelers, who dispatched him to Canaan." The prophecy occurred on the same night that I had booked passage on a freighter headed for Egypt. I had already loaded my possessions and was only waiting for it to get dark, so that I could smuggle my statue of Amon, patron of travelers, on board.

At that moment the harbor master came to me and said: "Tjerker Ba'al orders you to stay until tomorrow." I then replied: "Aren't you the same man who for the last twenty-nine days has ordered me to get out of your harbor? You are only ordering me to stay because you want me to miss my ship which is sailing tonight; then you will come back in the

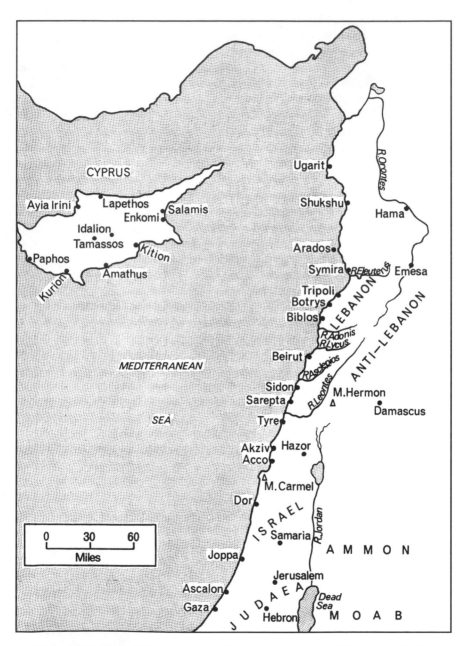

Map of the area of Phoenicia and Cyprus in the First Millennium, B.C.E.

morning and order me to get out." The harbor master reported my objection to Tjerker Ba'al who then ordered the captain of the freighter on which I had passage to remain at anchor until the next day.

The following morning Tjerker Ba'al sent for me. I left the statue in my tent at the harbor. As I entered, he was sitting in his upper room with his back to a window which overlooked the lapping waves of the Mediterranean Sea of Syria. I greeted him with a blessing from Amon and he asked me: "When did you leave the temple of Amon in Egypt?"

I replied that I had been away from home five months. Then he said: "May I see your letters of introduction from Amon Ra and his high priest?" I told him that I had given them to Smendes and his wife, Tanet Amon. Tjerker Ba'al became furious. "You have no papers? Where is the ship that Smendes gave you to transport the cedar timber and where is its Syrian crew? Is it not true that he plotted with the ship's captain to assassinate you and have your body thrown into the sea, so that there would be no trace of you or your statue of Amon, patron of travelers?" I objected: "Smendes outfitted me with an Egyptian, not a Syrian, ship and crew." Tjerker Ba'al was not convinced. "Why would Smendes send an Egyptian ship to Syria, when right now there are twenty Syrian ships in my harbor and there are another fifty Syrian ships docked in the harbor at Sidon ruled by Wekatara and under contract to him?"

ii: 200–80 (Josh 7:20–26; 1 Kgs 5:10–1; Acts 5:12–6)

When I kept silent he went on: "What are you really doing here?"

I answered: "I am here to buy timber for the great and noble ship of Amon-Ra, ruler of the divine assembly. Therefore you should do what your father and grandfather before you have done." Tjerker Ba'al replied: "Yes, they did supply timber for Amon-Ra. All you need do is pay me and I will also supply it. My predecessors did not carry out this commission until the pharaoh sent six freighters loaded with gifts from Egypt and these items had been placed in their storehouses. Tell me now, what have you brought me?"

At that point he sent for a scroll from the time of his predecessors and ordered it read aloud. It was a receipt for various items valued at 950,000 ounces of silver. Then he said: "If pharaoh were my lord and if I were his faithful servant, he would not have to pay me a monarch's ransom in silver and gold, as he paid my father to carry out the commission of Amon. In any case, I am not your servant, nor am I the servant of the one who sent you. I need only say the word and the heavens over the Lebanon mountains will open and wash their logs to the shore of the sea. But who will lash these logs in place and sail these freighters home to Egypt? Amon is the creator of every land which hears the thunder of Seth

Ba'al. Egypt, your land, was his first born. Only a fool would leave the land which invented ships, and which discovered how to navigate to come all the way here to me."

I replied: "You are wrong. My mission is not foolish. All of the ships on the Nile belong to Amon. The Mediterranean Sea and the Lebanon mountains do not belong to Syria, but to Amon. He planted forests on the Lebanon mountains as a source of timber to build the most sacred ship on the face of the earth, the *Amon User He*. It was Amon-Ra, ruler of the divine assembly, who ordered the high priest, Herihor, to dispatch me on this mission with the statue of Amon, patron of travelers. Now you have detained me and the statue of my divine patron for twenty-nine days in the harbor of Byblos. Surely, you knew Amon, the patron of travelers, was there. Amon-Ra is today what Amon-Ra has always been. How dare you bargain with the ruler of the divine assembly over the Lebanon? As for your statement that previous pharaohs had sent gold and silver, that was because they lacked the ability to send life and health. It was in place of life and health that they sent these paltry gifts to your predecessors. Amon-Ra is the giver of life and health, and it is he who was the lord of your predecessors. They made offerings to Amon throughout their reigns. You also are a client of Amon. If you agree to carry out the commands of Amon, then you and your entire land will be blessed with life and prosperity. If you refuse and withhold the timber which belongs to Amon-Ra, ruler of the divine assembly, he will attack you and your land like a lion protecting its lair. . . .

"Send for a scribe so that I may send a letter to Smendes and his wife, Tanet Amon, whom Amon-Ra appointed to care for northern Egypt. They will provide the ships and crews you need. I will tell the scribe: 'Write: When I return to southern Egypt, I will repay you for everything. . . .'" A messenger took my letter to Egypt along with seven gifts: a keel, a bow-post, a stern-post, and four hewn timbers.

The messenger returned from Egypt to Syria in the first month of winter. With him, Smendes and his wife, Tanet Amon, sent Tjerker Ba'al four priceless vases and one *kakmen*-vase, five silver vases, ten linen garments, ten bolts of linen fabric, five-hundred smooth linen mats, five-hundred ox-hides, five-hundred ropes, twenty sacks of lentils, and thirty baskets of fish. In addition, Tanet Amon sent me personally: five fine linen garments, five bolts of fine linen fabric, a sack of lentils, and five baskets of fish. Tjerker Ba'al was delighted and immediately dispatched three hundred loggers with three hundred oxen and their drivers to cut the timbers. The trees were felled and lay on the ground through the winter. During the third month of summer the logs were dragged to the seashore.

Tjerker Ba'al came out to inspect them and then said to me: "Come!"

When I stepped forward, the shadow of the Tjerker Ba'al's umbrella fell upon me and Pen-Amon the cupbearer shoved me aside, saying: "You are not worthy to bask in the shadow of pharaoh's beloved son." Tjerker Ba'al became angry and ordered the cupbearer to leave me alone.

I was then officially presented to Tjerker Ba'al who announced: "I have carried out the commission which my predecessors had previously carried out. You, however, have not done for me what your fathers had previously done for them. The final consignment of timber has now arrived and has been stacked. Obey my command. Load it and leave. Face bad weather at sea before facing my bad temper another day in port. You are lucky that I have not done to you what I did to the messengers of Khaemwase whom I detained seventeen years here in Syria until they died." At that point he directed the cupbearer: "Take him to see their graves." I pleaded: "Do not make me go see them. Khaemwase's messengers were merely humans, as was their patron. You do not have before you only a man, though you say: 'Go see your fellow humans.' You should now rejoice and erect a stele with the inscription: 'Amon-Ra, ruler of the divine assembly, sent Amon, patron of travelers, his divine messenger, and Wen-Amon, his human messenger, to obtain timber for the great and noble ship of Amon-Ra, ruler of the divine assembly. I felled the trees and loaded them on board my own ships worked by my own crews. I allowed them to return to Egypt so that they could request for me fifty more years of life from Amon.' Therefore, when another messenger comes from Egypt, who is skilled in writing and reads your name on the stele, you will drink from the fountain of life like the divine assembly who dwell in the west."

Tjerker Ba'al said: "That was quite a long speech." I replied: "I can assure you that when I return to the temple of Amon, the high priest, upon seeing your accomplishments, will grant you merit for them."

I left Tjerker Ba'al of Byblos and went down to the seashore to supervise the loading of the logs. At just that moment, eleven ships belonging to the Tjerker of Dor had dropped anchor. The commander of the fleet ordered his sailors: "Arrest him! Do not let his ship sail for Egypt." I sat down right there and wept.

The scribe of Tjerker Ba'al came to me and said: "What is it now?" I told him: "Birds have migrated to Egypt twice since I arrived. Watch them as they fly toward the land of cool waters. These men have come to arrest me? How long must I remain here?" He went and reported everything to Tjerker Ba'al and he wept also at this unfortunate turn of events. To comfort me he sent his scribe to me with two jars of wine and a sheep. He also sent Tanetne, an Egyptian singer, with this order: "Sing for him! Soothe his troubled spirit." He then sent word to me: "Eat, drink, and do not let your spirit be troubled. I will make a decision on this tomorrow."

The next morning, Tjerker Ba'al of Byblos convened the assembly to hear my case. He said to the Tjerker of Dor: "Why are you here?" They answered: "We have come in pursuit of the ships of our cursed enemy whom you are about to let escape to Egypt." Tjerker Ba'al instructed them: "I cannot arrest a messenger of Amon in my own country. I will send him away and you may then pursue and arrest him."

I was put on board my ship and sent away from that harbor. The winds carried me to Cyprus, the land of Alasiya, where a mob tried to murder me. I fought my way through the crowd toward the palace of Hatiba, ruler of Alasiya. As she walked from one building to another, I got her attention and then asked those crowding around me if anyone spoke Egyptian. One person said he did and I asked him: "Tell her majesty that even as far away as Thebes in the temple of Amon, Alasiya's reputation for justice is well known. Is she going to let an injustice like this ruin her country's reputation?"

Hatiba asked: "What is he saying?" I replied: "A raging sea and strong winds have driven me to your land. Will you allow me to be killed, despite the fact that I am a messenger of Amon? It is certain that a search will be made for me until the end of time. As for this crew of Tjerker Ba'al of Byblos, who are also in danger of being killed, surely he will find and kill ten crews of yours in revenge for their deaths." Then she warned the people not to harm us and granted us sanctuary for the night. . . .

YAVNE-YAM LETTER

Little remains of Hebrew manuscripts and writings because most of them were written on perishable materials such as papyrus or parchment. One nearly indestructible medium remains in fairly large quantities. Many short lists, notations, and letters were written on ostraca or broken pieces of pottery. The ostraca were always at hand and messages could easily be scratched or written on them with ink. They give us a record of the development of Hebrew script and grammar and are a wealth of personal names. Just before 600 BCE a farm worker sent a short message to the governor of the coastal region of Judah on an ostracon eight inches high and seven inches wide. This large ostracon was recovered by J. Naveh, an Israeli archaeologist, in 1960. It was in the guardroom of the gate in a small fortress five miles northwest of Jamnia and two miles south of the Wadi Rubin (Hebrew: nahal soreq*).*

The Yavne-Yam letter was probably dictated to a professional scribe. It is written in cursive style and contains a formal address in the first two lines, which was standard (1 Sam 26:19). The farm worker is asking the governor for the return of his outer garment, which was unjustly taken from him by an official. The garment had served as collateral to insure that the man would complete his work that day. However, by law and as a humanitarian gesture, it was to be returned to him at the end of the day. Otherwise, he would be left to shiver through the night and would be relegated to the status of a slave instead of a free day laborer.

Parallels to the Yavne-Yam letter appear in the book of Exodus (Exod 22:26-7) and the book of Amos (Amos 2:8)

Let my lord the governor pay heed to the words of his servant.

Your servant was harvesting in Hasar-asam. The work went as usual and your servant completed the harvesting and hauling which I was assigned. . . . Despite the fact that your servant had completed his assigned work, Hoshaiahu son of Shobai came and took your servant's garment. All my fellow workers will testify, all those who work in the heat of the day will surely certify that I am not guilty of any breach of contract.

Please intercede for me so that my garment will be returned and I will, as always, do my share of the work. The governor should see to it that the garment of your servant is returned and that no revenge be taken against your servant, that he not be fired.

Typical Philistine pottery from the coastal plain of Palestine showing a bird looking backward. Yavneh-Yam is located in this area.

OUTLINE OF
MESOPOTAMIAN HISTORY

2900–2400 **Sumerian Period**—city states: Kish, Uruk, Ur, Lagash. Gilgamesh, cuneiform, ziggurat

2400–2100 **Akkadian Period**—Sargon I (c. 2371–2316), Naram-Sin
(c. 2291–2255); Ebla rivals Akkad

2200–2113 **Ur III Period**—Sumerian Revival, Ur-Nammu (law code),
Shulgi

2006–1792 **Amorite Period**—struggle between Assyrians and new dynasties founded by Amorite leaders (Amurru) based at Larsa,
Mari, and Babylon

1792–1750 **Reign of Hammurabi,** who unified most of Mesopotamia
and compiled law code

1595–1168 **Kassites** ruled southern Mesopotamia for 400 little known
years; aided by the overthrow of Hammurabi's dynasty during the brief invasion of the Hittites

Hittites—centered in Asia Minor, they had two periods of
prominence: the Old Hittite Kingdom (c. 1600–1500) and
the New Hittite Kingdom (c. 1375–1200). Suppiluliumas,
Hattusilis

Hurrians—kingdom of Mitanni dominated western Syria
from c. 1500–1370; Nuzi; their defeat by the Hittites created
a political vacuum filled by the Hittites and Assyrians (Tigris
river area)

Ugarit—seacoast city in northern Syria, a trading center and
nominal go-between for the Hittites and Egyptians between
1600–1200. Its alphabetic cuneiform literary texts closely
parallel Old Testament poetic style: Aqhat, Ba'al and Anath.
This period of history was brought to an abrupt end with the
invasion of the Sea Peoples (including the Philistines) who
c. 1200 conquered the Hittites, destroyed Ugarit, and nearly
conquered Egypt.

883–612   **Neo-Assyrian Period**—conquer Mesopotamia and Syro-
          Palestine in savage campaigns; Tiglath-Pileser III, Shal-
          maneser III, Sargon II, Sennacherib, Ashurbanipal

612–539   **Neo-Babylonian (Chaldean) Period**—Nebuchadnezzar,
          Nabonidus, Belshazzar

539–331   **Persian Period**—Cyrus, Darius, Xerxes, Artaxerxes

331   **Alexander the Great** conquers Persians and Hellenistic
          Period begins; Ptolemies, Seleucids: Antiochus IV Epiphanes

OUTLINE OF
EGYPTIAN HISTORY
FROM 3100–332 BCE

3100–2700   **Early Dynastic Period**—dynasties 1–2
Memphite royal culture, Nome provincial centers
2700–2200   **Old Kingdom**—dynasties 3–6
Third Dynasty (2700–2650): Zoser and the step pyramid at Sakkarah
Fourth Dynasty (2650–2500): Pyramid Age, Giza pyramids of Cheops, Chephren, Mycerinus
Fifth–Sixth Dynasties (2500–2200): Pyramid Texts
2200–2050   **First Intermediate Period**—dynasties 7–10
2050–1800   **Middle Kingdom**—11th and 12th dynasties
1730–1570   **Second Intermediate Period**—dynasties 13–17
1570   **Hyksos expelled** from their capital, Avaris/Tanis, in the Delta region by Ahmose I, founder of the 18th dynasty
1570–1165   **New Kingdom**—dynasties 18–20: Empire period (1465–1165); Eighteenth Dynasty (1570–1305): Thutmose III (1490–1436), Akenaton (1369–1353), Tutankhamen (1352–1344), Haremhab (1342–1303); Nineteenth Dynasty (1303–1200): Ramses II (1290–1224), Merneptah (1224–1200); Twentieth Dynasty (1200–1090): Ramses III (1195–1164), attack of the Sea Peoples
1150–663   **Post-Empire Period**—dynasties 21–26; decline of power and culture, several non-Egyptian pharaohs: Sheshonk (945–924), Necho II (610–595)—battle of Carchemish in 605; story of Wen-Amon
525   **Persian Conquest** by Cambyses
332   **Conquest by Alexander the Great** and beginning of Hellenistic Period: founds Alexandria; Ptolemaic rulers until absorption by Rome in 30 BCE

OUTLINE OF ISRAELITE HISTORY

A. **Premonarchic periods portrayed in the biblical text:**
1. **Ancestral Period**—Abraham/Sarah, Isaac/Rebekah, Jacob/ Rachel and Leah (date uncertain)
2. **Movement of Jacob/Israel's family** into Goshen, Egypt, Joseph (perhaps dated to Hyksos Period, c. 1750–1570)
3. **Exodus from Egypt**—Moses and Aaron (perhaps in the reign of Rameses II, c. 1290–1226)
4. **Settlement Period**—Joshua, Merneptah Stele, incursions of the Sea Peoples, Philistines (c. 1250–1150)
5. **Judges Period**—Ehud, Deborah, Gideon, Jephthah, Samson (c. 1200–1020)

B. **Monarchy Period**
1. **Early Monarchy**—Samuel and Saul (c. 1020–1000)
2. **United Kingdom**—David and Solomon (c. 1000–922)
3. **Divided Monarchy**—Israel survives until 721 and Judah until 587
Names to remember in Israel: Jeroboam (1st king), Ahab and Jezebel. Prophets—Elijah, Elisha, Amos, Hosea. Capital city—Samaria. Conquered by Assyrian king Sargon II in 721—population deported.
Names to remember in Judah: Rehoboam (1st king), Jehoshaphat, Hezekiah, Josiah. Prophets—Isaiah, Micah, Jeremiah. Capital city— Jerusalem. Conquered by Nebuchadnezzar of Babylon in 597— Jehoiachin, Ezekiel and others taken into exile; final fall of Jerusalem in 587/6 with second deportation to Babylon.

C. **Exilic and Post-Exilic Period**
1. **Babylonian Exile** (597–538): Ezekiel, Isaiah of Exile
2. **Persian Period** (538–336): Cyrus, Darius, Xerxes, Artaxerxes. Temple rebuilt (515), Zerubbabel, Haggai. Jerusalem's walls rebuilt (c. 445), Nehemiah. Renewal of covenant by Ezra (c. 400)

D. Hellenistic and Roman Period

1. **Conquests of Alexander of Macedonia** (336–323) ended Persian control over Judah. All of Palestine became a part of the Hellenistic empire, ruled first by the Ptolemys and after 198 by the Seleucids. Maccabean revolt vs. Seleucid king Antiochus IV (Ephiphanes) in 168 brought brief independence period (Hasmoneans).

2. **Roman general Pompey captures Jerusalem** in 63 BCE. Two unsuccessful revolts against Roman rule in 66–73 CE (when Herod's temple is destroyed) and the Bar-Kochba revolt in 132–135 CE. Jews were scattered throughout the Roman empire in the Diaspora.

Bibliography of Texts in Transcription, Transliteration, and Translation

Hymn to Ptah:

J. Junker, *Die Gotterlehre von Memphis* (1940), no. 23.
M. Lichtheim, *Ancient Egyptian Literature. A Book of Readings, vol. 1* (1975), 51–57.
K. Sethe, *Das "Denkmal memphitishcher Theologie," der Schabakostein des Britischen Museums* (1928).

Stories of Ra and Apophis:

E.A.W. Budge, *Egyptian Hieratic Papyri in the British Museum.* First Series (1910).
R.O. Faulkner, *The Papyrus Bremner-Rhind* (1933).
———, "The Bremner-Rhind Papyrus—III," *Journal of Egyptian Archaeology* 23 (1937), 166–85.

Enuma Elish Stories:

S. Dalley, *Myths from Mesopotamia* (1989), 228–77.
A. Deimel, *Enuma Elis* (2nd ed., 1936).
A. Heidel, *The Babylonian Genesis* (1942).
L.W. King, *The Seven Tablets of Creation* (2 vols., 1902).
R. Labat, *Le poeme babylonian de la creation* (1935).

W.G. Lambert and S.B. Parker, *Enuma elis: The Babylonian Epic of Creation* (1966).
B. Landsberger and J.K. Wilson, "The Fifth Tablet of 'Enuma Elish'," *Journal of Near Eastern Studies* 20 (1961), 154–79.
S. Langdon, *The Babylonian Epic of Creation* (1923).

Stories of Gilgamesh:

S. Dalley, *Myths from Mesopotamia* (1989), 39–135.
A. Heidel, *The Gilgamesh Epic and Old Testament Parallels* (1946).
Peter Jensen, *Assyrisch-babylonische Mythen und Epen* (1900).
R. Campbell Thompson, *The Epic of Gilgamesh* (1930).
J.H. Tigay, *The Evolution of the Gilgamesh Epic* (1982).

Stories of Atrahasis:

S. Dalley, *Myths from Mesopotamia* (1989), 1–38.
W.G. Lambert, "A New Look at the Babylonian Background of Genesis," *Journal of Theological Studies* 16 (1965), 287–300.
W.G. Lambert and A.R. Millard, *Atra-Hasis: The Babylonian Story of the Flood* (1969).
A.R. Millard, "A New Babylonian Genesis Story," *Tyndale Bulletin* 18 (1967), 3–18.

Stories of Adapa:

F.M. Th. De Liagre Bohl, "Die Mythe vom weisen Adapa," *Die Welt des Orients* 2 (1959), 416–31.
S. Dalley, *Myths from Mesopotamia* (1989), 182–88.
A. Heidel, *Babylonian Genesis* (1942), 147–53.
J.A. Knudtzon, *Die El-Amarna-Tafeln* (1915), 965–69.
R. Campbell Thompson, *The Epic of Gilgamesh* (1930).

Nuzi Archives:

K. Grosz, "Dowry and Brideprice in Nuzi," in M.A. Morrison and D.I. Owen, eds., *Studies on the Civilization and Culture of Nuzi and the Hurrians* (1981), 161–82.
M. Morrison, "Urhi-kusuh DUMU LUGAL and the Family of Mus-apu: Texts from Group 19 (Part 1)," in *Nuzi and the Hurrians, IV: The Eastern Archives of Nuzi* (1993), 66–94.
E.A. Speiser, "A Significant New Will from Nuzi," *Journal of Cuneiform Studies* 17 (1963), 65–71.

Annals of Hatshepsut:

J. Breasted, *Ancient Records of Egypt,* II (1906).
H. Brunner, *Die Geburt des Gottkonigs,* Agyptologische Abhandlungen 10 (1964).

Annals of Dedumoses:

Josephus, *Against Apion* (i.14:73–89).
Manetho, *Aegyptiaca,* frag. 42, 1.75–89.

Stories of Anubis and Bata:

A.H. Gardiner, *Late-Egyptian Stories* (1932), 9–29.
M. Lichtheim, *Ancient Egyptian Literature. A Book of Readings,* vol. 2 (1976), 203–11.
G. Moller, *Hieratische Lesestucke,* II (1927), 1–20.
Select Papyri in the Hieratic Character from the Collections of the British Museum, II (1860), Pls. ix–xix.

Stories of Aqhat:

A. Caquot, M. Sznycer, and A. Herdner, *Textes ougaritiques, I. Mythes et legendes* (1974).
M.D. Coogan, *Stories from Ancient Canaan* (1978), 27–47.
J.C. De Moor, *An Anthology of Religious Texts from Ugarit* (1987), 224–69.
J.C. De Moor and K. Spronk, *A Cuneiform Anthology of Religious Texts from Ugarit* (1987), 102–121.
J. Obermann, *How Daniel Was Blessed with a Son* (1946).
C. Virolleaud, *La legende phenicienne de Danel* (1936).

Stories of Keret:

A. Caquot, M. Sznycer, and A. Herdner, *Textes ougaritiques, I. Mythes et legendes* (1974).
M.D. Coogan, *Stories from Ancient Canaan* (1978), 52–74.
J.C. De Moor, *An Anthology of Religious Texts from Ugarit* (1987), 191–223.
J.C. De Moor and K. Spronk, *A Cuneiform Anthology of ReligiousTexts from Ugarit* (1987), 78–101.
H.L. Ginsberg, *The Legend of King Keret* (1946).

Annals of Sargon I:

B.R. Foster, *Before the Muses: An Anthology of Akkadian Literature, vol. 2: Mature, Late* (1993), 819–20.

L.W. King, *Chronicles Concerning Early Babylonian Kings*, II (1907), 87–96.

B. Lewis, *The Sargon Legend* (1980).

A Treaty Between Ramses II and Hattusilis III:

G. Beckman, *Hittite Diplomatic Texts* (1996), 90–95.

E. Edel, *Der agyptisch-hethitische Korrespondenz aus Boghazkoi in babylonischer und hethitischer Sprache* (1994).

E.F. Weidner, *Politische Dokumente aus Kleinasien* (1923), 112–23.

Annals of Merneptah:

P. Lacau, *Steles du nouvel empire*, I (1909), pp. 52–59, Pls. xvii–xix.

M. Lichtheim, *Ancient Egyptian Literature. A Book of Readings,* vol. 2 (1976), 73–78.

W.M.F. Petrie, *Six Temples at Thebes* (1897), Pls. xiii–xiv.

Sumerian Code:

J.J. Finkelstein, "Sex Offenses in Sumerian Laws," *Journal of the American Oriental Society* 86 (1966), 355–72.

M. Roth, *Law Collections from Mesopotamia and Asia Minor* (1995).

Code of Ur-Nammu:

A.T. Clay, *Yale Oriental Series, Babylonian Texts,* Vol. I, no. 28.

J.J. Finkelstein, "Sex Offenses in Sumerian Laws," *JAOS* 86 (1966), 355–72.

———, "The Laws of Ur-Nammu," *JCS* 22 (1968–69), 66–82.

Code of Hammurabi:

E. Bergmann, *Codex Hammurabi: textus primigenius* (1953).

A. Deimel, *Codex Hammurabi, textus primigenius* (1930).

G.R. Driver and J.C. Miles, *The Babylonian Laws* (2 vols., 1952).

A. Finet, *Le Code de Hammurabi* (1973).

M. Roth, *Law Collections from Mesopotamia and Asia Minor* (1995).

Hittite Code:

J. Friedrich, *Die Hethitschen Gesetze* (1959).
F. Hrozny, *Code Hittite provenant de l'Asie Mineure (vers 1350 av. J.–C.), 1er partie, Transcription, traduction francaise* (1922).
E. Neufeld, *The Hittite Laws* (1951).
M. Roth, *Law Collections from Mesopotamia and Asia Minor* (1995).

Middle Assyrian Code:

G.R. Driver and J.C. Miles, *The Assyrian Laws, Edited with Translation and Commentary* (1935).
M. Roth, *Law Collections from Mesopotamia and Asia Minor* (1995).
R. Yaron, "Middle Assyrian Laws and the Bible," *Biblica* 51 (1970), 77–85.

Stories of Balaam:

J.A. Hackett, *The Balaam Text from Deir 'Alla* (1980).
J. Hoftijzer and G. van der Kooij, *Aramaic Texts from Deir 'Alla* (1976).
———, *The Balaam Text from Deir 'Alla Re-Evaluated* (1991).

Stories of Sinuhe:

A.M. Blackman, *Middle Egyptian Stories, Part I*, Bibliotheca Aegyptiaca 2 (1932).
A.H. Gardiner, *Notes on the Story of Sinuhe* (1916).
M. Lichtheim, *Ancient Egyptian Literature*, vol. 1 (1973), 222–35.
R. Parent, *L'affair Sinouhe* (1982).

Annals of Tuthmoses III:

M.S. Drower, "Inscriptions," in R. Mond and O.H. Myers, *Temples of Armant: A Preliminary Survey, The Text* (1940), 182–84.
C.R. Lepsius, *Denkmaler aus Aegypten und Aethiopien*, III (1849–50).

El Amarna Letters:

C. Bezold and E.A.W. Budge, *The Tell El-Amarna Tablets in the British Museum* (1892).
J.A. Knudtzon, *Die El-Amarna-Tafeln* (1907–1915).
W.L. Moran, *Les lettres d'el-Amarna* (1987).

Medinet Habu Annals of Ramses III:

J.A. Breasted, *Ancient Records of Egypt,* IV (1906).
W.F. Edgerton and J.A. Wilson, *Historical Records of Ramses III,* SAOC, 12 (1936).
Epigraphic Survey, *Medinet Habu, I. Earlier Historical Records of Ramses III* (1930).

Gezer Almanac:

W.F. Albright, "The Gezer Calendar," *Bulletin of the American Schools of Oriental Research* 82 (1943), 18–24.
J.C.L. Gibson, *Textbook of Syrian Semitic Inscriptions, I* (1971), 1–4.
S. Talmon, "The Gezer Calendar and the Seasonal Cycle of Ancient Canaan," *Journal of the American Oriental Society* 83 (1963), 177–87.

Archives of Babatha:

Y. Yadin, *The Finds from the Bar-Kokhba Period in the Cave of Letters* (1963).
———, "The Life and Trials of Babata," in *Bar-Kokhba: the Rediscovery of the Legendary Hero of the Second Jewish Revolt against Rome* (1971), 22–53 + 265.
———, J.C. Greenfield, and A. Yardeni, "Babatha's *Ketubba,*" *Israel Exploration Journal* 44 (1994), 75–101.

Annals of Tiglath-Pileser I:

M. Cogan, "'Ripping Open Pregnant Women' in Light of an Assyrian Analogue," *Journal of the American Oriental Society* 103/4 (1983), 755–57.
E. Ebeling, *Literarische Keilschrifttexte aus Assur,* #62 (1953), 82–83.
———, "Ein Heidenlied auf Tiglatpileser I. und der Anfang einer neuen Version von 'Istars Hollenfahrt' nach einer Schulertafel aus Assur," *Orientalia* 18 (1949), 30–39.

Annals of Mesha:

R. Dussaud, *Les monuments palestiniens et judaiques* (1912), 4–22.
J.C.L. Gibson, *Textbook of Syrian Semitic Inscriptions, I* (1971), 71–84.
K.P. Jackson, "The Language of the Mesha' Inscription," in *Studies in the Mesha Inscription and Moab* (1989), 96–130.

Tell Dan Annals of Hazael:

A. Biran and J. Naveh, "Aramaic Stele Fragment from Dan," *Israel Exploration Journal* 43 (1993), 81–98.

———, "The Tell Dan Inscription: A New Fragment," *Israel Exploration Journal* 45 (1995), 1–18.

Karatepe Annals of Azitawada:

H.T. Bossert and U.B. Alkim, *Karatepe* II (1947), Pls. xxix–xxxi, xl–xliv.

H.T. Bossert, et al., *Die Ausgrabungen auf dem Karatepe* (1950), Pl. xiv.

R.T. O'Callaghan, "The Phoenician Inscription on the King's Statue at Karatepe," *Catholic Biblical Quarterly* 11 (1949), 233–48.

J. Pedersen, "The Phoenician Inscription of Karatepe," *Acta Orientalia* 21 (1953), 33–56.

Annals of Shalmaneser III:

A.H. Layard, *Inscriptions in the Cuneiform Character* (1851).

———, *Monuments of Nineveh* I (1849), Pls. 53–56.

———, *Inscriptions in the Cuneiform Character from Assyrian Monuments* (1851), Pls. 87–98.

Nimrud Annals of Tiglath-Pileser III:

D.D. Luckenbill, *Ancient Records of Assyria and Babylonia, I* (1926).

P. Rost, *Die Keilschrifttexte Tiglat-Pilesers III nach den Papierabklatschen und Originalen des Britischen Museums* (1893).

Annals of Sargon II:

R. Borger, *Babylonisch-Assyrische Lesestucke* (1963), 54–58.

H. Winckler, *Die Keilschrifttexte Sargons* (1889), Pl. 38.

Annals of Sennacherib:

R. Borger, *Babylonisch-assyrische Lesestucke* (1963), 67–69.

F.M. Fales, *Assyrian Royal Inscriptions* (1981).

D.D. Luckenbill, *The Annals of Sennacherib* (1924).

Siloam Annals:

J.C.L. Gibson, *Textbook of Syrian Semitic Inscriptions, I* (1971), 21–23.
V. Sasson, "The Siloam Tunnel Inscription," *Palestine Exploration Quarterly* 114 (1982), 111–17.
K.A.D. Smelik, *Writings from Ancient Israel* (1991), 64–69.

Annals of Nebuchadnezzar:

A.K. Grayson, *Assyrian and Babylonian Chronicles, V* (1975).
D.J. Wiseman, *Chronicles of Chaldean Kings (626–556 B.C.) in the British Museum* (1956), 32–37, 73.

Arad Letters:

J.C.L. Gibson, *Textbook of Syrian Semitic Inscriptions, I* (1971), 49–54.
J.M. Lindenberger, *Ancient Aramaic and Hebrew Letters* (1994), 103–10.
K.A.D. Smelik, *Writings from Ancient Israel: A Handbook of Historical and Religious Documents* (1991), 101–15.

Lachish Letters:

A. Lemaire, *Inscriptions hebraiques, I: Les ostraca* (1977), 97–100.
J.M. Lindenberger, *Ancient Aramaic and Hebrew Letters* (1994), 110–16.
D. Pardee, *Handbook of Ancient Hebrew Letters* (1982), 78–81.
H. Torczyner, *Lachish I. The Lachish Letters* (1938), 33–43.

Visions of Neferti:

H. Goedicke, *The Protocol of Neferyt* (1977).
W. Golenischeff, *Les papyrus hieratiques no. 1115, 1116A, et 1116B de l'Ermitage Imperial a St. Petersbourg* (1913), Pls. 23–25.
M. Lichtheim, *Ancient Egyptian Literature. A Book of Readings*, vol. 1 (1975), 139–45.

Stories of Ishtar and Tammuz:

R. Borger, *Babylonisch–Assyrische Lesestucke, II* (1963), 86–93.
S. Dalley, *Myths from Mesopotamia* (1989), 154–62.
A. Heidel, *The Gilgamesh Epic and Old Testament Parallels* (1946), 121–28.

Mari Letters:

B. Batto, *Studies on Women at Mari* (1974).
F. Ellermeier, *Prophetie in Mari und Israel* (1968).
H.B. Huffmon, "Prophecy in the Mari Letters," *Biblical Archaeologist* 31/4 (1968), 101–24.
W.L. Moran, "New Evidence from Mari on the History of Prophecy," *Biblica* 50 (1969), 15–56.

Memoirs of Wen-Amon:

A.H. Gardiner, *Late-Egyptian Stories* (1932), 61–76.
H. Goedicke, *The Report of Wenamun* (1975).
G. Moller, *Hieratische Lesestucke*, II (1927), 29.

Yavne-Yam Letter:

J.C.L. Gibson, *Textbook of Syrian Semitic Inscriptions, I* (1971), 26–30.
J.M. Lindenberger, *Ancient Aramaic and Hebrew Letters* (1994), 96–98.
J. Naveh, "A Hebrew Letter from the Seventh Century B.C.," *Israel Exploration Journal* 10 (1960), 129–39.

A Decree of Cyrus:

R. Borger, *Handbuch der Keilschriftliteratur, I* (1967).
A. Kuhrt, "The Cyrus Cylinder and Achaemenid Imperial Policy," *Journal for the Study of the Old Testament* 25 (1983), 83–97.
F.H. Weissbach, *Die Keilinschriften der Achameniden* (1911), 2–9.

Elephantine Letters:

J.M. Lindenberger, *Ancient Aramaic and Hebrew Letters* (1994), 53–70.
B. Porten, *Archives from Elephantine* (1968), 278–98.
B. Porten and A. Yardeni, *Textbook of Aramaic Documents from Ancient Egypt: 1 Letters* (1986).

Laments for Ur:

I. Bernhardt, *Sumerische literarische Texte aus Nippur II* (1967), 16, tablets 18–25.
M.E. Cohen, *The Canonical Lamentations of Ancient Mesopotamia, I* (1988).
T. Jacobsen, *The Harps That Once: Sumerian Poetry in Translation* (1987).
S.N. Kramer, *The Lament Over the Destruction of Ur* (1940).

Hymn to Ninkasi:

M. Civil, "A Hymn to the Beer Goddess and a Drinking Song," in *Studies Presented to A. Leo Oppenheim: From the Workshop of the Chicago Assyrian Dictionary* (1964), 67–89.

A.L. Oppenheim and L.F. Hartman, *On Beer and Brewing Techniques in Ancient Mesopotamia: According to the XXIIIrd Tablet of the Series HAR.ra=hubullu* (Supplement to the *Journal of the American Oriental Society,* 10; 1950).

Ebla Archives:

G. Pettinato, *The Archives of Ebla: An Empire Inscribed in Clay* (1981).

Stories of Ba'al and Anat:

A. Caquot, M. Sznycer, and A. Herdner, *Textes ougaritiques, I. Mythes et légendes* (1974).

M.D. Coogan, *Stories from Ancient Canaan* (1978), 75–115.

J.C. De Moor, *An Anthology of Religious Texts from Ugarit* (1987), 20–109.

J.C. De Moor and K. Spronk, *A Cuneiform Anthology of Religious Texts from Ugarit* (1987), 1–44.

C.H. Gordon, *Ugaritic Literature* (1949), 9–56.

Hymn to the Aton:

N. de G. Davies, *The Rock Tombs of El-Amarna*, VI (1908), Pl. xxvii.

M. Lichtheim, *Ancient Egyptian Literature. A Book of Readings, II: The New Kingdom* (1976), 90–92.

Teachings of Ptah-Hotep:

E. Devaud, *Les maximes de Ptah-hotep* (1916).

G. Jequier, *Le Papyrus Prisse et ses variantes* (1911).

M. Lichtheim, *Ancient Egyptian Literature. A Book of Readings, I: The Old and Middle Kingdoms* (1975), 61–80.

Z. Zaba, *Les Maximes de Ptah-hotep* (1956).

Teachings of Khety:

H. Brunner, *Die Lehre des Cheti, Sohnes des Duauf* (1944).

M. Lichtheim, *Ancient Egyptian Literature,* vol. 1 (1973), 184–92.

Teachings of Amen-em-ope:

E.A.W. Budge, *Facsimiles of Egyptian Hieratic Papyri in the British Museum,* Second Series (1923), Pls. i–xiv.

——, *The Teachings of Amen-em-apt, Son of Kanakht* (1924).

I. Grumach, *Untersuchungen zur Lebenslehre des Amenope* (1972).

M. Lichtheim, *Ancient Egyptian Literature. A Book of Readings,* vol. 2 (1976), 146–63.

Teachings of Ahiqar:

J.M. Lindenberger, *The Aramaic Proverbs of Ahiqar* (1983).

T. Noldeke, *Untersuchungen zum Achiqar-Roman* (1914).

F. Stummer, *Der Kritische Wert der altaramaischen Ahikartexte aus Elephantine* (1914).

Teachings of Ankhsheshonqy:

S.R.K. Glanville, *The Instructions of 'Onchsheshonqy* (1955).

M. Lichtheim, *Ancient Egyptian Literature, III: The Late Period* (1980), 159–84.

Declarations of Innocence:

E.A.W. Budge, *The Egyptian Book of the Dead: (The Papyrus of Ani) Egyptian Text Transliteration and Translation* (1965).

L.H. Lesko, *The Ancient Egyptian Book of Two Ways* (1972).

M. Lichtheim, *Ancient Egyptian Literature,* vol. 2 (1976), 119–32.

A Sufferer and a Soul:

W. Barta, *Das Gesprach eines Mannes mit seinem Ba* (1969).

A. Erman, *Gesprach eines Lebensmuden mit seiner Seele* (1896).

H. Goedicke, *The Report about the Dispute of a Man with His Ba* (1970).

M. Lichtheim, *Ancient Egyptian Literature. A Book of Readings,* vol. 1 (1975), 163–69.

K. Sethe, *Aegyptische Lesestucke* (2nd ed., 1928), 43–46.

A Farmer and the Courts:

M. Lichtheim, *Ancient Egyptian Literature. A Book of Readings,* vol. 1 (1975), 169–84.

F. Vogelsang and A.H. Gardiner, *Die Klagen des Bauern* (1908).

A Sufferer and a Friend:

J.A. Craig, *Babylonian and Assyrian Religious Texts,* I (1895), Pls. 44–52.
W.G. Lambert, *Babylonian Wisdom Literature* (1960), 63–91.

Egyptian Love Songs:

E.A.W. Budge, *Facsimiles of Egyptian Hieratic Papyri in the British Museum,*
    Second Series (1923), Pl. xliii.
M.V. Fox, *The Song of Songs and the Ancient Egyptian Love Songs* (1985).
M. Lichtheim, *Ancient Egyptian Literature, A Book of Readings, vol. 2: The
    New Kingdom* (1976), 181–96.

BIBLIOGRAPHY OF
PICTURE SOURCES

Biran, A. and J. Naveh. "The Tell Dan Inscription: A New Fragment." *Israel Exploration Journal* 45/1, (1995): 1–18.

Castel, F. *The History of Israel and Judah in Old Testament Times* (Mahwah, N.J.: Paulist Press, 1985).

Contenau, G. *Everyday Life in Babylon and Assyria* (London: Edward Arnold Ltd., 1954).

Crawford, H. *Sumer and the Sumerians* (Cambridge: Cambridge University Press, 1991).

Fiore, S. *Voices from the Clay* (Norman, Okla.: University of Oklahoma Press, 1965).

Frankfort, H. *Cylinder Seals* (London: Gregg Press, 1939).

Gardiner, A. *Egypt of the Pharaohs* (New York: Oxford University Press, 1966).

Janssen, R. and J. *Egyptian Household Animals* (Aylesbury, UK: Shire Publications, 1989).

Manning, S. *The Land of the Pharaohs* (New York: Fleming H. Revell Company, 1924).

Maspero, G. *Manual of Egyptian Archaeology*, 6th ed. (New York: G. P. Putnam's Sons, 1926).

Michalowski, K. *Art of Ancient Egypt* (New York: Harry N. Abrams Inc., 1969).

Montet, P. *Lives of the Pharaohs* (Cleveland: The World Publishing Company, 1968).

Moortgat, A. *The Art of Ancient Mesopotamia* (London: Phaidon, 1969).

Murray, M. A. and J. C. Ellis. *A Street in Petra* (London: British School of Egyptian Archaeology, 1940).

Nelson, H. H. and U. Holshcher. *Work in Western Thebes 1931–33* (Chicago: University of Chicago Press, 1934).

Newsome, J. D., Jr. *By the Waters of Babylon* (Atlanta: John Knox Press, 1979).

Perrot, G. and C. Chipiez. *History of Art in Phoenicia and Its Dependencies* (London: Chapman and Hall Ltd., 1885).

Pettinato, G. *The Archives of Ebla: An Empire Inscribed in Clay* (Garden City, N.Y.: Doubleday, 1981).

Quirke, S. *Who Were the Pharaohs?* (London: British Museum Publications, 1990).

Rawlinson, F. *History of Ancient Egypt,* Vol. II (New York: John B. Alden, 1886).

———. *Ancient Egypt* (London: G. P. Putnam's Sons, 1904).

Saggs, H. W. F. *Everyday Life in Babylonia and Assyria* (London: B. T. Batsford Ltd., 1965).

Tadmor, M. *Inscriptions Reveal,* 2nd ed. (Jerusalem: Israel Museum, 1973).

Woldering, I. *The Art of Egypt: The Time of the Pharaohs* (New York: Crown Publishers, 1963).

ABBREVIATIONS

AA	Agyptologische Abhandlungen, Wiesbaden
AASOR	The Annual of the American Schools of Oriental Research
AO	tablets in the collections of the Louvre Museum
AP	Aramaic Papyri
ARI	Assyrian Royal Inscriptions. Grayson (1972–76)
ARM	Archives royales de Mari, Textes cuneiformes
BM	tablets in the collections of the British Museum
Cowley	A. Cowley, ed. *Aramaic Papyri of the Fifth Century B.C.* (Oxford, 1923)
CT	Cuneiform Texts from Babylonian Tablets in the British Museum (London, 1896)
CTA	A. Herdner, *Corpus des tablettes en cuneiformes alphabetiques decouvertes a Ras-Shamra-Ugarit de 1929–1939* (Paris, 1963)
EA	J.A. Knudtzon, *Die El-Amarna-Tafeln*
HSS	Harvard Semitic Series
IEJ	Israel Exploration Journal
JAOS	Journal of the American Oriental Society
JNES	Journal of Near Eastern Studies
KTU	*Die keilalphabetischen Text aus Ugarit.* Dietrich, Loretz and Sanmartin (1976)
KV	Valley of the Kings
Ni	tablets excavated at Nippur, in the collections of the Archaeological Museum of Istanbul
PAPS	Proceedings of the American Philosophical Society
TM	Siglum for tablets from Tell Mardikh (Ebla)
VAT	tablets in the collections of the Staatliche Museum, Berlin
WO	Die Welt des Orients
YOS	Yale Oriental Series, Babylonian Texts
ZA	Zeitschrift fur Assyriologie

TEXT ABBREVIATIONS

Adapa	Stories of Adapa
Ahiqar	Teachings of Ahiqar
Amarna	El Amarna Letters
Amen-em-ope	Teachings of Amen-em-ope
Ankhsheshonqy	Teachings of Ankhsheshonqy
Anubis	Stories of Anubis and Bata
Aqhat	Stories of Aqhat
Arad	Arad Letters
Aton	Hymn to the Aton
Atrahasis	Stories of Atrahasis
Ba'al	Stories of Ba'al and Anat
Babatha	Archives of Babatha
Balaam	Stories of Balaam
CH	Code of Hammurabi
Cyrus	A Decree of Cyrus
Declarations	Declarations of Innocence
Dedumoses	Annals of Dedumoses
Ebla	Ebla Archives
Elephantine	Elephantine Letters
Enuma	Enuma Elish Stories
Farmer	A Farmer and the Courts
Friend	A Sufferer and a Friend
Gezer	Gezer Almanac
Gilgamesh	Stories of Gilgamesh
Hatshepsut	Annals of Hatshepsut
Hazael	Tell Dan Annals of Hazael
Hittite	Hittite Code
Ishtar	Stories of Ishtar and Tammuz
Karatepe	Karatepe Annals of Azitawada
Keret	Stories of Keret
Khety	Teachings of Khety
Lachish	Lachish Letters
Love Songs	Egyptian Love Songs
MAL	Middle Assyrian Code
Mari	Mari Letters
Memphis	Memphis Stories
Merneptah	Annals of Merneptah
Mesha	Annals of Mesha
Nebuchadnezzar	Annals of Nebuchadnezzar
Neferti	Visions of Neferti
Ninkasi	Hymn to Ninkasi

Nuzi	Nuzi Archives
Ptah-Hotep	Teachings of Ptah-Hotep
Ra	Stories of Ra and Apophis
Ramses II	A Treaty Between Ramses II and Hattusilis III
Ramses III	Medinet Habu Annals of Ramses III
Sargon I	Annals of Sargon I
Sargon II	Annals of Sargon II
Sennacherib	Annals of Sennacherib
Shalmaneser	Annals of Shalmaneser III
Siloam	Siloam Annals
Sinuhe	Stories of Sinuhe
Soul	A Sufferer and a Soul
Sumerian	Sumerian Code
TP I	Annals of Tiglath-Pileser I
TP III	Nimrud Annals of Tiglath-Pileser III
Tuthmoses III	Annals of Tuthmoses III
Ur	Lament for Ur
Ur-Nammu	Code of Ur-Nammu
Wen-Amon	Memoirs of Wen-Amon
Yavne-Yam	Yavne-Yam Letter

INDEX

The following index provides a page and biblical citation index in conjunction with a text and parallel index. The scheme used for the parallels is as follows:

1 = genre: creation story, flood story, law, teaching
2 = verbal parallel: direct word or phrase parallels
3 = motif: barren wife, greed, widows & orphans, divine war
4 = social/scientific: anthropomorphism, taboo, propaganda
5 = plot parallel: similar action in both texts
6 = historical parallel: name, event, place

Citation	Page	Text	Parallel
2:7	33	Atrahasis	1 · creation story
			4 · anthropomorphism
	74	Aqhat	2 · breathe
2:7–15	17	Enuma	5 · humans
			4 · anthropomorphism
3:5	21	Gilgamesh	5 · gain knowledge
3:7	22	Gilgamesh	5 · make clothing
3:20	33	Atrahasis	2 · mother of living
3:20–1	22	Gilgamesh	5 · make clothing
3:22	44	Adapa	3 · divine food
4:3–16	61	Anubis	3 · sibling rivalry
4:3—5:32	74	Aqhat	1 · blessing
			2 · revenge
4:23–4	75	Aqhat	1 · boast
6—11	19	Gilgamesh	1 · flood story
6:1—11:26	32	Atrahasis	1 · flood story
6:14	38	Atrahasis	2 · pitch
6:14–6	26	Gilgamesh	2 · pitch
6:14–21	26	Gilgamesh	5 · ark
7:2–4, 7–9	26	Gilgamesh	5 · animals
7:11	259	Aton	2 · fountains of deep
7:11–2, 17–23	27	Gilgamesh	2 · darkness
7:13–6	26	Gilgamesh	5 · hatch
7:24—8:3	27	Gilgamesh	5 · aftermath
8:4	27	Gilgamesh	5 · landing
8:5–22	27	Gilgamesh	5 · release
8:20–1	27	Gilgamesh	5 · sacrifice
8:21	39	Atrahasis	2 · smell
8:21–2	27	Gilgamesh	3 · remorse
9:1–17	27	Gilgamesh	1 · covenant
			5 · hero's fate
			5 · rainbow
9:20–3	75	Aqhat	2 · drunk
10:9	70	Aqhat	2 · hunter
	155	Tiglath-Pileser I	2 · hunter
11:9	259	Aton	2 · languages
11:27—25:18	129	Sinuhe	1 · biography
			5 · immigrant
12:10–9	49	Nuzi	3 · wife/sister
13:5—14:24	241	Ebla	5 · negotiations
14:19	165	Karatepe	1 · blessing
			2 · creator

CITATION	PAGE	TEXT	PARALLEL
30:27–34	50	Nuzi	5 · herding contract
30:40–2	63	Anubis	5 · breeding
31:1–21	47	Nuzi	2 · idols
			4 · inheritance rights
31:19	324	Wen-Amon	2 · idol
31:19–35	323	Wen-Amon	2 · idol
31:39	109	CH	1 · contract
			2 · mangled animals
31:44–54	87	Ramses II	1 · covenant
			2 · "If you"
31:50–4	90	Ramses II	3 · curse
31:51–3	89	Ramses II	1 · covenant
			2 · God's witness
34	100	Sumer	5 · rape
34:1–12	100	Sumer	2 · rape
35:17	33	Atrahasis	2 · midwife
			3 · birthing
37:1—45:28	62	Anubis	3 · sibling rivalry
37:2—50:26	283	Ahiqar	1 · wisdom
			3 · restored fortune
38	112	Hittite	5 · levir
	252	Ba'al	1 · law (levir)
			3 · heir
			4 · mourning ritual
38:1–30	119	MAL	5 · household custody
			5 · levir
38:14–5	119	MAL	5 · veil
39:1–21	62	Anubis	5 · seduction
39:7–12	63	Anubis	5 · seduction
39:17–9	64	Anubis	5 · deception
41	129	Sinuhe	1 · biography
			5 · restored fortunes
41:9—47:12	58	Dedumoses	5 · foreign adviser
41:47–9	162	Karatepe	5 · storehouses
48:15–20	49	Nuzi	1 · blessing

EXODUS

1:16	33	Atrahasis	2 · birthstool/brick
1:22—2:10	85	Sargon I	5 · reed boat
			3 · miracle survival

CITATION	PAGE	TEXT	PARALLEL
22:16	100	Sumer	2 · seduce virgin
22:16–7	122	MAL	2 · seduce virgin
			4 · marriage law
22:18	121	MAL	2 · sorcery
	112	Hittite	2 · sorcery
22:26–7	331	Yavne-Yam	1 · law
			2 · pledge garment
	288	Ahiqar	1 · law
			2 · pledge garment
23:1–3	101	CH	2 · false witness
23:6–8	102	CH	2 · bribe
23:8	280	Amen-em-ope	2 · bribe
29:4	78	Keret	2 · washing
			4 · ritual cleansing
30:23–33	124	Balaam	2 · myrrh
			4 · anointing ritual
34:29–35	68	Aqhat	2 · shining face

LEVITICUS

CITATION	PAGE	TEXT	PARALLEL
10:9	238	Ninkasi	2 · beer
18:6–18	106	CH	2 · incest
			1 · decalogue
	110, 112–113	Hittite	4 · marriage taboos
18:8	106	CH	2 · incest with mother
			4 · marriage taboos
18:15	106	CH	2 · incest
			2 · daughter-in-law
			4 · marriage taboos
18:22	117	MAL	2 · homosexuality
19:11, 13	102	CH	2 · theft
19:15	102	CH	2 · unjust judge
19:20–1	98	Ur-Nammu	2 · slave woman
19:20–22	106	CH	2 · slave woman
20:10–21	106	CH	3 · illicit sex
	117	MAL	2 · adultery
20:11	106	CH	2 · incest with mother
			4 · marriage taboos
20:12	106	CH	2 · daughter-in-law
			2 · incest
			4 · marriage taboos
20:13	117	MAL	2 · homosexuality

CITATION	PAGE	TEXT	PARALLEL
19:16–9	101, 102	CH	2 · false witness
	98	Ur-Nammu	2 · false witness
19:21	107	CH	2 · talion
21:1–9	73	Aqhat	4 · forgiveness ritual
			5 · burial
	103	CH	2 · unknown murderer
21:18–21	99	Sumer	2 · prodigal son
	292	Ankhsheshonqy	2 · foolish child
22:1–4	102	CH	2 · property
			4 · social response
22:8	108	CH	2 · safe construction
			3 · liability
22:22	104	CH	2 · adultery
	115, 116	MAL	2 · adultery
22:22–7	113	Hittite	2 · rape
			4 · significant place
22:23–4	100	Sumer	2 · raped virgin
			4 · gate/justice of place
	98	Ur-Nammu	2 · raped virgin
22:23–7	105	CH	2 · raped virgin
			4 · justice of place
	115, 122	MAL	2 · raped virgin
22:28–9	122	MAL	2 · raped virgin
			4 · marriage law
23:15–6	88	Ramses II	2 · fugitive slaves
	98	Ur-Nammu	2 · fugitive slaves
	103	CH	2 · fugitive slaves
24:1	119	MAL	2 · divorce
24:1–4	105	CH	2 · divorce
24:7	103	CH	2 · kidnapping
24:16	114	MAL	2 · sentencing
24:20	145	Gezer	2 · olive harvest
25:5–10	112	Hittite	1 · law (will)
			5 · levir
	119	MAL	5 · levir
	252	Ba'al	1 · law (levir)
25:11–2	115	MAL	2 · genitalia
			4 · female taboo
26:5–11	145	Gezer	5 · harvest
25:13–5	104	CH	2 · false scales
27:20, 22–3	106	CH	2 · incest
29:6	238	Ninkasi	2 · beer

CITATION	PAGE	TEXT	PARALLEL
JUDGES			
1:4–11	91	Merneptah	1 · annal
			5 · campaign report
4:5	69	Aqhat	2 · tree/justice
			4 · justice site
4:17–22	75	Aqhat	3 · revenge
			5 · murder
4:19	75	Aqhat	4 · hospitality
			5 · drink request
5:24–7	74	Aqhat	3 · enemy defeated
			4 · gender reversal
5:27	250	Ba'al	5 · victim falls
7:12	244	Ba'al	2 · locusts
8:19	79	Keret	1 · oath
9:8–15	283, 287	Ahiqar	1 · fable
			5 · taunt
11:30–1	79	Keret	1 · oath
11:39–40	306	Ishtar	4 · mourning ritual
13:1–23	52	Hatshepsut	1 · annunciation
13:1—16:31	141	Ramses III	1 · annals
13:2–3	66	Aqhat	3 · barren wife
13:4	238	Ninkasi	2 · beer
14:11–20	306	Ishtar	5 · lovers' quarrel
15:1–8	299	Love Songs	5 · determined lover
16:3	255	Ba'al	4 · power struggle
			5 · gate posts removed
	308	Ishtar	5 · gate posts removed
16:4–22	306	Ishtar	5 · lovers' quarrel
19:22	162	Karatepe	2 · evil men
21:25	315	Neferti	2 · selfishness
			3 · anarchy
RUTH			
2:2–9	282	Amen-em-ope	1 · law
			3 · widows & orphans
			5 · widow gleaning
2:14	186	Arad	2 · sour wine
2:23	145	Gezer	2 · harvest
3:3	301	Love Songs	2 · anoint hair
	311	Ishtar	2 · anoint with oil
			5 · wash and anoint

CITATION	PAGE	TEXT	PARALLEL
3:13	79	Keret	1 · oath
4	112	Hittite	1 · law
			5 · levir
	252	Ba'al	1 · law (levir)
4:1	69	Aqhat	2 · gate
			4 · site of justice
4:11–2	80	Keret	1 · blessing

1 SAMUEL

CITATION	PAGE	TEXT	PARALLEL
1:1—4:1 +			
7:3—8:13	141	Ramses III	1 · annals
1:2–17	66	Aqhat	3 · barren wife
1:9–18	52	Hatshepsut	1 · annunciation
1:15	238	Ninkasi	2 · beer
1:21	162	Karatepe	2 · sacrifice
2:12—4:22	290	Ankhsheshonqy	1 · teaching
			3 · wise vs. fool
3:3–4	37	Atrahasis	1 · theophany
			5 · dream
4:20	33	Atrahasis	2 · midwife
6:13	145	Gezer	2 · reaping
8:4—2 Sam 8:13	141	Ramses III	1 · annals
9:9	124	Balaam	2 · seer
10:6	320	Mari	1 · prophecy
			2 · possession
12:14–5	320	Mari	1 · admonition
			2 · king's duty
			3 · obedience to God
12:24	223	Friend	2 · fear of God
14:24	79	Keret	1 · oath
15:27	254	Ba'al	1 · legal petition
			4 · hem = identity
16:14–23	324	Wen-Amon	5 · music
17:8–10	14	Enuma	1 · taunt
			5 · single combat
17:17–58	141	Ramses III	6 · Philistines
	129	Sinuhe	5 · duel
18:7	255	Ba'al	1 · song of praise
19:6	79	Keret	1 · oath
21:14	281	Amen-em-ope	2 · insanity
			4 · mental taboo

CITATION	PAGE	TEXT	PARALLEL
23:4	158	Mesha	1 · exhortation
			2 · Go!
			3 · divine war
24:5	320	Mari	2 · hem
			4 · identity
26:19	331	Yavne-Yam	1 · scribal address
28:3	112	Hittite	5 · witch
	121	MAL	5 · witch
30:27	185	Arad	6 · Ramoth-negeb

2 SAMUEL

1:27	73	Aqhat	1 · eulogy
			2 · mighty fallen
2:18–23	14	Enuma	1 · taunt
			5 · single combat
3:31	72	Aqhat	5 · tear robe
5:6–8	14	Enuma	1 · taunt
7:1–17	246	Ba'al	4 · propaganda
			5 · house for God
7:13	250	Ba'al	1 · covenant
			4 · divine right rule
7:14	77	Keret	4 · father role
8:1–12	243	Ebla	1 · royal annal
			5 · conquest list
	91	Merneptah	1 · royal annal
			5 · conquest list
8:2	158	Mesha	5 · sacrifice captives
10:1–4	327	Wen-Amon	1 · diplomacy
			5 · provocation
10:6–8	168	Shalmaneser	1 · annal
			5 · alliance
12:15–8	67	Aqhat	5 · seven day ritual
13:4–6	300	Love Songs	5 · fake illness
14:1–20	234	Ur	1 · petition
			3 · widows & orphans
15:1–6	77	Keret	5 · son's revolt
15:1–14	81	Keret	5 · king's flight
15:2	69	Aqhat	2 · gate
			4 · place of justice

CITATION	PAGE	TEXT	PARALLEL
22:10	69	Aqhat	2 · threshing floor
			4 · place of justice

2 KINGS

3:4	157	Mesha	6 · Mesha
3:8	185	Arad	6 · "Way of Edom"
3:15	324	Wen-Amon	1 · prophecy
			5 · ecstatic
	320	Mari	1 · prophecy
			5 · ecstatic
3:16	313	Neferti	2 · dry canals
4:8–17	66	Aqhat	3 · barren wife
4:34–7	80	Keret	1 · miracle story
			5 · cure
5:10–4	80	Keret	1 · miracle story
			5 · cure
8:11–2	155	Tiglath-Pileser I	2 · pregnant women
			5 · pillaging
8:25—10:36	161	Hazael	6 · Hazael
9:1—10:33	166	Shalmaneser	1 · annals
9:16–26	88	Ramses II	1 · covenant
			2 · chariots
			4 · reciprocity
9:30	244	Ba'al	5 · cosmetics
9:36	65	Anubis	1 · curse
9:37	306	Ishtar	1 · taunt
10:34	170	Shalmaneser	6 · Jehu
12:17–8	161	Hazael	6 · Hazael
14:9	287	Ahiqar	1 · fable
			5 · taunt
15:16	155	Tiglath-Pileser I	2 · pregnant women
			5 · pillaging
15:17–22	172	Tiglath-Pileser III	1 · annals
			5 · tribute
			6 · Menahem
17:1–41	160	Hazael	6 · Shalmaneser V
17:3–6	175	Sargon II	6 · fall of Samaria
17:6	175	Sargon II	5 · deportation
17:24	162	Karatepe	5 · deportation
18:1—20:21	177	Sennacherib	1 · annals
	181	Siloam	1 · annals

Citation	Page	Text	Parallel
28:9	227	Friend	2 · shepherd
29:10	247	Ba'al	2 · source of flood
31:9	227	Friend	2 · help in distress
34:9	223	Friend	2 · fear God
37:16	294	Ankhsheshonqy	1 · "Better" proverb
			3 · be satisfied
39:6	278	Amen-em-ope	3 · greed
42:1	251	Ba'al	2 · spring/deer
49:14	251	Ba'al	2 · lure of death
50	9	Enuma	1 · creation story
52:2	284	Ahiqar	2 · sharp words
52:7	278	Amen-em-ope	3 · greed
57:1	235	Ur	2 · storms
62:10	278	Amen-em-ope	2 · riches
			3 · greed
	287	Ahiqar	3 · greed
64:2, 7	286	Ahiqar	2 · shoot bow
68:4	250	Ba'al	2 · cloud rider
	72	Aqhat	2 · cloud rider
68:5	81	Keret	3 · widows & orphans
69:12	238	Ninkasi	3 · drunken fools
69:17	227	Friend	2 · distress
69:21	186	Arad	2 · sour wine
72:17	165	Karatepe	1 · blessing
			2 · name endure
74:13–4	14	Enuma	2 · sea serpent
94:19	213	Soul	2 · cares
			3 · consolation
95:3	247	Ba'al	2 · God is king
			3 · divine king
96:4	247	Ba'al	2 · God is king
			3 · divine king
97:9	247	Ba'al	2 · God is king
			3 · divine king
101:8	162	Karatepe	2 · destroy wicked
			4 · civil order
103:14	281	Amen-em-ope	1 · creation story
			2 · clay shapes
			4 · anthropomorphism
104	9	Enuma	1 · creation story
104:3	244	Ba'al	2 · cloud rider
	72, 73	Aqhat	2 · cloud rider

Citation	Page	Text	Parallel
104:5–9	241	Ebla	1 · creation hymn
104:10	260	Aton	2 · springs
104:11–4	259	Aton	2 · birds
104:20–3	258	Aton	2 · darkness
			5 · daily schedule
104:24	260	Aton	2 · sole power
104:25–7	259	Aton	2 · sea
104:27	259	Aton	2 · seasons
104:29–30	261	Aton	2 · reliance on God
124:1–5	255	Ba'al	1 · litany
			2 · "If not"
125:3	255	Ba'al	2 · broken scepter
126:4	254	Ba'al	2 · wadis
129:3	254	Ba'al	2 · plowing
			3 · affliction image
131:1	287	Ahiqar	2 · covet
132:7	251, 252	Ba'al	2 · footstool
132:18	254	Ba'al	2 · shame
137	232	Ur	1 · lament
137:7–9	187	Arad	6 · Edomite invasion
	198	Elephantine	1 · curse
			6 · Edomite invasion
139:13	259	Aton	2 · fetus
141:7	251	Ba'al	2 · mouth of death
145:13	250	Ba'al	2 · eternal kingdom

PROVERBS

Citation	Page	Text	Parallel
1:8	265	Ptah-Hotep	4 · title of teacher
1:12	251	Ba'al	2 · death swallows
1:17	265	Ptah-Hotep	1 · saying form
2:1–5	266, 269	Ptah-Hotep	1 · address form
			2 · seek wisdom
2:4	265	Ptah-Hotep	2 · good advice
3:10	164	Karatepe	1 · blessing
			2 · full barns
5:5	211	Soul	2 · path to death
6:1–5	287	Ahiqar	2 · pay debt
6:16–9	284	Ahiqar	2 · x/x + 1
			3 · number progression
6:23–9	268	Ptah-Hotep	2 · lust
6:24	265	Ptah-Hotep	2 · women

CITATION	PAGE	TEXT	PARALLEL
6:25–6	290, 294	Ankhsheshonqy	2 · another's wife
6:27–9	268	Ptah-Hotep	2 · lust
7:24–7	268	Ptah-Hotep	2 · lust
9:1	247	Ba'al	2 · seven pillars
9:17	265	Ptah-Hotep	1 · analogy
10:1	265	Ptah-Hotep	1 · analogy
11:21	266	Ptah-Hotep	2 · justice
12:4	269	Ptah-Hotep	2 · good wife
13:24	283	Ahiqar	2 · discipline
14:3	290	Ankhsheshonqy	2 · wise speech
14:5	279	Amen-em-ope	2 · false witness
14:7	278	Amen-em-ope	2 · fool
15:4	290	Ankhsheshonqy	2 · wise speech
15:16	277	Amen-em-ope	1 · "Better" proverb
			3 · be satisfied
15:17	277	Amen-em-ope	1 · "Better" proverb
			3 · be satisfied
15:27	216	Farmer	2 · bribes/greed
	268	Ptah-Hotep	2 · bribes/greed
16:1, 9	294	Ankhsheshonqy	2 · human/divine plans
16:8	277	Amen-em-ope	1 · "Better" proverb
			3 · be satisfied
	294	Ankhsheshonqy	1 · "Better" proverb
			3 · be satisfied
16:9	280	Amen-em-ope	2 · God's majesty
17:1	277, 279	Amen-em-ope	1 · "Better" proverb
			2 · eating
			3 · be satisfied
17:5	281	Amen-em-ope	2 · laugh/stricken
17:13	266	Ptah-Hotep	2 · evil
19:1, 22	277	Amen-em-ope	1 · "Better" proverb
			3 · be satisfied
19:18	283	Ahiqar	2 · discipline
19:20	278	Amen-em-ope	2 · advice
	266, 269	Ptah-Hotep	2 · advice
19:21	280	Amen-em-ope	2 · God's majesty
20:1	238	Ninkasi	2 · beer
20:4	145	Gezer	2 · planting
20:9	280	Amen-em-ope	2 · hypocrisy
	3	Memphis	4 · pure heart
20:20	287	Ahiqar	2 · honor parents
21:6	278	Amen-em-ope	2 · riches

CITATION	PAGE	TEXT	PARALLEL
31:27–31	269	Ptah-Hotep	2 · city gate
			3 · good wife
			4 · honored household

ECCLESIASTES

3:1–10	281	Amen-em-ope	2 · time
			3 · fate
3:3	14	Enuma	1 · covenant
			2 · build/break
3:12	210	Soul	2 · be content
3:12–3	24	Gilgamesh	3 · contentment
3:16	225	Friend	2 · inconsistencies
			3 · anarchy
3:20	251	Ba'al	2 · dust of grave
5:2	284	Ahiqar	2 · word
5:10	278	Amen-em-ope	2 · strive/greed
6:2–3	269	Ptah-Hotep	2 · wealth
6:10	284	Ahiqar	2 · obey authority
10:20	284	Ahiqar	2 · word like bird
11:1	292	Ankhsheshonqy	2 · good return
11:2	247	Ba'al	2 · x/x + 1
			3 · number progression
11:6	145	Gezer	2 · sowing

SONG OF SOLOMON

2:5	300	Love Songs	5 · lovesick
2:10–3	299	Love Songs	5 · fertile land
4:10	299	Love Songs	2 · love/wine
4:13–4	244	Ba'al	2 · henna
5:1	299	Love Songs	2 · intoxication
5:2–6	300	Love Songs	2 · door/latch
			3 · double entendre
5:8	300	Love Songs	5 · lovesick
7:5	298	Love Songs	2 · hair snare
			3 · trap
7:13	298	Love Songs	2 · mandrake
	299	Love Songs	2 · mandrake
			3 · love garden

CITATION	PAGE	TEXT	PARALLEL
63:3–6	244	Ba'al	3 · divine war
			5 · wading in blood
64:8	281	Amen-em-ope	1 · creation story
			2 · potter's clay
			4 · anthropomorphism

JEREMIAH

1:6–9	285	Ahiqar	2 · good sense
			3 · unexpected event
1:10	14	Enuma	1 · investiture
			2 · power
5:12	226	Friend	1 · false teaching
7:18	306	Ishtar	2 · Queen of Heaven
7:33	168	Shalmaneser	5 · unburied bodies
9:4–5	211	Soul	2 · neighbor
			3 · anarchy
9:21–2	236	Ur	5 · dead in squares
11:5	254	Ba'al	2 · land/honey
11:16	276	Amen-em-ope	2 · tree
11:19	237	Ur	2 · lamb/slaughter
	246	Ba'al	2 · lamb/slaughter
12:1	225	Friend	2 · wicked prosper
13:23	288	Ahiqar	2 · professions
			3 · order in life
15:7	254	Ba'al	2 · winnowing
16:4	236	Ur	5 · unburied bodies
16:6	252	Ba'al	4 · destruction ritual
			5 · mourning
	313	Neferti	2 · no mourners
17:5–8	276	Amen-em-ope	2 · tree
18:2–6	32	Atrahasis	1 · creation story
			2 · potter's clay
			4 · anthropomorphism
20:1	185	Arad	6 · Pashur
21:1–10	143	Ramses III	3 · divine warrior
26:16–9	249	Ba'al	4 · immune prophets
			5 · immunity
26:20–2	189	Lachish	6 · El-nathan
30:8–9	237	Ur	2 · restoration
31:38–40	237	Ur	1 · petition
			2 · restoration

CITATION	PAGE	TEXT	PARALLEL
DANIEL			
2—6	312	Neferti	3 · entertain king
5:12	312	Neferti	5 · summons
9:16–9	313	Neferti	1 · plea
			2 · restoration
11:2–4	315	Neferti	2 · divided land
11:14	315	Neferti	2 · take up arms
11:20–4	315	Neferti	2 · weak rulers
12:1	315	Neferti	5 · triumphant king
HOSEA			
2:9	36	Atrahasis	5 · withhold harvest
5:10	277	Amen-em-ope	2 · landmark
7:5	67	Aqhat	2 · drunkenness
11:1–9	320	Mari	2 · "raised you"
			3 · divine parent
13:15	251	Ba'al	2 · drying winds
14:9	269	Ptah-Hotep	1 · admonition
			2 · guidance
	282	Amen-em-ope	1 · admonition
			2 · study
JOEL			
2:7	314	Neferti	2 · scale walls
2:10	124	Balaam	2 · darkness
AMOS			
1:13	155	Tiglath-Pileser I	2 · pregnant women
			5 · pillaging
2:6–7	81	Keret	1 · law
			2 · hear poor
2:7	226	Friend	2 · trample needy
2:8	331	Yavne-Yam	1 · law
			2 · garment/pledge
	227	Friend	2 · fines
4:3	236	Ur	2 · breached wall

CITATION	PAGE	TEXT	PARALLEL
5:10	226	Friend	2 · honest quieted
5:10–3	216	Farmer	2 · criminals
			3 · anarchy
5:12	81	Keret	2 · failed justice
5:14	216	Farmer	2 · evil for good
5:14–5	211	Soul	2 · evil & good
			3 · anarchy
5:15	320	Mari	1 · admonition
			2 · justice
5:16	237	Ur	1 · lament
			2 · "Alas!"
5:18–20	233	Ur	3 · "Day of Lord"
8:1	145	Gezer	2 · summer fruit
8:5	216	Farmer	2 · false scales
	104	CH	2 · false scales

JONAH

2:1–10	41	Adapa	2 · sea calmed

MICAH

2:11	238	Ninkasi	2 · beer
4:9	27	Gilgamesh	2 · travail
5:5	77	Keret	2 · x/x + 1
6:3	139	Amarna	1 · petition
			2 · what done?
6:8	223	Friend	3 · humility
6:11	216	Farmer	2 · false scales
6:12	216	Farmer	2 · lying tongue

HABAKKUK

3:17	251	Ba'al	2 · produce dies

ZECHARIAH

7:1	182	Nebuchadnezzar	2 · month
8:16	216	Farmer	2 · truth
13:1–4	233	Ur	3 · "On that day"

CITATION	PAGE	TEXT	PARALLEL

MALACHI

1:11	162	Karatepe	1 · realm formula
			2 · rising sun
			4 · universal rule

TOBIT

1:1—14:15	283	Ahiqar	1 · wisdom
			3 · restored fortune
1:21–2	283	Ahiqar	2 · Ahiqar

JUDITH

13:2, 6, 9	75	Aqhat	3 · revenge
			5 · murder

THE WISDOM OF SOLOMON

1:15	215	Farmer	1 · teaching
			2 · justice
			3 · eternal things
8:13	215	Farmer	1 · teaching
			2 · justice
			3 · eternal things
10:21	285	Ahiqar	2 · child
			3 · unexpected wisdom
18:15–6	284	Ahiqar	2 · word like sword

SIRACH

3:1–16	287	Ahiqar	2 · honor parents
			4 · household honor
6:7	265	Ptah-Hotep	2 · friend
8:1	287	Ahiqar	2 · contend/powerful
9:1	265	Ptah-Hotep	2 · wife
19:7, 10	267	Ptah-Hotep	2 · repeat nothing
22:7	289, 291	Ankhsheshonqy	2 · fool
22:15	285	Ahiqar	2 · sand and salt
24:15	211	Soul	2 · myrrh
27:16–9	284	Ahiqar	2 · word
28:17	284	Ahiqar	2 · king's tongue